The Family Crochet Book

Shown in photograph on front cover.
Floral-patterned dress (see page 100); V-necked
sweater (see page 136); Pink and white dress (see
page 62).

Shown in photograph on back cover, from left to right:
Turquoise lampshade (see page 193); Matching tea
and egg cosies (see page 198); Round cushion (see
page 185); Striped cushion (see page 189); Pink
handbag (see page 146); Doll's outfit (see page 204);
Waste paper bin (see page 190); Slippers (see page
165).

Lamp base and egg cups by courtesy of Bentalls Ltd.,
Kingston-upon-Thames, Surrey.

The Family Crochet Book

HAMLYN
LONDON · NEW YORK · SYDNEY · TORONTO

Published by the Hamlyn Publishing Group Limited
London   New York   Sydney   Toronto
Hamlyn House, Feltham, Middlesex, England
© Copyright The Hamlyn Publishing Group Limited 1971
Second Impression January 1972
ISBN 0 600 33446 5

Printed in Holland by
N.V. Drukkerij Senefelder

Contents

Introduction

Crochet—like knitting—is believed to date back to the time of the Ancient Egyptians. In the sixteenth century, European nuns worked fine lace using crochet techniques, then in the nineteenth century the handicraft spread from Ireland to become popular in Victorian England—but then only in a limited way, as a form of decorative edging. It was not until recent years that the infinite possibilities of crochet work have been fully appreciated and a world-wide interest and enthusiasm for the hobby aroused.

For a start, crochet is supremely easy to learn: it consists of virtually one stitch only formed by inter-locking loops made with a single thread and a hook. But the variations on this one stitch, and the effects that can be achieved, are endless. And because you work with just one stitch on your hook at a time, in many ways crochet is simpler—and less tedious—than knitting. It also makes up with commendable speed, so you very soon can see the results of your efforts. The simplicity of the technique means it is easy to carry your work around with you to do on train or bus, on the beach, in the garden—or wherever you choose to relax.

The yarns used for crochet work vary almost as much as the garments themselves, from fine spidery cottons for summer clothes and delicate baby wear, to thick chunky wools for winter dresses, pullovers and sweaters, and easy-care synthetics for practical all-the-year-round use.

Crochet is for everyone. It is the modern handi-craft—and it is here to stay! This book will help you master the art in the shortest possible time.

Chapter One

All about crochet

THE MATERIALS YOU WILL NEED

The only basic materials you need to begin work are a *crochet hook* and *yarn*. You will probably however find the following items useful as well:

A tape measure.
Rustless steel dressmaking pins and safety pins.
Polythene bag or clean cloth to keep your work in.
Pencil and paper (to note down increases, decreases and number of rows worked).
Several sizes of large-eyed sewing needles (for making up).
Scissors.

Crochet hooks are available in steel for working with fine cotton yarns, and in aluminium or plastic for coarser cottons, wools and synthetic yarns. The size of hook you use depends on the weight and type of yarn you are working with, and crochet patterns usually recommend which size this should be. The important thing however is not necessarily to use the precise size of hook quoted, but to check your tension first by working a small sample in the stitch pattern (see notes on tension, page 14). Provided you achieve the correct tension as given in the instructions, it does not matter what size hook you use.

In the patterns throughout this book, the International Standard Sizes of crochet hooks only are given. The chart right indicates the equivalent sizes of hooks in other ranges, including the sizing system used previously for hooks made in the U.K.

Elegant for all seasons—instructions for this long jacket are on page 189.

INTERNATIONAL STANDARD SIZES	OLD U.K. SIZES		AMERICAN SIZES	
	Wool	Cotton	Wool	Cotton
7·00	2	—	K	—
—	3	—	—	—
6·00	4	—	—	—
5·50	5	—	—	—
5·00	6	—	J	—
4·50	7	—	I	—
4·00	8	—	H	—
3·50	9	—	G	—
3·00	10	3/0	F	2/0
—	11	2/0	E	0
2·50	12	0	D	1
—	13	1	C	2
—	—	—	—	3
2·00	14	$1\frac{1}{2}$	B	4
—	—	2	A	5
1·75	15	$2\frac{1}{2}$	—	6
—	—	3	—	—
1·50	16	$3\frac{1}{2}$	—	7
—	—	4	—	8
1·25	—	$4\frac{1}{2}$	—	9
—	—	5	—	10
1·00	—	$5\frac{1}{2}$	—	11
—	—	6	—	12
0·75	—	$6\frac{1}{2}$	—	13
0·60	—	7	—	14
—	—	$7\frac{1}{2}$	—	—

N.B. Australian, Canadian and South African sizes are the same as old U.K. sizes

HOW TO BEGIN

Crochet is really only one stitch—one loop pulled through another loop. If you have never attempted crochet before, then start by practising a simple chain, using a large size hook and fairly coarse yarn, so you can see clearly what you are doing. This will give you the feel of holding the hook and working with yarn.

The first loop

Make your first loop by lapping the long thread of yarn over short end. Hold in place between thumb and forefinger of the left hand (diagram 1). Grasp the bar of the hook like a pencil with your right hand. Insert the hook through the loop, under the long thread and pull it through the loop (diagram 2), to form loop on hook. Pull the short end and the ball thread in opposite directions to bring the loop close round the hook (diagram 3). You are now ready to begin working.

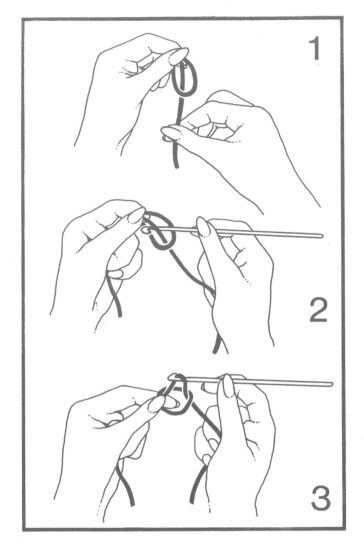

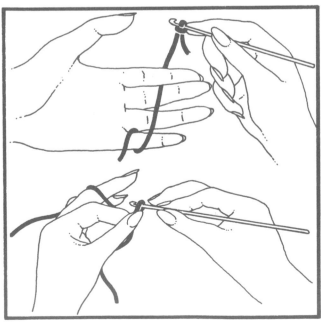

Holding the work

Loop the long thread round the little finger of your left hand, across the palm and behind the forefinger (see top diagram, left). This should keep tension of your work even. Catch the knot of the loop on the hook between the thumb and forefinger of left hand (as your work grows you will still continue to steady it by holding in this position). Hold the bar of the hook between thumb and forefinger of the right hand, as you would a pencil, and place the tip of the middle finger on head of hook to guide it (see diagram, left).

THE STITCHES YOU WILL USE

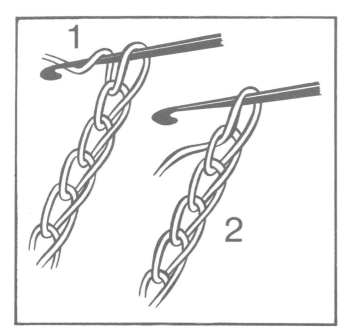

Chain

This is the foundation of all crochet work. With the yarn in position, and the first loop on hook, pass hook under the yarn held between left hand forefinger and hook, catch yarn with hook (diagram 1). Draw yarn and head of hook through loop already on hook (diagram 2). Each time you pull yarn through loop on hook counts as 1 chain. Continue until required number of chains are formed. Once you have mastered making a chain you are ready to practise the other basic crochet stitches.

Slip stitch

This stitch is used to give a firm edge, or for joining, fastening or re-positioning the yarn without adding to the dimension of your work.

Insert the hook into the stitch to the left of the hook, catch the long thread and draw it through the stitch and the loop already on the hook (see diagram above). This forms a flat chain and is sometimes called single crochet.

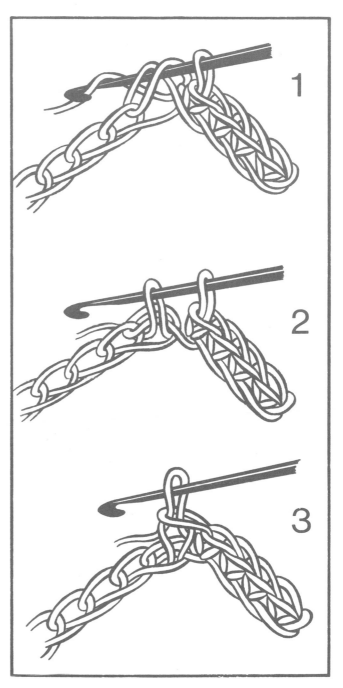

Double crochet

Insert the hook into the stitch to the left of the hook (under both top loops of the stitch) and catch yarn with hook (diagram 1). Draw yarn through stitch. You now have 2 loops on the hook (diagram 2). Put the yarn over the hook and draw it through the 2 loops. This leaves 1 loop on the hook (diagram 3).

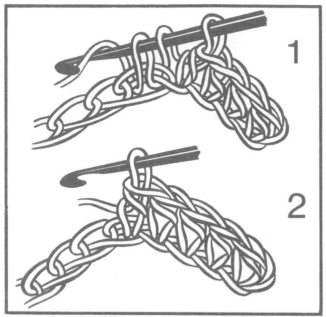

Half treble

Pass the hook under the yarn held in the left hand, insert the hook into the stitch to the left of the hook. Catch the yarn and draw it through the stitch. This gives you 3 loops on the hook. Put yarn over hook (diagram 1) and draw it through all loops on hook, leaving you with 1 loop (diagram 2).

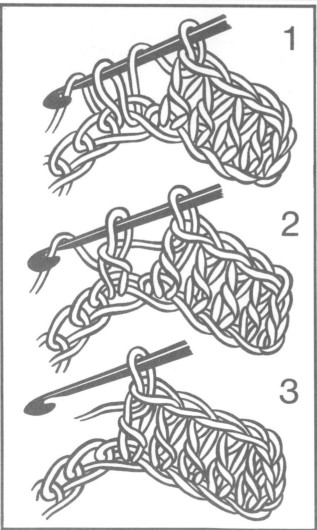

Treble

Pass the hook under yarn held in left hand, insert the hook into the stitch to the left of the hook and draw yarn through. You now have 3 loops on the hook. Put the yarn over the hook again (diagram 1) and pull it through the first 2 loops on the hook, leaving 2 loops on the hook. Put the yarn over the hook once more (diagram 2) and draw through the last 2 loops, leaving you with 1 loop on the hook (diagram 3).

Double treble

Pass the hook under the yarn held in left hand twice, put the hook into the next stitch, yarn over the hook and pull it through the stitch. This gives you 4 loops on the hook (see diagram, right). Put the yarn over the hook and pull it through 2 loops, leaving 3 loops, put yarn over the hook again and pull through the next 2 loops and finally put yarn over the hook and pull through the last 2 loops.

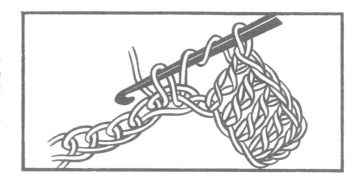

Triple treble

Pass the hook under the yarn held in left hand 3 times, put the hook into the next stitch and draw the yarn through. This gives you 5 loops on the hook (see diagram, right). Put yarn over the hook and draw through the first 2 loops (4 loops on hook), yarn over and draw through the next 2 loops (3 loops), yarn over and draw through next 2 loops (2 loops), yarn over and draw through last 2 loops.

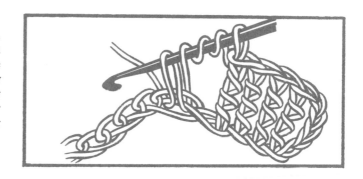

Quadruple treble

Pass the hook under the yarn held in left hand 4 times, insert hook into next stitch and draw the yarn through. This gives you 6 loops on the hook (see diagram, right). Pass the yarn over the hook and draw through the first 2 loops (5 loops on hook), pass yarn over hook and draw through next 2 loops (4 loops on hook), pass yarn over the hook and draw through next 2 loops (3 loops on hook), pass yarn over and draw through next 2 loops (2 loops), pass yarn over and draw through last 2 loops.

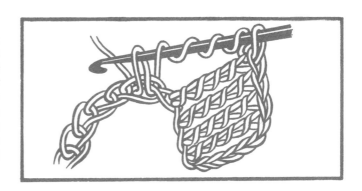

Picot

Work a chain of 3, 4 or 5 stitches, depending on size of picot wanted, form into a circle by working 1 double crochet into foundation of first chain (see diagram, right).

INCREASING

Normally, instructions for increasing are included in individual patterns, but as a general rule, increasing can be achieved by working the required number of times into the same foundation stitch. To increase the overall width more chain stitches can be worked between each group of the pattern. Alternatively, it is sometimes possible merely to change to a larger size hook.

DECREASING

Again, instructions for decreasing will be given in individual patterns to suit the particular stitch being worked. One method of decreasing is merely to omit a stitch, but this is only successful if the space created is not too obvious. Another method is to work 2 stitches together. Do not complete either of the stitches but leave the last loop on the hook in addition to the loop already on hook. Draw yarn through all the remaining loops to leave a single loop on hook.

At the beginning of rows for armhole and neck shaping decreasing can be achieved with slip stitch or alternatively stitches are left unworked.

TURNING

When crochet is worked straight (rather than in rounds) turning the work is not quite as simple as in knitting. This is because there is more depth to crochet stitches and as stitches are worked from the top down, the hook must first be taken up to the correct level.

Usually this is done by working a certain number of extra chains to form an upright stitch at the end of the row before turning the work. The exact number depends on which stitch you are using, but the following can be taken as a general guide: double crochet—1 turning chain; half treble—2 turning chain; treble—3 turning chain; double treble—4 turning chain; triple treble—5 turning chain; quadruple treble—6 turning chain.

JOINING

Never make knots in your work. When the yarn you are using is coming to an end, place the new yarn along the top of the work and crochet a few stitches over this. Before the old yarn has completely run out, change to the new yarn and work stitches over the old.

FINISHING

At the end of the last row, do not make any turning chain. Cut the yarn about 3 inches from the work. Draw the end through the last loop on hook and pull tight. Finally darn the loose end into the work so it is hidden.

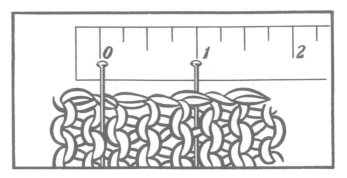

TENSION

The word "tension" in crochet—as in knitting—refers to the number of stitches and rows worked to each square inch of fabric. This measurement is a result of the combination of a particular weight and type of yarn with a suitable hook size, and can be varied by altering the yarn and/or hook used. It is possible, for instance, to work the same pattern in a variety of yarns and hook sizes and achieve entirely different results. For example, see the pattern for Three-way Poncho on page 126.

It is extremely important therefore before you embark on making up any pattern, to check that your work achieves the tension measurement quoted otherwise you will never produce finished work to the correct size. Check your tension by working about 4 in. of chain, using yarn and hook size recommended in pattern, and make up a sample of the stitch pattern (about 3 in. should be sufficient). Press the sample, following instructions for blocking and pressing on page 16, then using a ruler measure across 1 in. and mark this area with pins, as shown in diagram, above. Carefully count the number of stitches between the pins. If this comes to a greater number than quoted in the pattern, you are working too tightly—make another sample, trying a larger size hook. Alternatively, if you have fewer stitches in your inch than quoted in the pattern, you should try working with a smaller size hook. Keep on making sample pieces until you achieve the correct tension.

FILET CROCHET

This is a particular technique of crochet, based on forming designs from a series of solid and open squares, called "blocks" and "spaces". The effect of this work is similar to lace or net, and can be used to make attractive edgings for household items such as cloths, place mats, or even net curtains (see pattern, page 183).

Filet is worked in straight rows; the blocks of the pattern are formed by trebles; the spaces by chain and single trebles (see diagram, right). Patterns are usually given in the form of charts, one square on the chart equal to one stitch. Once you have mastered the technique, you can go on to devise your own designs on graph paper—the finished result will then be truly your own work!

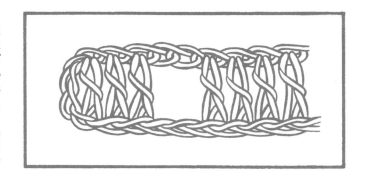

CROCHET WITH BEADS AND SEQUINS

Like knitting, crochet can have sequins or beads worked into it to achieve unusual and often stunning effects (see our pattern for evening bag and belt, page 148). Most haberdashery departments sell packets of beads and sequins, in a range of colours, sizes and types, specially for this purpose. Smooth yarns, fine enough to go through the chosen beads or sequins should be used, and the exact number of beads or sequins should be threaded on to your yarn before beginning work—patterns usually quote the number required. Beads are crocheted in from the wrong side of your work; sequins from the right.

Using beads

Count out the correct number of beads required, then cut a length of nylon thread long enough to take all the beads, with a good 6 in. over. Knot one end, thread the other on to a needle fine enough to go through the beads. String beads on to nylon. Remove needle, and tie end of nylon around crochet yarn. It is important to do it in this way, and not to tie yarn round nylon. Very carefully slide the beads over the knot and so on to the yarn (see diagram, right), taking care not to break the nylon. When all the beads are on yarn, remove nylon. The beads are worked into your pattern as and when required, usually with double crochet. Take the work to the point where a bead is to

be inserted, pull up a loop in the next double crochet, slip the bead up close to the hook, hold it in position on the side of the work away from you, put the yarn over hook and through the 2 loops (see bottom diagram). The bead is then positioned in your work.

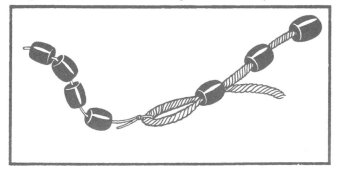

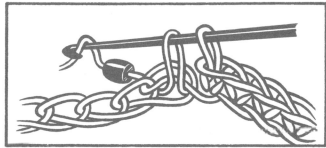

Using sequins

Thread sequins on to a length of double sewing thread and from there on to crochet yarn, in a similar way as described for threading beads on to nylon (see page 15). Always thread sequins so the right side faces needle (inside of cup is right side, if you are using cup sequins).

There are two methods of working sequins into crochet: either with trebles working double crochet on alternate non-sequin rows, or with one-chain loops.

Method 1 (trebles)

Each sequin requires three stitches and therefore each row must contain three times as many stitches as sequins. First work a row of double crochet. In the second row, push a sequin against the hook, put the yarn and the sequin over the hook as in treble, insert the hook in the second double crochet making certain the sequin is towards you and right side up.

Now continue to work treble in the normal way taking the loops off the hook two at a time from behind the sequin. Work 2 treble without sequins. The next row should be worked in double crochet.

Method 2 (chain loops)

In this method the sequin is worked in with the sequin side of the work away from you. Slide the sequin close to the hook with the back of the sequin to the hook Holding the sequin carefully in place and keeping the yarn taut so that the sequin will lie flat, make one double crochet into chain loop of the previous row; * chain 1 (chain 2 or 3 for larger sequins), slide next sequin close to the hook, double crochet into next chain, 1 space; repeat from * to the end of the row.

Sequins placed after the chain-one and before the double crochet will be raised to the top of the work which is suitable for an article worked from the top down. If the work is from the bottom up, the sequin should be placed after the double crochet and before the chain-one and the sequins will then be positioned towards the bottom of the work.

FINISHING DETAILS

Many a well-made crocheted garment has been spoiled by being carelessly finished off. Time and trouble spent on correct pressing and making-up are never wasted, for you will be rewarded with a neat, well-fitting, professional-looking garment.

Pressing

It is important to read any specific pressing instructions given in a pattern, as different yarns need different treatments. Acrylic fibres, for instance, do not require pressing at all. If, however, pressing is recommended, this should be carried out before

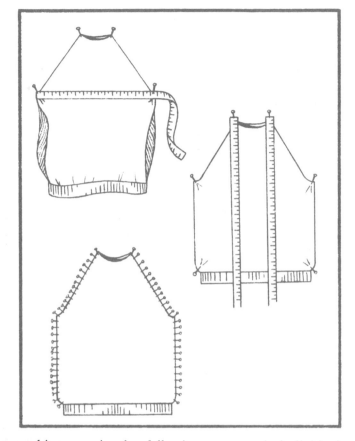

making up, in the following way: each individual piece of your work should be pinned out to the correct shape and size, right side downwards, on a thick pressing blanket, care being taken to keep stitches and rows running in straight lines. Plenty of pins should be used, and these should be inserted from the outer edge towards the centre of the work; the closer the pins are, the straighter the pressed edge will be (see diagram above). This process is called "blocking". When you are satisfied you have the pieces pinned sufficiently, to the right size, press the main part of the work using a warm iron over a damp cloth. Wait a few minutes until the steam has settled then remove the pins. Care should be taken not to overpress the main part of the work, especially when a fancy pattern has been used. Overpressing will flatten the fabric and can destroy the character of the stitch.

Although many man-made fibres should not be pressed, in order to ensure a perfect fit they should still be blocked. Pin out in a similar way as described above, then lay a damp cloth over the fabric, and leave until the cloth is completely dry.

Blouse-topped dress has a drawstring tie at waist. Instructions are on page 101.

Making-up

After the individual pieces of your work have been blocked and pressed they are stitched together. First make sure all loose ends are neatly darned in to the work, and then using the same yarn as you used for crocheting the item, stitch pieces together with either of the two following seams:

1. Flat seam

With right sides facing, place the 2 pieces of work together, edge to edge. Place the forefinger of your left hand just between these edges. Using an overcasting stitch draw the edges together over your finger (see diagram, right). Move finger along as work proceeds.

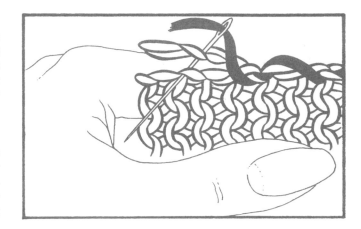

2. Backstitch seam

This seam should be used for edges where there will be extra pull or strain, or for joining edges which are heavily shaped or jagged. With right sides of work together, backstitch seam as close to the edges as possible (see diagram, right).
Press all seams flat to finish.

After-care

As with knitted garments, crocheted work should never be allowed to get too dirty before washing. Careful washing—no matter how frequent—will never harm wool, man-made fibres or the finest of cottons.

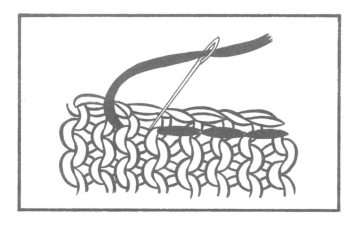

Cotton

Wash items made in crochet cotton in warm water and soap flakes; squeeze gently to remove dirt—never rub or twist. It may be necessary in the case of crochet worked to a specific shape such as a circle or a square, to pin it out again (see blocking instructions, page 16). If a light stiffening is required, use gum arabic or a solution of starch (1 dessertspoon to a pint of hot water); dab lightly over the article before pressing.

Wool

Wash woollen items gently in lukewarm soapy water; rinse thoroughly in at least three changes of warm water. Always support a woollen garment with both hands while it is wet or it will stretch out of shape from its own weight. Gently squeeze the garment after its final rinse, and roll it in a clean dry white towel without twisting. Leave to dry flat on a clean towel, away from direct sunlight or strong artificial heat. Ease it into its correct shape and size. When the garment is dry, press lightly on the wrong side with a medium hot iron over a damp cloth.

Man-made fibres

Wash as for wool, press with a warm iron over a dry cloth.
N.B. No pressing at all is required for Courtelle, Acrilan, Tricel or Orlon yarns.

LEFT-HANDED WORKERS

Follow instructions as given, but read right for left, and left for right. Where stitch diagrams occur, use a mirror to reflect them in reverse; follow this as a guide.

Smart for father and son—instructions for these zipped jerkins are on page 130.

ABBREVIATIONS

alt., alternate;
beg., beginning;
blk(s)., block(s);
ch., chain;
cl., cluster;
cont., continue;
d.c., double crochet;
dec., decreas(e)(ed)(ing);
d.tr., double treble;
foll., following;
gr(s)., group(s);
h.tr., half treble;
in., inch(es);
inc., increas(e)(ed)(ing);
p., picot;
patt., pattern;

qd.tr., quadruple treble;
rep., repeat;
sh., shell;
sp(s)., space(s);
s.s., slip stitch;
st(s)., stitch(es);
thr., through;
tog., together;
tr., treble;
t.tr., triple treble;
yd., yard;
y.o.h., yarn over hook.
Size note.
Instructions in every pattern are given in size order, with larger sizes in brackets. Where only one set of figures occurs this refers to all sizes.

WOOLS AND YARNS

All the crochet patterns in this book quote specific brand names and weights of wools and yarns, and for the best results it is recommended that these are used. However, in some countries a particular yarn may not be readily available, but a direct equivalent known by a different brand name is. Where no direct equivalent exists then a standard alternative can often be used. The following chart lists the direct and standard equivalents for yarns quoted in this book. If a yarn does not appear on the chart it can be assumed it is generally available in South Africa, Australia, Canada and USA as well as in the United Kingdom.

UNITED KINGDOM	SOUTH AFRICA	AUSTRALIA	CANADA	USA
COATS YARNS All yarns quoted are available in the United Kingdom, Canada, South Africa and Australia. USA equivalents are listed below:				
Mercer Crochet No. 10	—	—	—	J. & P. Coats 6/c Crochet Cotton No. 10 *or* 3/Mercerised Crochet Cotton No. 10
Mercer Crochet No. 20	—	—	—	J. & P. Coats 6/c Crochet Cotton No. 20 *or* 3/Mercerised Crochet Cotton No. 20
Mercer Crochet No. 40	—	—	—	3/Mercerised Crochet Cotton No. 40
Mercer Crochet No. 60	—	—	—	3/Mercerised Crochet Cotton No. 50 (This is slightly thicker yarn so fewer motifs may be needed to make the equivalent size of bedspread.)

UNITED KINGDOM	SOUTH AFRICA	AUSTRALIA	CANADA	USA

EMU YARNS Often available in all countries but in cases of difficulties use the following:

UNITED KINGDOM	SOUTH AFRICA	AUSTRALIA	CANADA	USA
4-ply	standard 4-ply	standard 4-ply	standard 4-ply	standard 4-ply
4-ply Tricel with Nylon	,,	,,	,,	,,
Supercrimp Bri-Nylon 4-ply	,,	,,	,,	,,
Scotch 4-ply	,,	,,	,,	,,
Super Crêpe	,,	,,	,,	,,
Bri-Nylon 4-ply	,,	,,	,,	,,
Diadem	,,	,,	,,	,,
Double Crêpe	standard double knitting	standard double knitting	standard double knitting	standard double knitting

HAYFIELD YARNS

UNITED KINGDOM	SOUTH AFRICA	AUSTRALIA	CANADA	USA
Courtier Bri-Nova Crêpe Double Knitting	High Crimp Bri-Nylon d.k.	standard d.k.	as for UK	standard d.k.
Bri-Nylon Double Knitting	High Crimp Bri-Nylon d.k.	,,	standard d.k.	,,
Beaulon 4-ply	High Crimp Bri-Nylon 4-ply	standard 4-ply	Courtier 4-ply	standard 4 ply

LEE TARGET YARN

UNITED KINGDOM	SOUTH AFRICA	AUSTRALIA	CANADA	USA
Motoravia Double Knitting	as for UK	standard d.k.	as for UK	standard d.k.

LISTER YARNS

UNITED KINGDOM	SOUTH AFRICA	AUSTRALIA	CANADA	USA
Lorette Double Crêpe	standard d.k.	standard d.k.	as for UK	standard d.k.
Lavenda Double Knitting	as for UK	,,	standard d.k.	as for UK
Bel Air Double Crêpe	standard d.k.	,,	as for UK	standard d.k.
Bel Air 4-ply	standard 4-ply	standard 4-ply	standard 4-ply	standard 4-ply
Bel Air Starspun	as for UK	standard 4-ply	standard 4-ply	standard 4-ply
Lavenda Double Crêpe	standard d.k.	standard d.k.	standard d.k.	standard d.k.
Velora Double Knitting	,,	,,	,,	,,
Bri-Nylon Double Knitting	,,	,,	,,	,,

PATONS YARNS

UNITED KINGDOM	SOUTH AFRICA	AUSTRALIA	CANADA	USA
Cameo Crêpe	as for UK	Bluebell Crêpe	Beehive Fingering or Patons Patwin 4-ply or Patons Atlantic Fingering or Patons Sterling Fingering	standard 4-ply
Piccadilly	Fiona	Swifta-Knit Bri-Nylon	Beehive Astra	standard 4-ply

UNITED KINGDOM	SOUTH AFRICA	AUSTRALIA	CANADA	USA

ROBIN YARNS Often available in all countries but in case of difficulties use the following:

	UNITED KINGDOM	SOUTH AFRICA	AUSTRALIA	CANADA	USA
Tricel-Nylon Perle	standard 4-ply	standard 4-ply	standard 4-ply	standard 4-ply
Vogue 4-ply	,,	,,	,,	,,
Casino Crêpe	,,	,,	,,	,,
Vogue Double Knitting	standard d.k.	standard d.k.	standard d.k.	standard d.k.
Bri-Nylon Double Knitting	,,	,,	,,	,,
Tricel-Nylon Double Knitting	,,	,,	,,	,,

SIRDAR YARNS

	SOUTH AFRICA	AUSTRALIA	CANADA	USA
Courtelle Crêpe Double Knitting	Double Crêpe	Double Crêpe	standard d.k.	standard d.k.
Double Knitting	as for UK	Double Crêpe	standard d.k.	standard d.k.
Talisman 4-ply	as for UK	Fontein Crêpe 4-ply	standard 4-ply	standard 4-ply

TWILLEY YARNS
All Twilley yarns quoted in this book should be readily available in the United Kingdom, South Africa, Australia, Canada and USA.

WENDY YARNS Often available in South Africa, Canada and USA, but not in Australia. In all cases of difficulty use the following:

	SOUTH AFRICA	AUSTRALIA	CANADA	USA
Carolette Double Knitting	standard d.k.	standard d.k.	standard d.k.	standard d.k.
Double Knit Nylonised	,,	,,	,,	,,
Diabolo	double d.k.	double d.k.	double d.k.	double d.k.
4-ply Nylonised	standard 4-ply	standard 4-ply	standard 4-ply	standard 4-ply
Peter Pan 3-ply Bri-Nylon	standard 3-ply	standard 3-ply	standard 3-ply	standard 3-ply

Important Note
Where the exact yarn given in a pattern is not available an equivalent may not work up to precisely the same measurements, therefore it is doubly important to make a tension check before beginning (see page 14). Yardage also varies with different yarns and you may find you need either more or less than the quantity specified in the pattern.

USEFUL FACTS AND FIGURES

Imperial Standard measurements are used throughout this book. If it is wished to convert these into the appropriate metric equivalents, follow the simple conversion tables below.

Weights

1 oz. = 28·35 grammes
4 oz. = 113·4 grammes
8 oz. = 226·8 grammes
1 lb. = 454 grammes
2 lb. 3 oz. (approx.) = 1 kilogramme

N.B. When buying knitting or crochet yarn, a 25-gramme ball of yarn will very approximately equal a 1-oz. ball. But as 1 oz. equals slightly over 25 grammes for larger quantities increase the number of gramme balls, e.g. if 12 oz. yarn is required, buy fourteen 25-gramme balls, and if 20 oz. is required, buy twenty-three 25-gramme balls.

Linear measures

1 inch = 2·54 centimetres
6 inches = 15·2 centimetres
1 foot (12 inches) = 30·48 centimetres
1 yard = 0·914 metre (just over 91 centimetres)
1 yard 4 in. (approximately) = 1 metre

The Patterns

93 easy-to-follow patterns
using the basic crochet stitches
and techniques described in the
previous chapter.

Chapter Two

Baby wear

White shawl

MATERIALS

10 oz. of Sirdar Sunshine 3-ply (see note on wools and yarns, page 22); crochet hooks International Standard Sizes 3.50 and 3.00 (see page 9).

MEASUREMENTS

44 in. square.

TENSION

1 patt. to 5½ in. (see note on tension, page 14).

ABBREVIATIONS

See page 20.

CENTRE

With No. 3.50 hook begin with 187 ch. loosely.

1st row: 1 tr. into 4th ch. from hook, 1 tr. into each ch.; turn: 185 tr.

2nd row: 3 ch., miss first tr., 1 tr. into each of next 2 tr., * 2 ch., miss 2 tr., 1 tr. into each of next 7 tr., 2 ch., miss 2 tr., 1 tr. into each of next 7 tr., 1 ch., miss 2 tr., 1 tr. into each of next 7 tr., 2 ch., miss 2 tr., 1 tr. into next tr.; rep. from * 5 times ending with 1 tr. into next tr., 1 tr. into 3rd of 3 ch.; turn.

3rd row: 3 ch., miss first tr., 1 tr. into each of next 2 tr., * 2 tr. into next sp., 1 tr. into next tr., 2 ch., miss 2 tr., 1 tr. into each of next 4 tr., 2 tr. into next sp., 1 tr., into next tr., 2 ch., miss 2 tr., 1 tr. into next tr., 2 ch., miss 2 tr., 1 tr. into next tr., 2 tr. into next sp., 1 tr. into each of next 4 tr., 2 ch.,

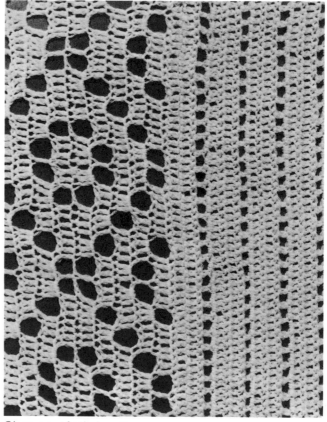

Close-up of stitch pattern.

The lacy patterned shawl can double as a warm pram cover.

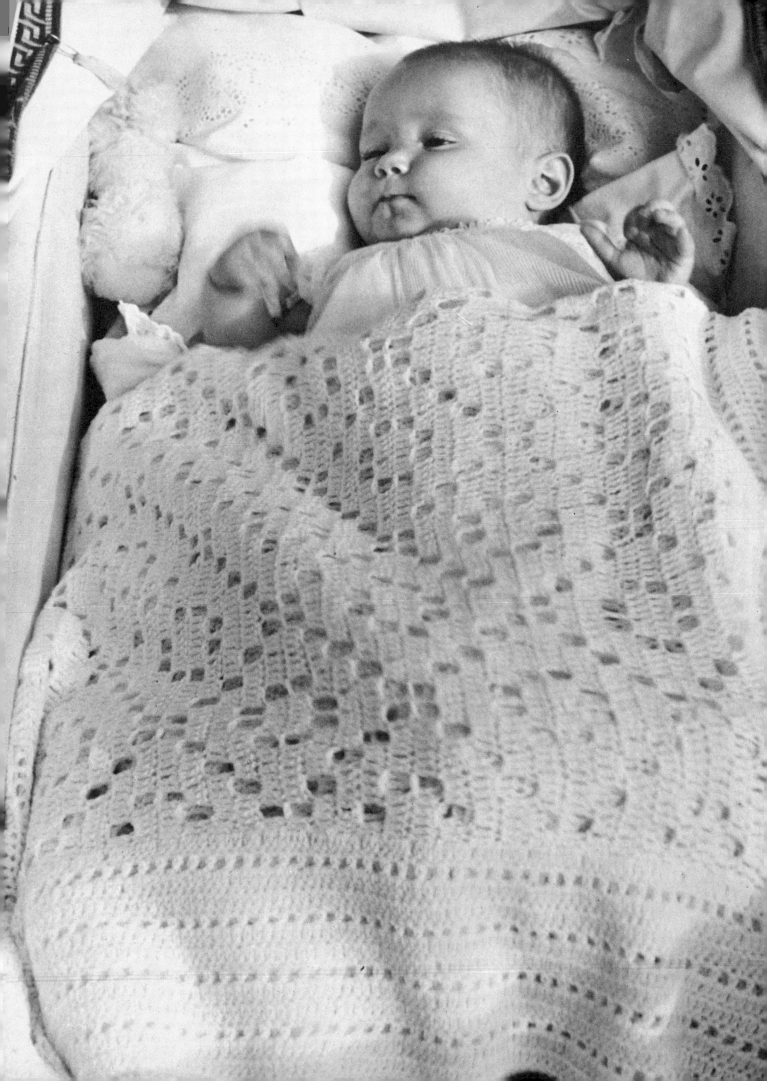

miss 2 tr., 1 tr. into next tr., 2 tr. into next sp., 1 tr. into next tr.; rep. from * ending with 1 tr. into next tr., 1 tr. into 3rd of 3 ch.; turn.

4th row: 3 ch., miss first tr., 1 tr. into each of next 2 tr., * 1 tr. into each of next 3 tr., 2 tr. into next sp., 1 tr. into next tr., 2 ch., miss 2 tr., 1 tr. into each of next 4 tr., 2 tr. into next sp., 1 tr. into next tr., 2 tr. into next sp., 1 tr. into each of next 4 tr., 2 ch., miss 2 tr., 1 tr. into next tr., 2 tr. into next sp., 1 tr. into each of next 4 tr.; rep. from * ending with 1 tr. into next tr., 1 tr. into 3rd of 3 ch.; turn.

5th row: 3 ch., miss first tr., 1 tr. into each of next 2 tr., * 2 ch., miss 2 tr., 1 tr. into each of next 4 tr., 2 tr. into next sp., 1 tr. into next tr., 2 ch., miss 2 tr., 1 tr. into each of next 7 tr., 2 ch., miss 2 tr., 1 tr. into next tr., 2 tr. into next sp., 1 tr. into each of next 4 tr., 2 ch., miss 2 tr., 1 tr. into next tr.; rep. from * ending with 1 tr. into next tr., 1 tr. into 3rd of 3 ch.; turn.

6th row: 3 ch., miss first tr., 1 tr. into each of next 2 tr., * 2 tr. into next sp., 1 tr. into next tr., 2 ch., miss 2 tr., 1 tr. into each of next 4 tr., 2 tr. into next sp., 1 tr. into next tr., 2 ch., miss 2 tr., 1 tr. into next tr., 2 ch., miss 2 tr., 1 tr. into next tr., 2 tr. into next sp., 1 tr. into each of next 4 tr., 2 ch., miss 2 tr., 1 tr., into next tr., 2 tr. into next sp., 1 tr. into next tr.; rep. from * ending with 1 tr. into next tr., 1 tr. into 3rd of 3 ch.; turn.

7th row: 3 ch., miss first tr., 1 tr. into each of next 2 tr., * 1 tr. into each of next 3 tr., 2 ch., 1 tr. into each of next 7 tr., 2 ch., 1 tr. into next tr., 2 ch., 1 tr. into each of next 7 tr., 2 ch., 1 tr. into each of next 4 tr.; rep. from * ending with 1 tr. into next tr., 1 tr. into 3rd of 3 ch.; turn.

8th row: 3 ch., miss first tr., 1 tr. into each of next 2 tr., * 2 ch., miss 2 tr., 1 tr. into next tr., 2 tr. into next sp., 1 tr. into each of next 4 tr., 2 ch., miss 2 tr., 1 tr. into next tr., 2 tr. into next sp., 1 tr. into next tr., 2 tr. into next sp., 1 tr. into next tr., 2 ch., miss 2 tr., 1 tr. into each of next 4 tr., 2 tr. into next sp., 1 tr. into next tr., 2 ch., miss 2 tr., 1 tr. into next tr.; rep. from * ending with 1 tr. into next tr., 1 tr. into 3rd of 3 ch.; turn.

9th row: 3 ch., miss first tr., 1 tr. into each of next 2 tr.,

* 2 tr. into next sp., 1 tr. into each of next 4 tr., 2 ch., miss 2 tr., 1 tr. into next tr., 2 tr. into next sp., 1 tr. into each of next 7 tr., 2 tr. into next sp., 1 tr. into next tr., 2 ch., miss 2 tr., 1 tr. into each of next 4 tr., 2 tr. into next sp., 1 tr. into next tr.; rep. from * ending with 1 tr. into next tr., 1 tr. into 3rd of 3 ch.; turn.

10th row: 3 ch., miss first tr., 1 tr. into each of next 2 tr., * 1 tr. into each of next 3 tr., 2 ch., miss 2 tr., 1 tr. into next tr., 2 ch., miss 2 tr., 1 tr. into each of next 4 tr., 2 ch., miss 2 tr., 1 tr. into next tr., 2 ch., miss 2 tr., 1 tr. into each of next 4 tr., 2 ch., miss 2 tr., 1 tr. into next tr., 2 ch., miss 2 tr., 1 tr. into each of next 4 tr.; rep. from * ending with 1 tr. into next tr., 1 tr. into 3rd of 3 ch.; turn.

11th row: as 8th row; turn.

Rep. 2nd to 11th rows 5 times (when repeating 2nd row 2 ch. will be worked over 2 ch. not over 2 tr.); turn.

Last row: 3 ch., miss first tr., 1 tr. into each of next 2 tr., * 2 tr. into next sp., 1 tr. into each of next 7 tr., 2 tr. into next sp., 1 tr. into each of next 7 tr., 2 tr. into next sp., 1 tr. into next tr.; rep. from * ending with 1 tr. into next tr., 1 tr. into 3rd of 3 ch.; turn. Do not fasten off.

EDGING

This is worked all round centre.

1st round: with No. 3.00 hook, work 3 ch., 3 tr. into first tr. (to form corner), then make 183 tr. evenly along first edge, * 4 tr. into next corner, 183 tr. along next edge; rep. from * all round, s.s. into 3rd of 3 ch.

2nd round: 4 ch., miss first tr., * miss 1 tr., 1 tr. into next tr., 1 ch.; rep. from * all round making 4 tr. into centre sp. at each of the 4 corners, s.s. into 3rd of 3 ch.

3rd round: 3 ch., miss first sp., * 1 tr. into next sp., 1 tr. into next tr.; rep. from * all round making 4 tr. into centre sp. at each of the 4 corners, s.s. into 3rd of 3 ch.

4th round: 3 ch., miss first tr., then work 1 tr. into each tr. all round making 4 tr. into centre sp. in each of the 4 corners, s.s. into 3rd of 3 ch.

Rep. 2nd to 4th edging rounds 3 times.

Fasten off.

Carrying cape

MATERIALS

9 oz. Sirdar 4-ply Fontein Crêpe (see note on wools and yarns, page 22); crochet hooks International Standard Sizes 3.00, 3.50, 4.00 and 4.50 (see page 9); 2 yd. narrow ribbon; 1 yd. ¾-in. lace.

MEASUREMENTS

Length from neck 20½ in.; width round lower edge 44 in.

TENSION

4 tr. and 2 rows to 1 in. with No. 4.50 hook; 4½ tr. and 3 rows to 1 in. with No. 4.00 hook; 5 tr. and 2½ rows to 1 in. with No. 3.50 hook; and 5½ tr. and 2½ rows to 1 in. with No. 3.00 hook (see note on tension, page 14).

The cape has a pretty lace-edged hood and a ribbon tie.

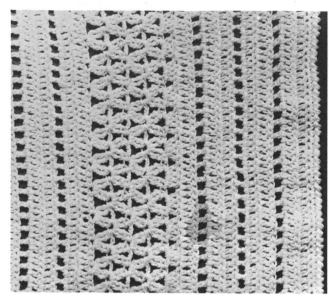

Close-up of stitch pattern.

ABBREVIATIONS

See page 20.

Cluster (cl.): y.o.h. twice, insert hook in next st., y.o.h. and draw thr., (y.o.h., draw thr. 2 loops) twice: 2 loops left on hook; y.o.h. twice, insert hook into same st., y.o.h. and draw thr., (y.o.h., draw thr. 2 loops) twice, y.o.h., draw thr. 3 loops. *Group* (gr.): 1 cl., 3 ch., 1 cl. For first row 1 cl. made into first st., miss 3 sts., 1 gr. into next st. In 2nd and 3rd rows groups are worked on the centre of 2 clusters.

MAIN SECTION

Begin at neck edge of cape and work downwards. With No. 3.00 hook make 97 ch.

1st row: 1 d.c. into 2nd ch. from hook, 1 d.c. into each ch. to end: 96 d.c.; 4 ch., turn.

Change to No. 3.50 hook.

2nd row: miss first st., * 1 tr. into next st., 1 ch., miss 1 st., rep. from * to end, 1 tr. into turning ch.: 48 sps.; 3 ch., turn.

3rd row: 1 tr. in first tr., * 2 tr. into next sp., 1 tr. into next tr., 1 tr. into next sp., 1 tr. into next tr., rep. from * to end: 120 tr.; 4 ch., turn.

4th row: 1 tr. into first st., * miss 1 st., (1 tr., 1 ch., 1 tr.) into next st., rep. from * to last 2 sts., miss 1 st., 1 tr. into turning ch.: 181 tr.; 2 ch., turn.

5th row: 1 h.tr. into each st. and sp. to end, 1 h.tr. into turning ch., 4 ch., turn.

6th row (lace pattern): 1 gr. into 3rd st., * miss 3 sts., 1 gr. into next st., rep. from * 43 times, 1 d.tr. in last st., 4 ch., turn.

7th row: 1 cl. in first st., * miss 3 ch., 1 gr. into next st., rep. from * 43 times, miss 3 ch., 1 cl. into next st., 1 ch., 1 d.tr. in last st., 4 ch., turn.

8th row: as 6th row working grs. on centre of two cl.: 45 grs.; 3 ch., turn.

9th row: 1 tr. into first st., * 3 tr. into 3-ch. sp., 1 tr. in cl., miss 1 cl., rep. from * to last cl., 1 tr. into last cl., 1 tr. into

turning ch.: 182 tr.; 3 ch., turn.

10th and 11th rows: 183 tr. in each row turning with 4 ch.

12th row: work 92 sps., 3 ch.; turn.

Change to No. 4.00 hook.

13th to 15th rows: 183 tr. in each row turning with 4 ch.

16th to 19th rows: work lace pattern as 6th and 7th rows twice: 46 grs.

20th row: work 185 tr. as in 9th row.

21st row: 185 tr., 4 ch.; turn.

22nd row: work 93 sps., 3 ch.; turn.

Work 2 rows of 185 tr. and 1 row of 93 sps. then a further 2 rows of 185 tr. turning with 4 ch.

28th to 31st rows: work 4 rows of lace pattern as 6th and 7th rows twice.

Change to No. 4.50 hook.

32nd to 42nd rows: work 2 rows tr. and 1 row sps. alternately ending with 2 tr. If a longer cape is required work the extra rows here. Fasten off.

BONNET

With No. 3.00 hook make 87 ch.

1st row: starting in the 2nd ch. from hook work 86 d.c., 3 ch., turn.

2nd row: 86 tr., 4 ch., turn.

3rd row: 43 sps., 3 ch., turn.

4th row: as 2nd row, 1 ch., turn.

5th row: as first row.

6th to 8th rows: work lace pattern: 21 grs.; 3 ch., turn.

Change to No. 3.50 hook.

9th and 10th rows: 86 tr., 3 ch., turn.

11th row: work 43 sps., 3 ch., turn.

12th and 13th rows: work 86 tr.

Change to No. 3.00 hook.

14th row: 86 tr., break yarn; turn.

Rejoin yarn to 32nd tr., 4 ch., miss 2 tr., 1 cl. into next st., miss 3 tr., work 4 more grs., miss 2 tr., 1 d.tr. into next st., 4 ch., turn.

Work 3 more lace pattern rows then work 2 rows tr., dec. 1 st. by leaving last st. of tr. on hook, work next tr. to last st., y.o.h. and draw thr. all 3 loops at each end of 2nd row: 19 tr., 4 ch., turn.

Next row: work 9 sps., 3 ch., turn.

Work 2 rows of tr., dec. 1 st. at each end of 2nd row: 17 tr.; 4 ch., turn.

Next row: 8 sps.

Work 2 rows of 15 tr. Fasten off.

TO COMPLETE

Press pieces lightly on the wrong side with a warm iron and damp cloth. Join side of bonnet to centre back. Sew neck edge to cape, leaving 7 sts. free each side of fronts. With right side facing work 1 row d.c. all round outer edge of cape and bonnet, working 3 d.c. into each corner on turning. Work back 1 row of reversed d.c. (d.c. worked from left to right) using No. 3.00 hook.

Thread ribbon through neck holes and round face of bonnet. Sew lace to first row of tr. round face of bonnet.

Blue and white pram set

(photographed in colour on page 36)

MATERIALS

10 oz. of Twilley's Cortina Super crochet wool in main shade and 2 oz. in contrast (see note on wools and yarns, page 22); one crochet hook International Standard Size 3.00 (see page 9); 4 small buttons; 2 yd. narrow ribbon.

MEASUREMENTS

Jacket: to fit chest size 19 (20, 21) in.; length from shoulder 10½ (11, 11½) in.; sleeve seam 5½ (6, 6½) in.
Bonnet: length of face edge 12 (13, 14) in.
Scarf: 6 in. by 24 in.
Bootees: length of foot 3½ (4, 4½) in.

TENSION

5 sts. and 6 rows to 1 in. over d.c. (see note on tension, page 14).

ABBREVIATIONS

See page 20; M., main shade; C., contrast shade.

JACKET

BACK

With M. commence with 81 (87, 93) ch. to measure 12½ (13½, 14½) in.

Foundation row: 1 tr. into 3rd ch. from hook, * miss 2 ch., 1 d.c. into next ch., miss 2 ch., 4 tr. into next ch.; rep. from * to within last 6 sts., miss 2 ch., 1 d.c. into next ch., miss 2 ch., 2 tr. into last ch. Fasten off; turn: 12 (13, 14) tr. gr. altogether.

1st patt. row: with C. attach yarn to first tr., 1 d.c. into same place, * 4 tr. into next d.c., 1 d.c. into centre sp. of next 4 tr. gr.; rep. from * working last d.c. of last rep. into 3rd of 3 ch. Fasten off; turn.

2nd patt. row: with M., attach yarn to first d.c., 3 ch., 1 tr. into same place as join, * 1 d.c. into next 4 tr. gr., 4 tr. into next d.c.; rep. from *, 1 d.c. into next 4 tr. gr., 2 tr. into last d.c. Fasten off; turn. Rep. last 2 rows 3 times, omitting last fasten off, then cont. working in patt. but using M. only until work measures 7 in. from beg.

Shape Armhole. 1st row: 1 s.s. into each of first 3 sts., 1 d.c. into each of next 6 sts., * miss next st., 1 d.c. into each of next 4 sts.; rep. from * to within last 6 sts., 1 d.c. into each of next 2 sts.; turn.

2nd row: 1 d.c. into first d.c., 1 d.c. into each d.c. to end, turn.

3rd row: 1 s.s. into first st., 1 d.c. into each st. to within last st.; turn. Rep. last 2 rows 14 (15, 17) times.
For size 20 only: work 2nd row once more.
For all sizes: fasten off.

RIGHT FRONT

With M., commence with 39 (39, 45) ch. to measure 6½ (6½, 7½) in., work as for Back until armhole shaping is reached.
Shape Armhole. 1st row: 1 s.s. into each of first 3 sts., 1 d.c. into each of next 6 sts., * miss next st., 1 d.c. into each of next 4 sts.; rep. from * to within last 5 sts., 1 d.c. into each st. to end; turn.
2nd row: 1 d.c. into first d.c., 1 d.c. into each d.c. to end; turn.
3rd row: 1 s.s. into first d.c., 1 d.c. into each d.c. to end; turn.
Rep. last 2 rows 11 (12, 13) times.
Shape Neck. 1st row: 1 s.s. into each of first 4 sts., 1 d.c. into each d.c. to end; turn.
2nd row: as 3rd row of Back armhole shaping; turn.
3rd row: as 2nd row of Right Front armhole shaping; turn.
For size 20 only: work 3rd row once. **For size 21 only:** work 2nd and 3rd rows once each. **For all sizes:** work 3 more rows dec. at armhole edge where necessary. Fasten off.

LEFT FRONT

Work as for Right Front until armhole shaping is reached.
Shape Armhole. 1st row: 1 d.c. into each of first 9 sts., * miss next st., 1 d.c. into each of next 4 sts.; rep. from * to within last 5 sts., 1 d.c. into each of next 2 sts.; turn.
2nd row: as 2nd row of Right Front armhole shaping.
3rd row: 1 d.c. into first d.c., 1 d.c. into each d.c. to within last d.c.; turn.
Rep. last 2 rows 11 (12, 13) times.
Shape Neck. 1st row: 1 d.c. into first d.c., 1 d.c. into each d.c. to within last 4 sts.; turn.
2nd row: as for 3rd row of Back armhole shaping; turn.
3rd row: as for 2nd row of Left Front armhole shaping; turn.
For size 20 only: work 3rd row once. **For size 21 only:** work 2nd and 3rd rows once. **For all sizes:** work 3 rows dec. at armhole edge where necessary. Fasten off.

SLEEVES (make 2 alike)

With M., commence with 51 (57, 63) ch. to measure 8 (9, 10) in. Work in patt. as for Back until work measures 5½ (6, 6½) in. from beg.
Shape Sleeves. Work as for Back armhole shaping. Fasten off.

TO COMPLETE

Join raglan seams, join side and sleeve seams.
Edging
1st row: with right side facing and M, attach yarn to corner of Right Front, then work d.c. evenly up front, 3 d.c. into corner, d.c. evenly round neck, 3 d.c. into corner, 1 d.c. into each d.c. down 2nd front; turn.
For size 20 only. 2nd row: 1 d.c. into first d.c., * 1 d.c. into each d.c. until 2nd d.c. at corner is reached, 3 d.c. into next d.c.; rep. from * once, 1 d.c. into each d.c. to end; turn. Rep. last row once.
For all sizes. 1st buttonhole row: 1 d.c. into each d.c. to within 33 d.c. before first corner, * 3 ch., miss 3 d.c., 1 d.c. into each of next 7 d.c.; rep. from *, 3 ch., miss 3 d.c., 3 d.c. into centre d.c. at corner, complete as 2nd row; turn.
2nd buttonhole row: 1 d.c. into first d.c., 1 d.c. into each d.c., working 3 d.c. into centre d.c. at each corner and 3 d.c. into each buttonhole; turn.
Last row: as 2nd row. Fasten off.
Sew buttons to correspond with buttonholes.

SCARF

With M., commence with 45 ch. to measure 7 in. Work as for Jacket Back until work measures 22¾ in., ending with 2nd patt. row. Using C. and M. alternately work first and 2nd patt. rows of Jacket 4 times. Fasten off.

BOOTEES (make 2 alike)

With M., commence with 27 (29, 31) ch. to measure 5½ (5¾, 6) in.
Foundation row: 2 d.c. into 2nd ch. from hook, 1 d.c. into each of next 10 (11, 12) ch., 2 d.c. into each of next 2 ch., 1 d.c. into each of next 10 (11, 12) ch., 2 d.c. into next ch., 1 d.c. into last ch.; turn.
1st row: 1 d.c. into first d.c., 2 d.c. into next d.c., 1 d.c. into each d.c. until 2nd d.c. of first 2 d.c. gr. is reached, 2 d.c. into each of next 2 d.c., 1 d.c. into each d.c. to within last 2 d.c., 2 d.c. into next d.c., 1 d.c. into next d.c.; turn.
Rep. last row 1 (2, 3) times more then work 1 d.c. into first d.c., 1 d.c. into each d.c. to end; turn—until work measures 1½ (1¾, 2) in. from beg.
Shape Foot. 1st row: 1 s.s. into each of first 2 sts., patt. to within last 2 sts.; turn.
2nd row: as first row.
3rd row: 1 s.s. into each of first 2 (3, 4) sts., patt. to within last 2 (3, 4) sts.; turn.
4th row: 4 ch., miss 2 d.c., * 1 tr. into next d.c., 1 ch., miss next d.c.; rep. from * 1 tr. into last d.c. Fasten off; turn: 12 (14, 16) sps.
5th row: with C. attach yarn to first tr., 1 d.c. into same place, * 4 tr. gr. into next tr., 1 d.c. into next tr.; rep. from * making tr. of last rep. into 3rd of 3 ch. Fasten off; turn.
Work patt. rows of Jacket until work measures 2 (2, 2½) in. from beg. of 5th row ending with M. Fasten off.

TO COMPLETE

Join seams and thread ½ yd. ribbon through sps. on each bootee.

Ribbon-trimmed and lacy-patterned—instructions for this matinee jacket are on page 34.

BONNET

Work exactly as for Jacket Back until work measures 6 (6½, 7) in. from beg. Fasten off.

TO COMPLETE

Fold work in half and sew a 3-in. seam along edges opp fold, on M. colour section only. Gather up open edges between seamed edge and fold, and draw tight (this forms top of bonnet). Make a pompon in C. and M. (follow instructions on page 69, making card circle 2 in.) and attach to gathers. Cut rem. ribbon in half, sew one half to each corner to tie under chin.

Ribbon-trimmed matinee jacket

(photographed in black and white on page 33)

MATERIALS

3 oz. of Patons Cameo Crêpe (see note on wools and yarns, page 21); one crochet hook International Standard Size 3.00 (3.50) (see page 9); 2 yd. narrow ribbon.

MEASUREMENTS

To fit first baby size (second baby size).

TENSION

12 tr. to 2 in. with No. 3.00 hook; 11 tr. to 2 in. with No. 3.50 hook (see note on tension, page 14).

ABBREVIATIONS

See page 20.

BACK AND FRONT (worked tog.)

Yoke. Starting at neck, made 51 ch. loosely.

1st row: 1 d.c. in 3rd ch., 1 d.c. in each ch. to end: 50 d.c.

2nd row: 3 ch. for first tr., * 1 ch., miss 1 d.c., 1 sh. in next d.c., 1 ch., miss 1 d.c., 1 tr. in next d.c., rep. from * 11 times.

3rd row: 3 ch., inc. by working into first tr., * 1 ch., 1 sh. in ch. sp. of sh., 1 ch., inc. by working 2 tr. in next tr., rep. from * 11 times, working last 2 tr. in top of 3 ch. at end.

4th row: 3 ch., 1 tr. in next tr., * 1 ch., sh. in sh., 1 ch., inc. in next tr., 1 tr. in next tr., rep. from * 10 times, 1 ch., sh. in sh., 1 ch., 2 tr. in ch.

5th row: 3 ch., 1 tr. in first tr., 1 tr. in next tr., * 1 ch., sh. in sh., 1 ch., 1 tr., inc. 2 by working 3 tr. in next tr., 1 tr., rep. from * 10 times, 1 ch., sh. in sh., 1 ch., 1 tr. in next tr., 2 tr. in ch.

6th row: 3 ch., 2 tr., * 1 ch., sh. in sh., 1 ch., 5 tr., rep. from * 10 times, 1 ch., sh. in sh., 3 tr.

7th row: 3 ch., 1 tr. in first tr., 2 tr., * 1 ch., sh. in sh., 1 ch., 2 tr., inc. 2, 2 tr., rep. from * 10 times, 1 ch., sh. in sh., 2 tr., inc. 1.

Cont. in this way for 6 more rows, inc. 2 at centre of tr. group on each alt. row and inc. 1 each end of alt. rows.

Main Part. 1st row: 3 ch., 6 tr., 1 ch., sh. in sh., 1 ch., 13 tr., * 1 ch., 1 tr. in next sh., now work 1 tr. inserting hook in same sh. and in 3rd sh. along row to draw them together, 1 ch., 2 tr. in sh. just worked into (missed sts. are for sleeve) *, (1 ch., 13 tr., 1 ch., sh. in sh.) twice, 1 ch., 13 tr., rep. from * to * once, 1 ch., 13 tr., 1 ch., sh. in sh., 1 ch., 7 tr.

Cont. in patt. on these sts. for 13 more rows, on first and every 4th row inc. 2 as before in centre of tr. groups and inc. 1 at each end.

Next (edging) row: 3 ch., 1 tr., 1 ch., 2 tr. in first tr., * (1 ch., miss 3 tr., 1 sh. in next tr.) twice, 1 ch., sh. in sh., 1 ch., miss 2 tr. of tr. group, sh. in next tr., (1 ch., miss 3 tr., sh. in next tr.) twice; rep. from * to end of lower edge. Cont. up right front thus: 1 ch., sh. in end of 2nd row of tr., (1 ch., miss 1 row, sh. in next row) 12 times. Cont. round neck thus: 1 ch., 1 tr. in first foundation ch., (1 ch., sh. in d.c. at base of sh., 1 ch., 1 tr. in d.c. at base of tr.) 12 times (last tr. will be into end ch.). Cont. down left front thus: 1 ch., sh. in first row of tr., (1 ch., miss 1 row, sh. in next row) 12 times, 1 ch., join to top of 3 ch. and fasten off.

SLEEVES (make 2 alike)

1st row: with wrong side of last row of yoke facing, join to first of 13-tr. group at underarm, 3 ch. for first tr., patt. without inc. as far as last tr. of 3rd 13-tr. group, 1 ch., 2 tr. in sh. already worked into in first row of main part, 2 tr. in next sh. already worked into, thus completing a sh., 1 ch., join to top of 3 ch.; turn.

2nd row: 4 ch., sh. in sh., 1 ch., patt. to end: join to 3rd of 4 ch.; turn.

Cont. in patt. on these sts. without inc. for 10 more rows; turn.

EDGING

S.s. along to 3rd tr. of group, 3 ch., (1 tr., 1 ch., 2 tr.) all in 3rd tr., * (1 ch., miss 3 tr., sh. in next tr.) twice, 1 ch., sh. in sh., 1 ch., miss 2 tr., sh. in next tr., rep. from * twice,

continued on page 39

Matching dress, coat and hat outfit—instructions on page 48.

Above: blue and white pram set (instructions on page 31).

Opposite: turquoise two-piece bolero and skirt suit (instructions on page 64).

The dainty matinee jacket has a picot trimming in pink round lower edge.

omitting last sh. in last rep., 1 ch., join and fasten off.

TO COMPLETE
Press on wrong side. Cut ribbon into 1-yd. and two ½-yd. lengths. Thread long ribbon through holes at neck, over tr. and under sh., and tie in bow at front; thread a short length of ribbon through each wrist edging, draw up and tie in bow at top of sleeve edge.

Pink-edged matinee jacket

MATERIALS
6 balls of Robin Bri-Nylon Double Knitting in white and oddment of similar yarn in pink (see note on wools and yarns, page 22); crochet hooks International Standard Sizes 5.00, 4.50, 4.00 and 3.00 (see page 9); 1 yd. pink ribbon ¼ in. wide.

MEASUREMENTS
To fit chest size 18 in.; length from shoulder 9½ in.; length of sleeve 5½ in.

TENSION
5½ tr. and 3 rows to 1 in. (see note on tension, page 14).

ABBREVIATIONS
See page 20; W., white; P., pink.

SKIRT (worked in one piece from top)
With No. 4.00 hook and W., commence with 115 ch. worked loosely.
Foundation row (right side): into 3rd ch. from hook, work 2 tr., 1 ch. and 2 tr., * miss 3 ch., 2 tr., 1 ch. and 2 tr. into next ch.: gr. made; rep. from * to end, 3 ch.; turn: 29 tr.gr.
1st row: 2 tr., 1 ch. and 2 tr. into ch.sp. in centre of each tr.gr. of previous row, ending with 1 tr. into last tr. of previous row, 3 ch.; turn.
2nd row: 2 tr., 1 ch. and 2 tr. into ch.sp. in centre of each tr.gr. of previous row ending with 1 tr. into top of turning ch., 3 ch.; turn.
The last row forms the skirt patt. Change to No. 4.50 hook and work 4 more rows in patt.
Next row: change to No. 5.00 hook and work as 2nd row, but working 3 tr., 1 ch. and 3 tr. into each ch.sp. Cont. in this way for 3 more rows.
Next row: as 2nd row but working 4 tr., 1 ch. and 4 tr. into each ch.sp.
Cont. working 4 tr., 1 ch. and 4 tr. into each ch.sp. until skirt measures 6 in. from beg.
Fasten off.
Press skirt lightly on wrong side, using a warm iron over a damp cloth. Ch. edge at top should measure 20 in.

RIGHT FRONT
With No. 4.00 hook and W. and right side of work facing, rejoin yarn to top of ch. edge.
1st row: * 1 tr. into first small hole (made when 2 tr., 1 ch. and 2 tr. were worked into 1 ch. on foundation row), 3 tr. into next 3-ch. sp.; rep. from * 4 times, 3 ch.; turn: 20 tr.
Next row: ** keeping armhole edge straight, work in tr. to last 2 tr., miss next tr., 1 tr. into last tr.: 1 dec. Working in tr., dec. 1 st. at front edge only on every row until 11 tr. rem. and ending at front edge, 3 ch.; turn.
Shape Shoulder. Next row: 1 tr. into first tr., 1 tr. into next 5 tr., s.s. over last 5 tr.; fasten off.

LEFT FRONT
With No. 4.00 hook and W. and right side of work facing, rejoin yarn to top of ch. edge at the fifth 3-ch. sp. from centre front.
1st row: * 3 tr. into 3-ch. sp., 1 tr. into small hole; rep. from * to end: 20 tr.
Now work to match Right Front from ** reversing shapings.

BACK
With No. 4.00 hook and W. and right side of work facing, rejoin yarn to top of ch. edge of Skirt at 5th small hole from right armhole edge.
1st row: * 1 tr. into small hole, 3 tr. into 3-ch.sp.; rep. from * 9 times, 1 tr. into next small hole, 3 ch.; turn: 41 tr.
Work 10 rows straight on these 41 tr. but do not work turning ch. at end of last row
Shape Shoulder. Next row: s.s. over first 5 tr., work in tr. to last 5 tr., s.s. to end; fasten off.

SLEEVES (make 2 alike)
With No. 4.00 hook and W., commence with 30 ch.
Foundation row (right side): 1 tr. into 3rd ch. from hook, 1 tr. into each ch. to end, 3 ch.; turn: 28 tr. Work 2 more rows in tr.
Cont. in tr. inc. (by working 2 tr. into 1 tr.) at each end of the next and the following alt. row: 32 tr. Now inc. as before at each end of every following 4th row until there are 38 tr.
Work 4 rows straight on these 38 tr. Fasten off.

TO COMPLETE

Press work lightly on wrong side using a warm iron over a damp cloth. Backstitch shoulder and sleeve seams, omitting the last 4 rows at top of sleeves. Set in sleeves placing centre of sleeve top to shoulder seam, and the 4 rows open at sleeve top to armhole shaping, joining with backstitch. Press seams, keeping front edges straight and allowing fullness to fall to sides, giving flared effect.

Edging. With No. 3.00 hook and P. and right side of work facing, rejoin yarn to first tr. of gr. at lower edge of Left Front, s.s. into each tr. and 1-ch. sp., work 4 ch., s.s. to first of 4 ch., 1 d.c. into same sp.: p. made. Cont. in this way all round lower edge; fasten off. With W., rejoin yarn to lower edge of Right Front and work 1 row of d.c. evenly up Right Front, across Back neck and down Left Front; fasten off.

Thread ribbon through holes along ch. edge between skirt and top and sew ribbon in place under arms.

Cotton coat

MATERIALS

7 (8) oz. of Twilley's Lyscordet (see note on wools and yarns, page 22); one crochet hook International Standard Size 2.00 (see page 9); three ⅜-in. buttons.

MEASUREMENTS

To fit chest size 18 (20) in.; length from shoulder 14 in.; sleeve seam 4½ (5½) in.

TENSION

7. d.c. to 1 in. (see note on tension, page 14).

ABBREVIATIONS

See page 20.

YOKE

Commence with 82 (90) ch. tightly to measure 10 (11) in.
Foundation row: 1 d.c. into 2nd ch. from hook, 1 d.c. into each of next 17 (19) ch., 2 d.c. into next ch., 1 d.c. into each of next 3 ch., 2 d.c. into next ch., 1 d.c. into each of next 35 (39) ch., 2 d.c. into next ch., 1 d.c. into each of next 3 ch., 2 d.c. into next ch., 1 d.c. into each of next 18 (20) ch.; turn.
1st row: 1 d.c. into first d.c., * 1 d.c. into each d.c. until until first d.c. of next 2-d.c. gr. is reached, 2 d.c. into next d.c.; rep. from * ending with 1 d.c. into each d.c. to end; turn.
Rep. last row 15 (17) times: 149 (165) d.c. on last row.

RIGHT FRONT

1st row: 3 ch., 2 tr. into first d.c., * 3 ch., 1 s.s. into top of last tr.: a p. made, miss 2 d.c., 6 tr. into next d.c.: a sh. made; rep. from * 7 (8) times, 3 ch., 1 s.s. into top of last tr., miss 2 d.c., 3 tr. into next d.c.; turn.
Patt. row: 3 ch., 2 tr. into first tr., * 3 ch., 1 s.s. into top of last tr., a 6-tr. sh. into centre sp. of next sh.; rep. from * ending with 3 ch., 1 s.s. into top of last tr., 3 tr. into 3rd of 3 ch.; turn.
Rep. last row until work measures 14 in. from commencing ch. (or length required). Fasten off.

BACK

Miss next 19 (20) d.c. for armhole and attach yarn to next d.c.
1st row: as first row of Right Front but work rep. until 17 (19) 6-tr. shs. have been made, and as first row of Right Front; turn.
Complete as Right Front. Fasten off.

LEFT FRONT

Miss next 19 (21) d.c. for armhole and attach yarn to next d.c. Work as Right Front to end. Fasten off.

SLEEVES (make 2 alike)

With right side facing attach yarn to 5th row of Back for right sleeve, 3 ch., 2 tr. into same place, then work patt. evenly up 5 rows of Back, along Yoke and down 5 rows of Right Front until seven 6-tr. shs. have been formed, ending with 3 ch., 1 s.s. into top of last tr., 3 tr. into same place as join; turn.
Work in patt. until sleeve measures 4 (5) in. from beg.
Next row: 3 ch., 2 tr. into first tr., a 6-tr. sh. into each sh., 3 tr. into 3rd of 3 ch.; turn.
Next row: 1 d.c. into each of first 2 tr., * miss next tr., 1 d.c. into each of next 2 tr.; rep. from * to end; turn.
Next row: 1 d.c. into first d.c., * 3 ch., 1 s.s. into top of first d.c. (a p. made), 1 d.c. into each of next 2 d.c.; rep. from * to end; fasten off.
Work left sleeve as right sleeve but attach yarn to 5th row of Left Front.

TO COMPLETE

Press work lightly on the wrong side with a warm iron over a damp cloth. Join side and sleeve seams. Press seams.
Edging. 1st row: with right side facing attach yarn to lower corner of Right Front, then work d.c. up front, round neck and down Left Front, having a multiple of 2 d.c.; turn.
2nd row: as last row of sleeve but making 6 p. of 7 ch. to form 3 buttonholes down Right Front. Sew on buttons.

The yoke of the coat is worked in double crochet, the rest in shell pattern.

Chapter Three

Children's garments

Drawstring dress

MATERIALS
7 (8, 9) oz. Sirdar 4-ply Fontein Crêpe (see note on wools and yarns, page 22); one crochet hook International Standard Size 4.00 (see page 9); four $\frac{1}{2}$-in. buttons.

MEASUREMENTS
To fit chest size 22 (24, 26) in.; length from shoulder 16 (18, 20) in.

TENSION
5 d.c. and 6 rows to 1 in. (see note on tension, page 14).

ABBREVIATIONS
See page 20.

BACK
Bodice. Make 62 (68, 74) ch. to measure $12\frac{1}{2}$ ($13\frac{1}{2}$, $14\frac{1}{2}$) in.

Foundation row: 1 d.c. into 2nd ch. from hook, 1 d.c. into each ch. to end; turn.

Next row: 4 ch., miss 2 d.c., * 1 tr. into next d.c., 1 ch., miss next d.c., rep. from * ending with 1 tr. into last d.c.; turn.

Next row: 1 d.c. into first tr., * 1 d.c. into next sp., 1 d.c. into next tr., rep. from * to end making 1 d.c. at end of last rep. into 3rd of 4 ch.; turn.

Patt. row: 1 d.c. into first d.c., 1 d.c. into each d.c. to end; turn.

Rep. last row until work measures 2 ($2\frac{1}{2}$, 3) in. from beg.

Shape Armholes and Back Opening. 1st row: miss first st., 1 s.s. into each of next 4 d.c., 1 d.c. into each of next 24 (27, 30) d.c. then working into front loops only make 1 d.c. into each of next 3 d.c., marking first loop; turn.

2nd row: patt. to within last d.c.; turn.

3rd row: miss first d.c., 1 d.c. into each d.c. to end; turn. Rep. 2nd row once more. **For sizes 24 and 26 only:** rep. 3rd row once more. **For all sizes:** rep. patt. row until armhole measures 4 ($4\frac{1}{2}$, 5) in. from beg. of armhole shaping. Fasten off.

Complete Second Side. 1st row: attach yarn to marked loop, 1 d.c. into same place, 1 d.c. into each of next 2 loops, 1 d.c. into each d.c. to within last 4 d.c.; turn. Work 3rd and 2nd rows of first side of Back 1 (2, 2) times. **For size 22 only:** rep. 3rd row once more. **For all sizes:** complete as for first side. Fasten off.

Skirt. Foundation row: working along other side of commencing ch., attach yarn to first ch., 3 ch., 1 tr. into first ch., * 3 ch., miss 2 ch., 1 tr. into next ch., 3 ch., miss 2 ch., 4 tr. into next ch.; rep. from * finishing with 3 ch., miss 2 ch., 1 tr. into next ch., 3 ch., miss 2 ch., 2 tr. into last ch.; turn.

1st row: 3 ch., 1 tr. into first sp., 3 ch., 1 s.s. into last tr. formed (a p. made), 2 tr. into same sp., 2 ch., * 1 tr. into next single tr., 2 ch., 2 tr. into sp. between next 2 tr., 1 p., 4 tr. between 2nd and 3rd tr. of previous row, 1 p., 2 tr. between 3rd and 4th tr. 2 ch., rep. from * finishing with 1 tr. into next single tr., 2 ch., miss next tr., 2 tr. into last sp., 1 p.,

A cool and pretty summer dress for a toddler.

2 tr. into turning ch.; turn.

2nd row: 6 ch., miss first 4 tr., * 4 tr. into next single tr., 3 ch., 1 tr. into centre sp. of next sh., 3 ch., rep. from * finishing with 4 tr. into last single tr., 3 ch., 1 tr. into 3rd of 3 ch.; turn.

3rd row: 3 ch., miss first tr., * 2 ch., miss next tr., 2 tr. between next 2 tr., 1 p., 4 tr. between 2nd and 3rd tr. of previous row, 1 p., 2 tr. between 3rd and 4th tr., 2 ch., 1 tr. into next single tr., rep. from * to end working 1 tr. at end of last rep. into 3rd of 6 ch.; turn.

4th row: 3 ch., 1 tr. into first tr., * 3 ch., 1 tr. into centre sp. of next sh., 3 ch., 4 tr. into next single tr., rep. from * finishing with 3 ch., 1 tr. into centre sp. of last sh., 3 ch., 2 tr. into 3rd of 5 ch.; turn. Rep. last 4 rows until back measures 16 (18, 20) in. from shoulder. Fasten off.

FRONT

Bodice. Same as for Back Bodice until Armhole Shaping is reached.

Shape Armholes. 1st row: miss first st., 1 s.s. into each of next 4 sts., patt. to within last 4 sts.; turn.

2nd row: 1 s.s. into first st., patt. to within last st.; turn. Rep. last row 2 (3, 3) times, then work patt. row until armholes measure $2\frac{1}{2}$ ($2\frac{3}{4}$, 3) in. from beg.

Shape Neck. 1st row: 1 d.c. into first d.c., 1 d.c. into each of next 14 (15, 16) d.c.; turn.

Work 3rd and 2nd rows of first side of Back Armhole Shaping 3 times, then work patt. row until total number of rows from beg. of armhole is same as for Back. Fasten off.

Complete Second Side of Neck. 1st row: attach yarn to 15 (16, 17) d.c. counting from opposite edge, patt. to end; turn.

Work 2nd and 3rd rows of first side of Back Armhole Shaping once; turn.

Complete as for first side of neck. Fasten off.

Skirt. Same as for Back Skirt.

TO COMPLETE

Join side and shoulder seams.

Back Opening Edging. With right side facing attach yarn to back corner of outside edge of opening, 1 d.c. into same place as join, 5 d.c. evenly into edge, (3 ch., miss 3 rows, 6 d.c. evenly into edge) twice, 3 ch., miss 3 rows, 1 d.c. into edge. Fasten off.

Neck Edging. 1st row: with right side facing attach yarn to neck corner, 4 ch., (1 tr., 1 ch., miss 2 d.c.) 20 (22, 24) times evenly round edge, 1 tr. into 2nd corner; turn.

2nd row: 1 d.c. into first tr., * 1 d.c. into next sp., 1 d.c. into next tr., rep. from * to last tr., 1 d.c. into next sp., 1 d.c. into 3rd of 4 ch.; turn.

3rd row: 1 d.c. into first d.c., * 3 ch., 1 s.s. into last d.c. made, 1 d.c. into each of next 2 d.c.; rep. from * ending with 3 ch., 1 s.s. into last d.c. made, 1 d.c. into last d.c. Fasten off.

Armhole Edgings (both alike). With right side facing attach yarn to edge, then work d.c. evenly round, s.s. into first d.c. Fasten off.

Tie. With double thickness of yarn make a length of ch. 30 in. long and thread this through sps. at waist to tie at front. Fasten off.

Bobbles (make 2 alike). With double thickness of yarn wrap yarn round finger once to form a ring, 3 ch., 11 tr. into ring, s.s. into 3rd of 3 ch. Fasten off, leaving a long thread hanging. Draw commencing ring tight. Thread remaining yarn through the top of each tr., draw tight and fasten off. Attach a bobble to each end of tie.

Sew buttons to back opening and use spaces in back opening edging and 2nd row of neck edging as buttonholes.

Button-up dress

MATERIALS

5 (6, 7) oz. of Sirdar Talisman 4-ply (see note on wools and yarns, page 22); one crochet hook International Standard Size 4.00 (see page 9); button moulds each $\frac{5}{8}$-in. in diameter.

MEASUREMENTS

To fit chest size 22 (24, 26) in.; length from shoulder 14 (17, 20) in.

TENSION

5 d.tr. to 1 in. (see note on tension, page 14).

ABBREVIATIONS

See page 20.

FRONT AND BACK (worked in one piece)

Working from neck down, commence with 69 ch. made tightly to measure 12 in.

Foundation row: 3 d.tr. into 7th ch. from hook, * 1 ch., miss next ch., 1 d.tr. into next ch., 1 ch., miss 1 ch., 3 d.tr. into next ch.; rep. from * to within last 3 ch., ending with 1 ch., miss 1 ch., 1 d.tr. into last ch.; turn: 16 3-d.tr. grs.

The lacy dress fastens at the back with five buttons.

1st row: 5 ch., * miss next sp., 2 d.tr. into sp. between first 2 d.tr. of 3-d.tr. gr., 2 d.tr. into sp. between 2nd and 3rd d.tr. of 3-d.tr. gr., 1 ch., 1 d.tr. into next single d.tr., 1 ch.; rep. from * to end, working 1 d.tr. at end of last rep. into 4th of 5 ch.; turn: 1 d.tr. inc. in each gr.

2nd row: 5 ch., * miss next sp., into sp. between first and 2nd d.tr. of 4-d.tr. gr. work 1 d.tr., 3 ch., 1 s.s. into last d.tr.: a p. made, 1 d.tr., into sp. between 2nd and 3rd d.tr. of 4-d.tr. gr. work 1 d.tr., into sp. between 3rd and 4th d.tr. of 4-d.tr. gr. work 1 d.tr., a p. and 1 d.tr., 1 ch., 1 d.tr. into next single d.tr., 1 ch.; rep. from * to end, working 1 d.tr. at end of last rep. into 4th of 5 ch.; turn: 1 d.tr. inc. in each gr.

3rd row: 4 ch., * 1 ch., miss sp., into sp. between 2nd and 3rd d.tr. work 1 d.tr., a p. and 2 d.tr., into sp. between 3rd and 4th d.tr. work 2 d.tr., a p. and 1 d.tr., 1 ch., 1 d.tr. into next single d.tr.; rep. from * to end, working 1 d.tr. at end of last rep. into 4th of 5 ch.; turn: 1 d.tr. inc. in each gr.

4th row: 4 ch., * 2 ch., miss sp., into sp. between 2nd and 3rd d.tr. work 1 d.tr., a p. and 2 d.tr., into sps. between each d.tr. until 3 d.tr. remain work 1 d.tr., into sp. after next d.tr. work 2 d.tr., a p. and 1 d.tr., 2 ch., 1 d.tr. into next single d.tr.; rep. from * to end, working 1 d.tr. at end of last rep. into 4th of 6 ch.; turn: 1 d.tr. inc. in each gr.

5th row: 4 ch., * 2 ch., miss 2 d.tr., into next d.tr. work 1 d.tr., a p. and 2 d.tr., 1 d.tr. into each d.tr. until 3 d.tr. remain, into next d.tr. work 2 d.tr., a p. and 1 d.tr., 2 ch., 1 d.tr. into next single d.tr.; rep. from * ending with 2 ch., 1 d.tr. into 4th of 6 ch.; turn. Rep. last row an odd number of times until work measures 5½ (6, 6½) in.; turn.

Divide for Armholes. 1st row: 4 ch., work rep. of 4th row twice, * * 2 ch., miss 2 d.tr., into sp. after 2nd d.tr. work 1 d.tr., a p. and 2 d.tr., into each sp. between 2 d.tr. to centre of gr. work 1 d.tr., miss 2 whole grs. for armholes, 1 d.tr.

at centre of next gr., into each sp. between 2 d.tr. work 1 d.tr. until 3 d.tr. remain, into sp. after next d.tr. work 2 d.tr., a p. and 1 d.tr. * *; work rep. of 4th row 4 times, rep. from * * to * * once, then work rep. and ending of 4th row; turn. * * * **2nd row:** as 5th row.

Rep. last row 3 times, then 4th row once; rep. from * * * until dress measures 13½ (16½, 19½) in. from beg. Fasten off.

SLEEVES (make 2 alike)

1st row: attach yarn to a single d.tr., work as 5th row to end, but working 1 d.tr. at end of last rep. into same place as join; turn. * * * * Rep. 2nd row of armholes 3 times, then 4th row once. Rep. from * * * * until sleeve measures 4½ (5, 5½) in. from beg. Fasten off.

TO COMPLETE

Join sleeve seams.

Edging. 1st round: with right side facing attach yarn to lower edge then work d.c. all round garment, making 3 d.c. into each of the corners, 1 d.c. into first d.c.

2nd round: make 1 d.c. into each d.c. and 3 d.c. at centre d.c. at each corner, 1 d.c. into first d.c.

3rd round: * 3 ch., 1 s.s. into first d.c. formed, 1 d.c. into each of next 3 d.c.; rep. from * all round omitting 1 d.c. at end of last rep., s.s. into first d.c.; fasten off.

Buttons. Wind yarn round finger to form a ring.

1st round: 7 d.c. into ring; draw commencing ring tight.

Next round: working in a continuous round, make * 2 d.c. into next d.c., 1 d.c. into next d.c.; rep. from * until work is large enough to cover button mould. Fasten off. Attach cover to mould. Make 4 more buttons in same way. Sew buttons down left back and use spaces in patt. on right back as buttonholes.

Sleeveless cotton dress

MATERIALS

7 (8, 10, 11, 13) oz. of Twilley's Crysette (see note on wools and yarns, page 22); one crochet hook International Standard Size 3.50 (see page 9).

MEASUREMENTS

To fit chest size 22 (24, 26, 28, 30) in.; length from shoulder 14 (17, 20, 23, 26) in.

TENSION

5½ sts. to 1 in. (see note on tension, page 14).

ABBREVIATIONS

See page 20.

FRONT

Make 90 (95, 104, 109, 120) ch. to measure 16½ (18, 19, 20½, 22) in.

Foundation row: 1 tr. into 6th ch. from hook, * 1 ch., miss next ch., 1 tr. into next ch., rep. from * 16 (18, 20, 22, 25) times, 1 tr. into each of next 10 (11, 12, 13, 14) ch., then work rep. to end; turn: 18 (20, 22, 24, 26) sps. either side of centre band.

1st patt. row: 3 ch., 1 tr. into each 1-ch. sp. and tr. all along, 1 tr. into 3rd of 4 ch.; turn.

2nd patt. row: 4 ch., miss first 2 trs., * 1 tr. into next tr., 1 ch., miss next tr., rep. from * until centre band is reached, 1 tr. into each of next 10 (11, 12, 13, 14) tr., then work rep. to within last 2 sts., 1 tr. into 3rd of 3 ch.; turn.

This shift dress is easy and quick to make.

Rep. last 2 rows 1 (2, 1, 1, 1) times.

* * **Dec. row:** 3 ch., (1 tr. into next sp., 1 tr. into next tr.) 3 times, make 1 tr. into next sp. and 1 tr. into next tr., leaving last loop of each tr. on hook, yarn over hook and draw through all loops on hook (one dec. formed). patt. to within last sp. before centre band, one dec. over next sp. and tr., 1 tr. into each of next 9 (10, 11, 12, 13) tr., a dec. over next tr. and sp., patt. to within last 9 sts., a dec. over next tr. and sp., patt. to end; turn. Work 3 (3, 5, 5, 5) rows in patt.

Rep. from * * 3 (3, 4, 4, 5) times then work dec. row once more. Work in patt. until work measures 9½ (12, 14½, 17, 19½) in. from beg.

Shape Armholes. 1st row: 1 s.s. into each of first 4 sts., patt. to within last 4 sts.; turn.

2nd row: 1 s.s. into each of first 2 sts., patt. to within last 2 sts.; turn.

Rep. last row 1 (2, 2, 3, 3) times.

Work in patt. until armholes measure 4 (4½, 5, 5½, 6) in. from beg. ending with 2nd patt. row. Fasten off.

BACK

Make 90 (96, 104, 110, 120) ch. to measure 16½ (18, 19, 20½, 22) in.

Foundation row: 1 tr. into 6th ch. from hook, * 1 ch., miss next ch., 1 tr. into next ch., rep. from * to end; turn.

Work 1st patt. row of front once; turn.

2nd patt. row: 4 ch., miss first 2 tr., * 1 tr. into next tr., 1 ch., miss next tr., rep. from *, 1 tr. into 3rd of 3 ch.; turn.

Rep. last 2 rows 1 (2, 1, 1, 1) times.

* * **Dec. row:** 3 ch., (1 tr. in next sp., 1 tr. in next tr.) 3 times, a dec. over next sp. and tr., (1 tr. into next sp., 1 tr. into next tr.) 8 times, a dec. over next sp. and tr., patt. to within last 27 sts., a dec. over next tr. and sp., (1 tr. into next tr., 1 tr. into next sp.) 8 times, a dec. over next tr. and sp., patt. to end; turn.

Work 3 (3, 5, 5, 5) rows in patt.

Rep. from * * 3 (3, 4, 4, 5) times then work dec. row once more. Work in patt. until same number of rows are completed as for Front.

Shape Armholes. Work as for Front.

TO COMPLETE

Join side seams, join shoulder seams to measure 1¼ (1¼, 1½, 1½, 1¾) in. each.

Edgings (all alike). 1st round: with right side facing attach thread to edge, then work d.c. evenly round, 1 d.c. into first d.c.

2nd and 3rd rounds: working in continuous rounds make 1 d.c. into each d.c., s.s. into first d.c. of last round. Fasten off.

Matching dress, coat and hat

(photographed in colour on page 35)

MATERIALS

For dress: 13 (14, 15, 16) oz. Twilley's Cortina (see note on wools and yarns, page 22); one crochet hook International Standard Size 3.00 (see page 9); three ⅜-in. buttons.

For coat: 23 (24, 26, 27) oz. Twilley's Cortina (see note on wools and yarns, page 22); one crochet hook International Standard Size 3.00 (see page 9); four ⅜-in. ball buttons.

For hat: 3 (3, 3, 3) oz. Twilley's Cortina.

MEASUREMENTS

Dress: to fit chest size 22 (24, 26, 28) in.; length 16 (18, 20, 22) in. (adjustable); sleeve seam 1½ in. **Coat:** to fit chest size 22 (24, 26, 28) in.; length 17 (19, 21, 23) in.; sleeve seam 10 (11½, 13, 14½) in. **Hat:** to fit average size head.

TENSION

5 sts. to 1 in. over patt. (see note on tension, page 14).

ABBREVIATIONS

See page 20.

DRESS

FRONT

Make 67 (73, 79, 85) ch. loosely for lower edge of yoke.

1st row: 1 d.c. in 2nd ch. from hook, (1 d.c. in next ch.) to end; turn.

2nd row: 1 ch., 1 d.c. in each d.c. to end; turn. Rep. last row once more.

Shape Armhole. S.s. across first 6 sts., d.c. to last 6 sts.; turn.

Work 1 row straight in d.c.; turn.

Next row: s.s. across first 2 sts., d.c. to last 2 d.c.; turn.

Rep. last 2 rows once more: 46 (52, 58, 64) sts. * * * Cont. straight in d.c. until work measures 3 (3½, 4, 4½) in. from beg.

Shape Neck. Next row: 1 ch., 16 (18, 20, 22) d.c.; turn.

Work 1 row on these sts.

* * **Next row:** 1 ch., d.c. to last 2 sts.; turn.

Work 1 row straight, * * then rep. last 2 rows twice more. Fasten off.

Leave centre 14 (16, 18, 20) sts., rejoin yarn to rem. 16 (18,

The dress from the matching set has neat short sleeves and a double crochet yoke.

48

20, 22) sts. and d.c. across them.

Rep. from * * to * * 3 times then work 1 row more. Fasten off. * * * * With right side facing rejoin yarn and work across lower ch.-edge for skirt as follows: (1 d.c. in each of first 2 ch., 2 d.c. in next ch.) to last 6 (3, 0, 6) ch., 1 d.c. in each of these 6 (3, 0, 6) ch.: 86 (95, 104, 110) sts.; turn.

Next row: 1 ch., 1 d.c. in each st. to end; turn.

1st patt. row: 1 ch., 1 d.c. in first st., * (y.o.h., insert hook into next st., y.o.h., draw through loop, y.o.h., draw through 2 loops) 5 times, y.o.h., draw through 6 loops, 1 d.c. in each of next 2 sts., * rep. from * to * to last st., 1 d.c. in last st.; turn.

2nd patt. row: 1 ch., 1 d.c. in each st. to end; turn.

3rd patt. row: 1 ch., 1 d.c. in each of first 2 sts., rep. from * to * as first patt. row to end; turn.

4th patt. row: as 2nd patt. row.

5th patt. row: 1 ch., 1 d.c. in each of first 3 d.c., rep. from * to * as first patt. row, ending 1 d.c. instead of 2 d.c.; turn.

6th patt. row: as 2nd patt. row.

Cont. in patt. until work measures 16 (18, 20, 22) in. from shoulder (adjust length here if required). Fasten off.

BACK

As front to * * *.

Divide for Opening. 1 ch., 23 (26, 29, 32) d.c.; turn. Work on these sts. only until work measures 4 (4½, 5, 5½) in. from beg. Fasten off.

Complete other side of back to match. Work skirt as Front from * * * *.

SLEEVES (make 2 alike)

Make 49 (55, 61, 67) ch.

Next row: 1 d.c. in 2nd ch. from hook, 1 d.c. in each ch. to end; turn.

Next row: 1 ch., 1 d.c. in each d.c. to end; turn. Rep. last row for 1½ in.

Next row: s.s. across first 2 sts., d.c. to last 2 sts.; turn. Work 1 row straight then rep. last 2 rows 7 times more. Fasten off.

TO COMPLETE

Join shoulders. Work 4 rows d.c. around neck edge. Work 2 rows d.c. around back opening on 2nd row making three 5-ch. buttonhole loops missing 1 d.c. each time, at top and 1-in. intervals down right side of opening. Do not press. Set in sleeves. Join side and sleeve seams. Press seams only. Sew on buttons.

COAT
BACK

Start at shoulder and work downwards. Make 54 (60, 66, 72) ch.

Foundation row: 1 d.c. in 2nd ch. from hook, (1 d.c. in next ch.) to end; turn: 53 (59, 65, 71) sts.

1st patt. row: 1 ch., 1 d.c. in first st., * (y.o.h., insert hook into next st., y.o.h., draw through loop, y.o.h., draw through 2 loops) 5 times, y.o.h., draw through 6 loops, 1 d.c. in

each of next 2 d.c., * rep. from * to * to last st., 1 d.c. in last st.; turn.

2nd patt. row: 1 ch., 1 d.c. in each st. to end; turn.

3rd patt. row: 1 ch., 1 d.c. in each of first 2 d.c., rep. from * to * as first patt. row to end of row; turn.

4th patt. row: as 2nd patt. row.

5th patt. row: 1 ch., 1 d.c. in each of first 3 d.c., rep. from * to * as first patt. row, ending 1 d.c. instead of 2 d.c.

6th patt. row: as 2nd patt. row.

Cont. in patt. until work measures 3½ (4, 4½, 5) in. from beg.

Shape Armhole. Next row: 6 ch., work 1 d.c. into each of 6 ch., patt. to end; turn.

Rep. last row 3 times more, taking extra sts. into patt.

Next row: 9 ch., work 1 d.c. into each of 9 ch., patt. to end; turn.

Rep. last row once more: 21 sts. inc. at each side, 95 (101, 107, 113) sts.

Cont. straight in patt. until work measures 17 (19, 21, 23) in. from beg. (adjust length here if required). Fasten off.

RIGHT FRONT

Make 18 (21, 24, 27) ch.

Foundation row: 1 d.c. in 2nd ch. from hook, (1 d.c. in next ch.) to end. Work 3 rows in patt. as Back.

Shape Neck Edge. Next row: 6 ch., work 1 d.c. in each of 6 ch., patt. to end; turn.

Work 1 row straight, rep. last 2 rows once more then inc. row again: 18 sts. inc. at neck edge, 35 (38, 41, 44) sts. Work 4 rows straight in patt.

Next row (buttonhole row): patt. to last 9 sts., s.s. loosely across next 3 sts., patt. 6; turn.

Next row: patt. 6, 3 ch., miss 3 s.s., patt. to end; turn. Cont. in patt., making 2nd buttonhole 1¾ (2, 2¼, 2¾) in. from first buttonhole, until work measures 3½ (4, 4½, 5) in. from beg., ending at side edge.

Shape Armhole. Next row: 6 ch., work 1 d.c. in each of 6 ch., patt. to end.

Work 1 row straight then rep. last 2 rows once more.

Next row: 9 ch., work 1 d.c. in each of 9 ch., patt. to end: 21 sts. inc. at side edge, 56 (59, 62, 65) sts. Cont. in patt., making 2 more buttonholes 1¾ (2, 2¼, 2½) in. apart, until work measures 17 (19, 21, 23) in. from beg. (adjust length here if required). Fasten off.

LEFT FRONT

As Right Front, reversing shapings and omitting button-holes.

SLEEVES (make 2 alike)

Make 12 (18, 12, 18) ch.

Next row: 1 d.c. in 2nd ch. from hook, (1 d.c. in next ch.) to end. Work 2 rows in patt. as Back.

Next row: 6 ch., work 1 d.c. in each of 6 ch., patt. to end. Rep. last row 7 (7, 9, 9) times more: 59 (65, 71, 77) sts. Work 9½ (11, 12½, 14) in. straight in patt. at same time dec. 1 st. each end of every 6th row until there are 6 decs. at each side (adjust length here if required). Fasten off.

COLLAR

Make 72 (72, 78, 78) ch.

Next row: 1 d.c. in 2nd ch. from hook, (1 d.c. in next ch.) to end; turn.

Work 2½ (2¾, 3, 3¼) in. in patt. as Back.

Next row: s.s. across first 3 sts., patt. to last 3 sts; turn.

Work 1 row straight then rep. last 2 rows twice more. Fasten off.

TO COMPLETE

Borders. Work 3 rows d.c. along straight front edges of Fronts, around lower edges of Sleeves and around 3 sides of Collar, excluding ch. edge.

Do not press. Join shoulder, side and sleeve seams. Set in sleeves. Sew ch. edge of collar to neck, beg. and ending 1 in. from front edges. Press seams only. Sew on buttons.

HAT
MAIN PIECE

Make 78 (84, 90, 96) ch.

Next row: 1 d.c. in 2nd ch. from hook, (1 d.c. in next ch.) to end; turn.

Work 4¾ (5, 5¼, 5½) in. in patt. as Coat Back.

Next row: s.s. across first 27 (30, 33, 36) sts., patt. 23; turn. Work on these centre sts. only for 5 (5½, 6, 6½) in. Fasten off.

TO COMPLETE

Sew sides of extension to 27 (30, 33, 36)-st. edges. Work 3 rows d.c. all around outer edge, inc. 2 sts. at each front corner on 2nd and 3rd rows and dec. 5 sts. evenly across centre back panel in 3rd row.

Fasten off.

Boy's jacket

(photographed in black and white on page 53)

MATERIALS

7 (8, 9, 10, 11, 12) oz. Twilley's Crysette (see note on wools and yarns, page 22); crochet hooks International Standard Sizes 4.00 and 3.00 (see page 9); 5 (5, 5, 6, 6, 6) button moulds ⅝-in. in diameter.

MEASUREMENTS

To fit chest size 22 (24, 26, 28, 30, 32) in.; length from shoulder 11 (13, 15, 17, 19, 21) in.; sleeve seam 7 (9, 11, 13, 15, 17) in.

TENSION

5 sts. to 1 in. with No. 4.00 hook (see note on tension, page 14).

ABBREVIATIONS

See page 20.

BACK

With No. 4.00 hook commence with 63 (67, 73, 77, 83, 87) ch. to measure 12½ (13½, 14½, 15½, 16½, 17½) in.

Foundation row: 1 h.tr. into 5th ch. from hook, * 1 ch., miss next ch., 1 h.tr. into next ch.; rep. from * to end; turn: 30 (32, 35, 37, 40, 43) sp.

1st patt. row: 2 ch., * 1 h.tr. into next sp., 1 h.tr. into next h.tr.; rep. from * working last h.tr. of last rep. into 2nd of 3 ch.; turn.

2nd patt. row: 3 ch., miss first 2 h.tr.; * h.tr. into next h.tr., 1 ch., miss next h.tr.; rep. from * ending with 1 h.tr. into 2nd of 2 ch.; turn.

Rep. last 2 rows until work measures 6½ (8, 9½, 11, 12½, 14) in. from beg. ending with 1st patt. row.

Shape Armholes. 1st row: 1 s.s. into each of first 4 sts., patt. to within last 4 sts.; turn.

2nd row: 1 s.s. into each of first 2 sts., patt. to within last 2 sts.; turn.

Rep. last row 0 (0, 1, 1, 2, 2) times, then work patt. rows until armholes measure 4½ (5, 5½, 6, 6½, 7) in. from beg., ending with patt. row; fasten off.

LEFT FRONT

With No. 4.00 hook commence with 37 (39, 41, 43, 47, 49) ch. to measure 7¼ (7¾, 8¼, 8¾, 9¼, 9¾) in. Work as Back until armhole shaping is reached, ending with 1st patt. row.

Shape Armhole. 1st row: 1 s.s. into each of first 4 sts., patt. to end; turn.

2nd row: patt. to within last 2 sts.; turn.

For sizes 26 (28, 30, 32) only. 3rd row: 1 s.s. into each of first 2 sts., patt. to end; turn.

For sizes 30 and 32 only. Rep. 2nd row once.

For all sizes. Work in patt. until 2 (2, 2, 4, 4, 4) rows less than Back are completed, ending with 1st patt. row.

Shape Neck. 1st row: patt. to within last 12 (14, 14, 16, 14, 16) sts.; turn.

Work 3rd row of armhole shaping once, then work 1 patt. row. **For sizes 28 (30, 32) only.** Rep. last 2 rows once. **For all sizes:** Fasten off.

RIGHT FRONT

Work as Left Front until armhole shaping is reached, ending

with 1st patt. row.

Shape Armhole. 1st row: patt. to within last 4 sts.; turn.

2nd row: 1 s.s. into each of first 2 sts., patt. to end; turn.

For sizes 26 and 28 only. Work 2nd row of Left Front armhole shaping once.

For sizes 30 and 32 only. Work 2nd and 3rd rows of Left Front armhole shaping once.

For all sizes. Cont. as for Left Front until neck shaping is reached. Fasten off.

Shape Neck. 1st row: miss first 12 (14, 14, 16, 14, 16) sts., attach yarn to next st. and patt. to end; turn. Work 2nd row of Left Front armhole shaping once, then work 1 patt. row.

For sizes 28 (30, 32) only. Rep. last 2 rows once. Fasten off.

SLEEVES (make 2 alike)

With No. 4.00 hook commence with 37 (39, 41, 45, 47, 49) ch. to measure $7\frac{1}{2}$ (8, $8\frac{1}{2}$, 9, $9\frac{1}{2}$, 10) in. Work as Back until work measures 2 (2, 3, 3, 4, 4) in., ending with 1st patt. row.

Inc. row: 3 ch., 1 h.tr. into first h.tr., * 1 ch., miss next h.tr., 1 h.tr. into next h.tr.; rep. from * to within last 2 sts., 1 ch., 1 h.tr. into 2nd of 3 ch., 1 ch., 1 h.tr. into same place as last h.tr.; turn. Work in patt. until work measures 5 (6, 8, 9, 11, 12) in. from beg., ending with 1st patt. row.

Work inc. row once, then cont. in patt. until work measures 7 (9, 11, 13, 15, 17) in. from beg., ending with 1st patt. row.

Shape sleeve. 1st and 2nd rows: as 1st and 2nd rows of Back armhole shaping.

3rd row: patt. to end; turn.

4th row: as 2nd row.

Rep. last 3 rows until work measures $2\frac{1}{4}$ ($2\frac{1}{2}$, $2\frac{3}{4}$, 3, $3\frac{1}{4}$, $3\frac{1}{2}$) in. from beg. of shaping. Fasten off.

TO COMPLETE

Join side and shoulder seams; set in sleeves; join sleeve seams.

Edgings. With No. 3.00 hook and with right side facing attach thread to corner of Right Front. Work 1 row d.c. evenly up Right Front, round neck, down Left Front and along bottom edge, s.s. into first d.c.; fasten off.

Buttons. Wind yarn round finger to form a ring.

1st round: with No. 3.00 hook, 1 d.c. into ring; draw commencing ring tight.

Next rounds: working in continuous rounds, work * 2 d.c. into next d.c., 1 d.c. into next d.c.; rep. from * until work is large enough to cover button mould. Fasten off.

Attach cover to mould. Make 4 more buttons in same way. Sew buttons evenly down Right Front and use sps. between patt. on Left Front as buttonholes.

Press lightly.

This useful jacket for a little boy has crochet-trimmed buttons.

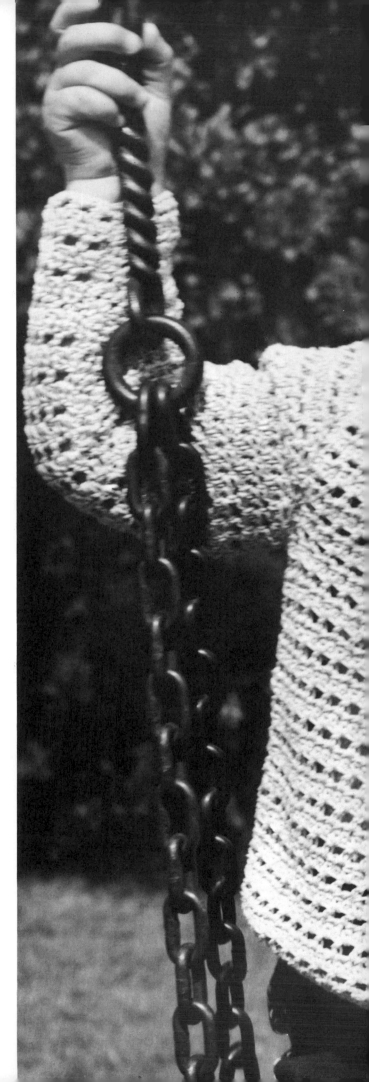

Boy's jumper and trousers

MATERIALS
3 (3, 4) balls (2-oz.) of Twilley's Stalite in white, 1 ball (2-oz.) of Twilley's Stalite in turquoise and 3 balls (2-oz.) of Twilley's Stalite in kingfisher (see note on wools and yarns, page 22); one crochet hook International Standard Size 3.00 (see page 9); 3 buttons each $\frac{3}{8}$-in. in diameter; waist length of shirring elastic.

MEASUREMENTS
To fit chest size 20 (22, 24) in.; length of jumper from shoulder 11 (12½, 14) in.; length of sleeve 9 (10½, 12) in.; length of trousers 7 (8, 9) in.

TENSION
5 tr. to ½ in. (see note on tension, page 14).

ABBREVIATIONS
See page 20; W., white; T., turquoise; K., kingfisher.

JUMPER
FRONT
With K. commence with 56 (60, 68) ch.
* * Work 2 rows in tr.
3rd row (right side facing): join in T., * work 1 tr., with T. work 1 tr. but work last loop with K., with K. work 1 tr., with K. work 1 tr. but work last loop with T.; rep. from * to end; break off K. With T. work 3 rows in tr.
7th row: Join W., work as 3rd row, but work W. for T. and T. for K.; break off T. * *
Cont. in tr. with W., working 1 tr. more at each end of every 6th row until there are 60 (66, 72) tr. Cont. until work measures 7½ (8½, 9½) in. from beg.
Armhole shaping. Leave 7 (8, 9) tr. at beg. of next 2 rows, then dec. 1 tr. at each end of next 4 rows: 38 (42, 46) tr. Cont. until work measures 9½ (11, 12½) in.
Neck Shaping. Next row: work 13 (14, 15) tr.; turn. Work 4 rows tr., leaving 1 tr. at neck on each row. Work 1 row more. Fasten off.
Leave 12 (14, 16) tr. at centre then complete other side of neck to match first side.

BACK
Work as Front until work measures 7½ (8½, 9½) in.
Shape Armholes. Leave 7 (8, 9) tr. at beg. of next 2 rows, then dec. 1 tr. at each end of next 4 rows: 38 (42, 46) tr.
Back Dividing. Work 19 (21, 23) tr.
Work on these sts. only until Back is same length as Front. Fasten off. Complete other side of Back to match.

SLEEVES (make 2 alike)
With K. commence with 32 (36, 40) ch. Work as Front from * * to * *. Cont. in tr. with W., work 1 tr. more each end of every 6th row until there are 38 (44, 48) tr. Cont. until work measures 9 (10½, 12) in.

Shape Top. Leave 7 (8, 9) tr. at end of next 2 rows, then dec. 1 tr. at each end of every row until 8 (8, 9) tr. remain. Fasten off.

TO COMPLETE
Borders. Join shoulder seams. With W., work d.c. evenly around neck edge. Break off W. and join in T., work 4 rows d.c. in T. Fasten off. With T., work 2 rows of d.c. into edge along right side of Back opening. With T., work 1 row of d.c. along left side of Back opening; work 1 more row in d.c. on left side but leave 3 sps., made by working 2 ch. over 2 d.c., evenly spaced for buttonholes.
Press work lightly on the wrong side with a warm iron over a damp cloth. Set in sleeves. Join side and sleeve seams. Sew buttons on right side of Back opening. Press seams.

TROUSERS
RIGHT AND LEFT SIDES (work 2 alike)
With K. commence with 65 (70, 75) ch.
Work 3 rows tr., turning with 2 ch. Leave 2 tr. at end of next 2 rows, then cont. in tr. Dec. 1 tr. at each end of every 3rd row until 51 (56, 61) sts. remain. Cont. until work measures 6 (7, 8) in. from beg. Fasten off.

TO COMPLETE
Waistband. Join sides together to form back seam. With K. work 20 d.c. into centre of top edge, by working into 10 tr. each side of seam; turn.
1st row: 20 d.c., then work 10 d.c. into next 10 tr. along top edge; turn.
2nd row: 30 d.c., work 10 d.c. into next 10 tr. along top edge; turn.
3rd row: 40 d.c., work 10 d.c. into next 10 tr. along top edge; turn.
4th row: 50 d.c., work 10 d.c. into next 10 tr. along top edge; turn.
5th row: 60 d.c., work 20 (25, 30) d.c. into top edge, to end.
6th row: 80 (83, 85) d.c., work 20 (25, 30) d.c. into top edge, to end.
Work 5 rows more in d.c., across all sts. Fasten off. Press work lightly on the wrong side with a warm iron over a damp cloth. Join front and leg seams. Press seams. Thread shirring elastic through wrong side of waistband.

The top is white, banded with the trouser colour and a light tone of the same shade.

Above: daisy-trimmed party dress (see page 61) and pink and white belted dress (page 60).

Opposite: a sparkling jumper and dress from the same pattern (see page 88).

Yellow dressing-gown

MATERIALS
14 (15, 16) oz. of Sirdar Double Knitting (see note on wools and yarns, page 22); one crochet hook International Standard Size 4.50 (4.00, 4.50) (see page 9); 3 button moulds, each 1 in. in diameter.

MEASUREMENTS
To fit chest size 22 (24, 26) in.; length from shoulder 26 (28, 30) in.; length of sleeve $7\frac{1}{2}$ ($8\frac{1}{2}$, $9\frac{1}{2}$) in.

TENSION
1 patt. to 1 in. with No. 4.50 hook; 7 patt. to $6\frac{1}{2}$ in. with No. 4.00 hook (see note on tension, page 14).

ABBREVIATIONS
See page 20.

BACK
Commence with 71 (79, 79) ch. to measure $17\frac{1}{2}$ ($18\frac{1}{2}$, $19\frac{1}{2}$) in.

Foundation row: 1 tr. into 3rd ch. from hook, * miss 3 ch., 4 tr. into next ch.; rep. from * ending with miss 3 ch., 2 tr. into last ch.; turn: 16 (18, 18) 4-tr. shs.

1st patt. row: 4 ch., * 1 tr. into sp. before next sh., 1 ch., 1 tr. into centre of next sh., 1 ch.; rep. from * ending with 1 tr. into 3rd of 3 ch.; turn.

2nd patt. row: 3 ch., 1 tr. into first tr., * miss next tr., 4 tr. into next tr.; rep. from * ending with miss next tr., 2 tr. into 3rd of 4 ch.; turn.

Rep. last 2 rows until work measures 7 (8, 9) in. from beg., ending with 2nd patt. row.

Dec. row: 4 ch., (1 tr. into sp. before next sh., 1 ch., 1 tr. into centre of next sh., 1 ch.) twice, leaving last loop of each tr. on hook make 1 tr. into sp. before next sh., 1 tr. into centre of next sh., 1 tr. into sp. before next sh., y.o.h. and draw through all loops on hook (a dec. made), 1 ch., * 1 tr. into centre of next sh., 1 ch., 1 tr. into sp. before next sh., 1 ch.; rep. from * to within last 4 shs., ending with 1 tr. into centre of next sh., 1 ch., a dec. over next sh., 1 ch., 1 tr. into centre of next sh., 1 ch., then work rep. and ending of first patt. row; turn.

Rep. 2nd and first patt. rows until work measures 16 (17, 18) in. from beg., ending with 2nd patt. row. Work dec. row once then rep. 2nd and first patt. rows until work measures $21\frac{1}{2}$ (23, $24\frac{1}{2}$) in. from beg., ending with first patt. row.

Shape Armholes. 1st row: miss first tr., 1 s.s. into each of next 4 sts., 3 ch., 1 tr. into same place as s.s., then work rep. of 2nd patt. row to within last 8 sts., ending with miss next tr., 2 tr. into next tr.; turn.

Rep. first patt. row once, then rep. first row of armhole

Warm for bedtime—in a snug, shell-patterned dressing-gown.

shaping once. Rep. patt. rows until armholes measure 4 ($4\frac{1}{2}$, 5) in. from beg., ending with 2nd patt. row. Fasten off.

RIGHT FRONT
Commence with 39 (43, 43) ch. to measure $9\frac{1}{2}$ (10, $10\frac{1}{2}$) in.

Foundation row: as Back foundation row: 8 (9, 9) patt. Cont. as for Back to dec. row.

Dec. row: 4 ch., (1 tr. into sp. before next sh., 1 ch., 1 tr. into centre of next sh., 1 ch.) twice, a dec. over next sh., 1 ch., 1 tr. into centre of next sh., 1 ch., then work rep. and ending of first patt. row; turn. Cont. as for Back to next dec. row. Rep. dec. row of Right Front once, then cont. as for Back to armhole shaping.

Shape Armhole. 1st row: same as 2nd patt. row, but work rep. to within last 8 sts., ending with miss next tr., 2 tr. into next tr.; turn.

Work first patt. row once, then first row of armhole shaping once. Cont. as for Back to within last 2 rows.

Shape Neck. 1st row: as first patt. row but work rep. to within last 2 shs., 1 tr. into sp. before next sh.; turn.

2nd row: miss first st., 1 s.s. into each of next 4 sts., 3 ch., 1 tr. into same place as s.s., then work rep. and ending of 2nd patt. row; turn. Work first patt. row. Fasten off.

LEFT FRONT
As Right Front to dec. row.

Dec. row: 4 ch., * 1 tr. into sp. before next sh., 1 ch., 1 tr. into centre of next sh., 1 ch.; rep. from * to within last 4 shs., 1 tr. into centre of next sh., 1 ch., a dec. over next sh., 1 ch., 1 tr. into centre of next sh., 1 ch., then work rep. and ending of first patt. row; turn.

Cont. as for Back to next dec. row. Rep. dec. row once, then cont. as for Back to armhole shaping.

Shape Armhole. 1st row: miss first tr., 1 s.s. into each of next 4 sts., 3 ch., 1 tr. into same place as s.s., then work rep. and ending of 2nd patt. row; turn. Work first patt. row once then rep. first row of Left Front armhole shaping once. Cont. as for Right Front to neck shaping.

Shape Neck. 1st row: miss first st., 1 s.s. into each of next 8 sts., 3 ch., 1 tr. into same place as s.s., then work rep. and ending of first patt. row; turn.

2nd row: as 2nd patt. row, but work rep. to within last 8 sts., ending with miss next tr., 2 tr. into next tr.; turn. Rep. first patt. row once. Fasten off.

SLEEVES (make 2 alike)
Commence with 39 (43, 43) ch. to measure $9\frac{1}{2}$ (10, $10\frac{1}{2}$) in. Cont. as Right Front working patt. rows until sleeve measures 7 (8, 9) in. from beg., ending with first patt. row.

Shape top. 1st row: * * rep. first row of Back armhole shaping once then first patt. row once. * *
Rep. from * * to * * 1 (1, 2) times.

For second size only: rep. first row of Back armhole

shaping once.
For all sizes: fasten off.

TO COMPLETE
Join side and shoulder seams, set in sleeves, join sleeve seams.

Edging. 1st round: with right side facing attach yarn to edge then work d.c. evenly round bottom, front and neck edges, having a multiple of 4 sts., 1 d.c. into first d.c.

2nd round: make 1 d.c. into each d.c., 2 d.c. into each corner d.c., s.s. into first d.c.; fasten off.

3rd round: attach yarn to first d.c. at a corner, 3 ch., into same place as join work 1 tr., 3 ch., 1 s.s. into last tr. made, 2 tr., * into next d.c. work 2 tr., 3 ch., 1 s.s. into last tr. made, 2 tr., miss 3 d.c.; rep. from * to next corner, into each of next 2 d.c. work 2 tr., 3 ch., 1 s.s. into last tr. made, 2 tr.; cont. all round, s.s. into first st.; fasten off.

Work edging round cuffs but omit corner incs.

Buttons. Wind yarn round finger to form a ring.

1st round: 7 d.c. into ring; draw commencing ring tight.

Next round: working in a continuous round, make * 2 d.c. into next d.c., 1 d.c. into next d.c.; rep. from * until work is large enough to cover button mould. Fasten off. Attach cover to mould. Make 2 more buttons in same way. Sew buttons evenly down Left Front and use spaces in pattern on Right Front as buttonholes.

Belt. Commence with 10 ch. to measure 2 in.

Foundation row: 1 tr. into 6th ch. from hook, 1 ch., miss next ch., 1 tr. into next ch., 1 ch., miss 1 ch., 1 tr. into last ch.; turn.

Next row: 3 ch., miss first tr., (1 tr. into next tr., 1 ch.) twice, 1 tr. into 3rd of 4 ch.; turn.

Rep. last row until work measures 36 in. from beg. Gather up each end and make a tassel.

Belted dress

(photographed in colour on page 56)

MATERIALS
12 (14) balls Hayfield Courtier Bri-Nova Crêpe Double Knitting in main shade, 2 balls in contrast shade (see note on wools and yarns, page 21); crochet hooks International Standard Sizes 3.50 and 3.00 (4.50, 4.00, 3.50 and 3.00) (see page 9); a 1-in. belt buckle.

MEASUREMENTS
To fit chest size 24 (26) in.; length 19 (22) in.; sleeve seam 10 (11) in.

TENSION
6 sts. (2 Vs) to 1 in. with No. 3.00 hook (see note on tension, page 14).

ABBREVIATIONS
See page 20; M., main shade; C., contrast shade.

BACK
With No. 4.00 (4.50) hook and M. make 87 ch.

1st row: (1 tr., 1 ch., 1 tr.) in 6th ch. from hook: V made; 1 ch., * miss 2 ch., (1 tr., 1 ch., 1 tr.) in next ch., 1 ch. Rep. from * ending with 1 tr. in last ch., 4 ch.; turn.

2nd row: * (1 tr., 1 ch., 1 tr.) in centre of V, 1 ch. Rep. from * ending with 1 tr. in 3rd of turning ch., 4 ch.; turn. Rep. 2nd row 8 (10) times. Change to No. 3.50 (4.00) hook and work 10 (12) more rows. Change to No. 3.00 (3.50) hook and work 10 (12) more rows; 3 ch.; turn.

Next row: * (1 tr., 1 ch., 1 tr.) in centre of V. Rep. to end of row. Rep. last row till work measures 14½ (17) in.

Shape Armhole. S.s. 6 sts., work in patt. to last 6 sts., 3 ch.; turn. Cont. in patt. till armhole shaping measures 4¼ (4¾) in.

Shape Neck. Cont. in patt. till 6 Vs have been worked, 1 tr. in next V. Fasten off.

Count Vs at opposite side, and joining yarn at neck edge, work other shoulder to match.

FRONT
Work as for Back until armhole shaping is reached.

Armhole and Neck Opening. Next row: s.s. 6 sts., patt. to centre of work, 3 ch.; turn.

Cont. in patt. till armhole is 5 rows shorter than Back.

Shape Neck. Work in patt. till 8 Vs are made, 1 tr. in next V, 3 ch.; turn.

Next row: 1 tr. in first V, cont. in patt. to end.

Next row: work in patt. till 7 Vs are made, 1 tr. in next V, 3 ch.; turn.

Next row: 1 tr. in first V, cont. in patt. to end.

Next row: work in patt. till 6 Vs are made, 1 tr. in next V. Fasten off. Rejoin yarn at centre opening and work other side to match.

SLEEVES (make 2 alike)
With No. 3.00 (3.50) hook and M., make 45 ch.

1st row: (1 tr., 1 ch., 1 tr.) in 6th ch. from hook, * miss 2 ch., (1 tr., 1 ch., 1 tr.) in next ch. Rep. from * ending with 1 tr. in last ch., 3 ch.; turn.

2nd row: * (1 tr., 1 ch., 1 tr.) in V. Rep. from * ending with 1 tr. in 3rd turning ch.

Cont. in patt. but inc. by 1 ch., 1 tr. at each end of every 4th row 8 times. Cont. straight till work measures 10 (11) in.
Shape Top. S.s. 6 sts., work in patt. to last 6 sts. ending with 1 tr., 3 ch.; turn.
Next row: * (1 tr., 1 ch., 1 tr.) in next V. Rep. from * ending with 1 tr. in last V.
Rep. last row 5 times. Fasten off.

TO COMPLETE
Join shoulder seams and work 1 row of d.c. round neck edge. Stitch in sleeves, and join sleeve and side seams.
Collar. With No. 3.00 (3.50) hook and C., make 75 ch.
1st row: as first row of Back.
Change to No. 3.50 (4.00) hook and work 4 rows as for

2nd row of Back.
Fasten off.
Cuffs. With No. 3.00 (3.50) hook and C., make 39 ch. and work in patt. as for Collar.
Belt. With No. 3.00 (3.50) hook and C. make 7 ch.
1st row: 1 tr. in 3rd ch. from hook, 1 tr. in each ch. to end, 2 ch.; turn.
2nd row: 1 tr. in each tr. to end of row.
Rep. 2nd row till belt measures 26 (27) in.
Next row: dec. at each end of row. Fasten off. Stitch buckle to one end of belt. Stitch collar and cuffs in place on dress. With No. 3.00 hook and C., make a chain 25 in. long. Lace this through front opening to tie in bow at neck. Neaten ends of chain.

Daisy-trimmed dress
(photographed in colour on page 56)

MATERIALS
11 (12, 13) oz. of Hayfield Courtier Bri-Nova Crêpe Double Knitting (see note on wools and yarns, page 21); one crochet hook International Standard Size 3.00 (see page 9); 1½ yd. daisy trimming in contrasting colour to yarn; 6 press studs; approx. 5 in. narrow elastic.

MEASUREMENTS
To fit chest size 22 (24, 26) in.; length 18 (21, 24) in.

TENSION
6 sts. to 1 in. of bodice patt. (see note on tension, page 14).

ABBREVIATIONS
See page 20.

FRONT
Skirt. Starting at waist edge of skirt, make 116 (124, 132) ch.
Foundation row: * * (1 tr., 1 ch., 1 tr.) in 8th ch. from hook, 2 ch., * miss 3 ch., (1 tr., 2 ch., 1 tr.) in next ch. Rep. from * to last 4 ch., miss 3 ch., 1 tr. in last ch., 4 ch.; turn.
1st patt. row: miss the first ch.-sp., * (1 d.c., 2 ch.) 3 times and 1 d.c. all into next ch.-sp., 2 ch., miss next ch.-sp. Rep. from * to end, finishing with 1 tr. into 3rd of turning ch., 4 ch., turn.
2nd patt. row: * (1 tr., 2 ch., 1 tr.) all into centre loop of next shell, 2 ch. Rep. from * to end, finishing with 1 tr. into 3rd of turning ch., 4 ch.; turn. Rep. these 2 rows 8 (11, 12) times. Fasten off.
Bodice. Rejoin yarn at waist edge and work 1 d.c. in each sp.
Next row: work in d.c. across row, but work 2 d.c. in the

3rd and every foll. 5th st. Work 2 rows in d.c., 3 ch.; turn.
1st patt. row: (1 tr., 1 ch., 1 tr.) in 3rd d.c.: V made; * miss 2 d.c., make V in next d.c. Rep. from * to end of row, ending with 1 tr. in 2nd of turning ch., 3 ch.; turn.
2nd patt. row: * 1 d.c. in first sp., 2 d.c. in next sp. Rep. from * to end of row.
Rep. these 2 rows 10 (13, 15) times.
Shape Armhole. S.s. 6 sts., work in patt. to last 6 sts., 3 ch., turn. Cont. in patt. for 5 (6, 7) patts.: 16 (20, 22) patts. in all. * *
Divide for Neck. 1st row: work in patt. till 5 Vs are made, miss 2 d.c., 1 tr. in next d.c., 3 ch.; turn.
2nd row: as 2nd patt. row.
3rd row: as 1st patt. row.
4th row: as 2nd patt. row.
5th row: 7 d.c. in next 7 d.c., 3 ch., miss 1 d.c., 3 d.c. in next 3 d.c., 3 ch., miss 1 d.c., 1 d.c. in each d.c. to end. Fasten off.
Join yarn at neck edge, and work other side to match. Work 2 rows d.c. round neck edge, then work picot row: * 4 ch., 1 s.s. in 2nd ch., 1 ch., 1 s.s. in next 2 ch. Rep from * to end of row. Fasten off.

BACK
Work exactly as for Front from * * to * *.
Work 2 further patt. rows. Divide for neck as for front, but working the 2 patt. rows once only, then 1 row of d.c. to form facing for shoulder fastening. Fasten off. Complete neck edging as for Front.

SLEEVES (make 2 alike)
Stitch shoulders together at sleeve edge, overlapping front to back. Work 1 row d.c. round armhole edge making sure

number of sts. will divide by 4, 4 ch.; turn.

1st row: as foundation row for Skirt.

Work the 2 patt. rows as for Skirt 4 (4, 5) times, then first row once.

Next row: 1 d.c. in every alt. loop to end of row, 3 ch.; turn.

Next row: 1 d.c. across row, 3 ch.; turn.

Next row: (1 tr., 1 ch., 1 tr.) in 2nd d.c., * miss 2 d.c., (1 tr., 1 ch., 1 tr.) in next d.c. Rep. from * to end of row, 3 ch.; turn.

Next row: * 1 d.c. in first sp., 2 d.c. in next sp. Rep. from * to end of row. Fasten off.

TO COMPLETE

Do not press. Join side and sleeve seams with a flat edge-to-edge stitch. Sew 3 press fasteners to each shoulder opening. Stitch daisy trimming round lower edge of bodice and in a straight line down front, starting 1 in. to the left of neckline and following a row of sts. down to meet waist trimming.

ALICE BAND
TO MAKE

Make 52 ch.

Work foundation row and first patt. row, as for Skirt. Fasten off. Rejoin yarn at cast-on edge and rep. foundation row inserting hook in same place as before.

Next row: as first patt. row. Fasten off. Stitch daisy trimming along centre of work. Stitch to length of elastic to form Alice band.

Pink and white dress

(photographed in colour on the front cover and in black and white opposite)

MATERIALS

7 (7, 8) oz. of Wendy 4-ply Nylonised in pink and 2 (2, 2) oz. in white (see note on wools and yarns, page 22); crochet hooks International Standard Sizes 3.50 and 3.00 (see page 9); 3 pink buttons each ¼ in. in diameter.

MEASUREMENTS

To fit chest sizes 23–24 (25–26, 27–28) in.; length, 17½ (19½, 21½) in.

TENSION

2 tr.gr. to 1 in. approx., 1 motif—2¼ in. in diameter, with No. 3.00 hook (see note on tension, page 14).

ABBREVIATIONS

See page 20; P., pink; W., white.

BODICE BACK

With No. 3.00 hook and P., make 98 (106, 114) ch.

Foundation row: 1 d.c. into 2nd ch. from hook, * 3 ch., miss 3 ch., 1 d.c. into next ch.; rep. from * to end.

1st patt. row (right side): 4 ch., * 3 tr. into next loop, 1 ch.; rep. from * to end, 1 tr. into last d.c.: 24 (26, 28) tr.gr.

2nd patt. row: 1 ch., 1 d.c. in first 1-ch. sp., * 3 ch., 1 d.c. into next sp.; rep. from * to end. These 2 rows form patt. Cont. in patt. until back measures 5½ (6½, 7½) in., ending with a 1st patt. row.

Shape Armholes. 1st row: s.s. over first tr.gr. and into next ch.sp., * 3 ch., 1 d.c., into next sp.; rep. from * until 1 tr.gr. rem., turn.

2nd row: s.s. to centre of first loop, 4 ch., * 3 tr. into next loop, 1 ch.; rep. from * until 1 loop rem., 1 tr. into last loop; turn.

3rd row: as 2nd patt. row.

4th row: as 2nd armhole shaping row: 18 (20, 22) tr.gr.

Divide for Opening. Next row: 1 ch., 1 d.c. into first 1-ch. sp., (3 ch., 1 d.c. into next sp.) 9 (10, 11) times; turn and work on these sts. only. Cont. straight until armhole measures 4¼ (4¾, 5¼) in.; fasten off. Rejoin wool to inner edge of rem. sts.

Next row: 1 d.c. into centre ch. sp., patt. to end. Cont. straight until armhole measures 4¼ (4¾, 5¼) in.; fasten off.

BODICE FRONT

Work as for Back until work measures 3 (4, 5½) in. approx. ending with a 1st patt. row.

Divide for Front Opening. Next row: 1 ch., 1 d.c. into first ch.sp., (3 ch., 1 d.c. in next sp.) 10 (11, 12) times; turn and work on these sts. only. Cont. straight until front measures 5½ (6½, 7½) in., ending with a 1st patt. row.

Shape Armhole. 1st row: s.s. over first tr.gr. and into next ch.sp., * 3 ch., 1 d.c. into next sp.; rep. from * to end.

2nd row: patt. until 1 loop remains, 1 tr. into last loop; turn.

3rd row: as 2nd patt. row.

4th row: as 2nd armhole shaping row: 7 (8, 9) tr.gr. Cont. straight until armhole measures 3¼ (3¾, 4¼) in., ending with a 2nd patt. row.

Shape Neck. 1st row: s.s. to centre of 2nd loop, 4 ch., * 3 tr. in next loop, 1 ch.; rep. from * to end, 1 tr. into last d.c.

2nd row: as 2nd patt. row.

Big flower motifs trim the waist and neck edge of this pretty summer dress.

3rd row: s.s. to centre of next loop, 4 ch., * 3 tr. into next loop, 1 ch.; rep. from * to end, 1 tr. into last d.c.; fasten off. Leave the centre 4 tr.gr. free for opening. Rejoin wool to next ch.sp.

Next row: 1 d.c. into this sp., patt. to end. Cont. straight until front measures 5½ (6½, 7½) in., ending with a 1st patt. row.

Shape Armhole. 1st row: patt. until 1 tr.gr. remains; turn.

2nd row: s.s. to centre of first loop, 4 ch., * 3 tr. into next loop, 1 ch.; rep. from * to end, 1 tr. into last d.c.

3rd row: as 2nd patt. row.

4th row: as 2nd armhole shaping row: 7 (8, 9) tr.gr. Cont. straight until armhole measures approx. 3¾ (3¾, 4¼) in., ending with a 2nd patt. row.

Shape Neck. 1st row: patt. until 2 loops rem., 1 tr. into next loop; turn.

2nd row: as 2nd patt. row.

3rd row: patt. until 1 loop remains, 1 tr. into last loop; fasten off.

SKIRT BACK AND FRONT (make 2 pieces alike)

With No. 3.50 hook and P., make 130 (138, 146) ch. Work foundation row as for bodice back; continue in patt.: 32 (34, 36) tr.gr. Work until skirt measures 2½ (3, 3½) in. Change to No. 3.00 hook and cont. in patt. until skirt measures approx. 5¾ (6¼, 6¾) in., ending with a 1st patt. row.

Next row: 1 d.c. into first tr., * miss ch. sp., 1 d.c. into next tr., miss 1 tr., 1 d.c. into next tr.; rep. from * until turning ch. remains, 1 d.c. into turning ch.

Next row: 1 d.c. into each d.c. of previous row; fasten off.

FLOWER MOTIFS (make 14 (15, 16) alike)

With No. 3.00 hook and W., make 7 ch. and join with s.s. to form a ring.

1st round: 16 d.c. into ring, s.s. into first d.c.

2nd round: 5 ch., * miss 1 d.c., 1 tr. into next d.c., 2 ch.; rep. from * to end, s.s. into 3rd ch.

3rd round: into every ch. sp. work 1 d.c., 1 tr., 3 d.tr., 1 tr. and 1 d.c., ending with 1 s.s. into first d.c.; fasten off.

TO COMPLETE

Press. Join side seams of bodice and skirt, then join shoulder seams. With No. 3.00 hook and P., work a row of d.c. along lower edge of bodice and skirt, working 2 d.c. into each loop and 1 d.c. into each d.c. Turn and work a 2nd row of d.c. Fasten off. With P. work a row of d.c. along back opening, round neck and along front opening edge. Turn and work a 2nd row, working 3 d.c. into corners at neck to keep work flat and making three 3-ch. loops evenly along right back opening edge. With P. work 2 rows of d.c. round armhole edges. Join 3 motifs together and sew into front opening. Join the remaining 11 (12, 13) motifs together into a round. Sew one long edge to lower part of bodice and other long edge to top of skirt. Press seams. Sew buttons on left back opening opposite ch. loops.

Turquoise two-piece

(photographed in colour on page 37)

MATERIALS
8 (8, 10) balls (1-oz.) of Twilley's Cortina Super crochet wool (see note on wools and yarns, page 22); crochet hooks International Standard Sizes 3.50 (4.00, 4.50) and 3.00 (3.50, 4.00) (see page 9); 3 small buttons.

MEASUREMENTS
To fit chest size 24 (26, 28) in.; jacket length 15½ (16¼, 18) in.; skirt length 10½ (12½, 13½) in. (adjustable).

TENSION
2 patts. to 3 (3¼, 3½) in. and 4 rows to 1½ (1⅝, 1¾) in. (see note on tension, page 14).

ABBREVIATIONS
See page 20.

JACKET
BACK

With No. 3.50 (4.00, 4.50) hook make 66 ch. loosely.

Foundation row: 1 d.c. into 2nd ch. from hook, (miss 3 ch., 7 d.tr. into next ch.: d.tr.gr. worked; miss 3 ch., 1 d.c. into next ch.) to end: 8 d.tr.gr.

1st row: 5 ch., 1 tr. into first d.c., * 3 ch., 1 d.c. into centre of d.tr.gr., 3 ch., (1 tr., 2 ch., 1 tr.) into d.c.; rep. from * to end.

2nd row: 4 ch., 3 d.tr. into 2-ch.sp., (1 d.c. into d.c., 7 d.tr. into next 2-ch.sp.) to end, finishing 4 d.tr. into last ch.sp.

3rd row: 1 ch., 1 d.c. into first d.tr., * 3 ch., (1 tr., 2 ch., 1 tr.) into d.c., 3 ch., 1 d.c. into centre of d.tr.gr., rep. from * to end, finishing 1 d.c. into 4th ch.

4th row: 1 ch., 1 d.c. into d.c., (7 d.tr. into next 2-ch.sp., 1 d.c. into d.c.) to end. Rep. these 4 patt. rows 5 times.

Armhole Shaping. Next row: s.s. to centre of first d.tr.gr., 1 ch., 1 d.c. into centre of gr., patt. to within last d.tr.gr. 3 ch., 1 d.c. into centre of gr.; turn. Patt. 13 rows straight.
Neck Shaping. Next row: 5 ch., 1 tr. into first d.c., * 3 ch., 1 d.c. into centre of d.tr.gr., 3 ch., (1 tr., 2 ch., 1 tr.) into d.c., rep. from * once. Fasten off. Miss centre 3 d.tr.gr., join yarn to next d.c., 5 ch., 1 tr. into same d.c., patt. to end. Fasten off.

LEFT FRONT
With No. 3.50 (4.00, 4.50) hook make 34 ch. loosely. Work foundation row as back: 4 d.tr.gr. Now rep. 4 patt. rows of Back 6 times.
Armhole and Front Shaping. Next row: as armhole shaping row of Back. Work 1 row straight.
Next row: patt. to within last d.tr.gr., 3 ch., 1 d.c. into centre of gr.; turn. Rep. last 2 rows once. Work 10 rows straight. Fasten off.

RIGHT FRONT
As Left Front, reversing armhole and front shapings.

SKIRT
With No. 3.00 (3.50, 4.00) hook make 154 ch. loosely. Work foundation row as for Back of jacket: 19 d.tr.gr. Now rep. 4 patt. rows of jacket twice, then s.s. into first d.c., thus forming work into a round; turn. Change to No. 3.50 (4.00, 4.50) hook.
1st round: 6 ch., * 1 d.c. into centre of d.tr.gr., 3 ch., (1 tr., 2 ch., 1 tr.) into d.c., 3 ch., rep. from * 17 times, 1 d.c. into centre of d.tr.gr., 3 ch., 1 tr. into same sp. as 6 ch., 2 ch., s.s. into 3rd of 6 ch.; turn.
2nd round: 4 ch., 3 d.tr.gr. into same sp., patt. to end, finishing 3 d.tr. into same sp. as 4 ch. and 3 d.tr., s.s. into 4th ch.; turn.
3rd round: 1 ch., 1 d.c. into same sp., patt. to end, finishing s.s. into first d.c.; turn.
4th round: 1 ch., 1 d.c. into first d.c., patt. to end, finishing s.s. into first d.c.; turn. Rep. last 4 rounds until work measures 10 (11, 12) in. (adjust length here) ending with

a first round.
Picot round: 7 ch., s.s. into 3rd ch. from hook, 3 d.tr. into same sp., * (1 d.c., 1 ch., 1 d.c.) into next d.c., (4 d.tr., 3 ch., s.s. into 3rd ch. from hook: a picot formed; 3 d.tr.) into 2-ch.sp., rep. from * 17 times, (1 d.c., 1 ch., 1 d.c.) into next d.c., 3 d.tr. into same sp. as 7 ch., and 3 d.tr. s.s. into 4th ch. Fasten off.

TO COMPLETE
With wrong side of work facing block jacket and skirt out to correct measurements (see page 16). Press work firmly and carefully with a warm iron over a damp cloth, then lightly press with a cool iron over a dry cloth. Join shoulders of jacket.
Armhole Edging. With right side facing, join yarn to underarm and with No. 3.00 (3.50, 4.00) hook work 50 d.c. evenly around armhole.
Next row: 1 ch., 1 d.c. into each d.c. to end. Fasten off. Join side seams.
Front Border. Join yarn to right shoulder. Make 7 ch., s.s. into 3rd ch. from hook, 3 d.tr. into same sp., (1 d.c., 1 ch., 1 d.c.) into corner of back neck, * (4 d.tr., 3 ch., s.s. into 3rd ch. from hook, 3 d.tr.: picot tr.gr. worked) into d.c., (1 d.c., 1 ch., 1 d.c.) into centre of d.tr.gr.; rep. from * twice, 1 picot tr.gr. into shoulder, ** (1 d.c., 1 ch., 1 d.c.), 1 picot tr.gr., rep. from ** 3 times along shaped edge of left front, then rep. from ** evenly along straight edge, finishing (1 d.c., 1 ch., 1 d.c.). Work 1 picot tr.gr. into corner, then along lower edge work (1 d.c., 1 ch., 1 d.c.) into base of d.tr.gr., 1 picot tr.gr. into d.c. to end. Work along right front edge of jacket to match other side, finishing 4 d.tr. into same sp. as 7 ch., and 3 d.tr., s.s. to 4th ch. Fasten off.
Skirt Waistband. With right side facing and No. 3.00 (3.50, 4.00) hook work 80 d.c. evenly along foundation ch.
Next row: 1 ch., 1 d.c. into each d.c. to end. Rep. last row 5 times. Fasten off. With right side facing, work 24 d.c. along each side of back opening.
Next row: 1 ch., 1 d.c. into first d.c., (3 ch., miss 2 d.c., 1 d.c. into 7 d.c.) twice, 3 ch., miss 2 d.c., d.c. to end. Fasten off. Sew on buttons opposite buttonholes.

Girl's gloves
(photographed in black and white on page 67)

MATERIALS
1 ball main colour and 1 ball contrast Coats Mercer-Crochet No. 40 (20 grm.) (see note on wools and yarns, page 20); one crochet hook International Standard Size 1.00 (see page 9).

MEASUREMENTS
From base of thumb to tip of middle finger 5 in.

TENSION
First 7 rows and 5 patts. to 1 in. (see page 14).

ABBREVIATIONS

See page 20, M., main colour; C., contrast colour.

LEFT HAND
PALM

Little Finger. With M., commence with 80 ch.

1st row: 1 tr. into 3rd ch. from hook, 1 ch. *, 1 tr. into each of next 2 ch., 1 ch.; rep. from * ending with 1 tr. into each of last 2 ch., 5 ch.; turn.

2nd row: 1 d.c. into first sp., * 5 ch., 1 d.c. into next sp.; rep. from * ending with 1 ch., miss 1 tr., 1 d.tr. into next ch., 3 ch.; turn.

3rd row: 1 tr. into loop just formed, * 1 ch., 2 tr. into next loop; rep. from * working last tr. into 3rd of 5 ch., 5 ch.; turn.

4th row: 1 d.c. into first sp., * 5 ch., 1 d.c. into next sp.; repeat from * ending with 2 ch., 1 tr. into 3rd of 3 ch., 2 ch.; turn.

5th row: 1 tr. into loop just formed, * (2 tr. into next loop, 1 ch.) 8 times, 1 d.c. into next loop, 33 ch.

Third Finger. 1st row: 1 tr. into 3rd ch. from hook, 1 ch. (1 tr. into each of next 2 ch., 1 ch., miss 1 ch.) 10 times, 2 tr. into same loop as d.c., * 1 ch., 2 tr. into next loop; rep. from * working last tr. into 3rd of 5 ch., 5 ch.; turn.

2nd to 4th row: as 2nd to 4th row of little finger.

5th row: 1 tr. into loop just formed, (2 tr. into next loop, 1 ch.) 9 times, 1 d.c. into next loop, 33 ch.

Middle Finger. 1st row: 1 tr. into 3rd ch. from hook, 1 ch. (1 tr. into each of next 2 ch., 1 ch., miss 1 ch.) 10 times, 2 tr. into same loop as d.c., * 1 ch., 2 tr. into next loop; rep. from * working last tr. into 3rd of 5 ch., 5 ch.; turn.

2nd to 4th row: as 2nd to 4th row of little finger.

5th row: 1 tr. into loop just formed, (2 tr. into next loop, 1 ch.) 10 times, 1 d.c. into next loop, 30 ch.

Forefinger. 1st row: 1 tr. into 3rd ch. from hook, 1 ch., (1 tr. into each of next 2 ch., 1 ch., miss 1 ch.) 9 times, 2 tr. into same loop as d.c., * 1 ch., 2 tr. into next loop; rep. from * working last tr. into 3rd of 5 ch., 5 ch.; turn.

2nd to 4th row: as 2nd to 4th row of little finger.

5th row: 1 tr. into loop just formed, (2 tr. into next loop, 1 ch.) 16 times, 1 d.c. into next loop, 24 ch.

Thumb. 1st row: 1 tr. into 3rd ch. from hook, 1 ch., (1 tr. into each of next 2 ch., 1 ch., miss 1 ch.) 7 times, 2 tr. into same loop as d.c., 1 ch., 2 tr. into next loop, 1 ch., 1 tr. and 1 h.tr. into next loop, 1 ch., 1 d.c. into next loop, 4 ch.; turn.

2nd row: miss first sp., 1 d.c. into next sp., (5 ch., 1 d.c. into next sp.) 9 times, 1 ch., miss 1 tr., 1 d.tr. into next ch., 3 ch.; turn.

3rd row: 1 tr. into loop just formed, (1 ch., 2 tr. into next loop) 9 times, 1 ch., 2 tr. into next 4 ch. loop, 1 ch., 2 tr. into same loop as d.c., 1 ch., 2 tr. into next loop, 1 ch., 1 tr. and 1 h.tr. into next loop, 1 ch., 1 d.c. into next loop, 4 ch.; turn.

Cotton gloves with a contrast trimming are cool and smart for special occasions.

4th row: miss first sp., 1 d.c. into next sp., (5 ch., 1 d.c. into next sp.) 12 times, 2 ch., miss 1 tr., 1 tr. into next ch., 2 ch.; turn.

5th row: 1 tr. into loop just formed, (2 tr. into next loop, 1 ch.) 12 times, 2 tr. into next 4 ch. loop, 1 ch., 2 tr. into same loop as d.c., (1 ch., 2 tr. into next loop) 5 times working last tr. into 3rd of 5 ch. Fasten off.

BACK

With M., work a length of 51 ch. and leave aside. Work as Palm until 3rd row of Third Finger has been completed ending last row with 3 ch.; turn.

4th row: 1 d.c. into first sp., (3 ch., 1 d.c. into next sp.) 16 times, (5 ch., 1 d.c. into next sp.) 11 times, 2 ch., 1 tr. into 3rd of 3 ch., 2 ch.; turn.

5th row: as 5th row of Third Finger.

Middle Finger. 1st row: 1 tr. into 3rd ch. from hook, 1 ch., (1 tr. into each of next 2 ch., 1 ch., miss 1 ch.) 10 times, 2 tr. into same loop as d.c., 1 ch., 1 tr. into next loop, 1 tr. into 3rd ch. of same 5 ch. loop, 5 ch.; turn.

2nd row: as 2nd row of Little Finger.

3rd row: 1 tr. into loop just formed, 1 ch., (2 tr. into next loop, 1 ch.) 11 times, 1 tr. into next loop, 1 tr. into 3rd ch. of same 5-ch. loop, 1 ch., attach length of chain already worked to base of last tr., (miss 1 ch., 1 tr. into each of next 2 ch., 1 ch.) 16 times, miss 1 ch., 1 tr. into each of next 2 ch., 5 ch., turn and complete as for Palm.

Attach main M. to same place as ch. worked at beg. and work loops along chain as follows: 1 d.c. into next sp., (3 ch., 1 d.c. into next sp.) 16 times, 3 ch., 1 s.s. into base of last tr. Fasten off.

TO COMPLETE

Back Trimming. With right side facing attach C. to first 3-ch. loop at wrist, 1 d.c. into same loop, * (4 ch., leaving last loop of each on hook work 2 tr. into 4th ch. from hook,

yarn over and draw through all loops on hook—a 2 tr. cluster made) twice, miss next 3-ch. loop, 1 d.c. into next loop; rep. from * 7 times more, 4 ch., a 2 tr. cluster into 4th ch. from hook, 1 d.c. into row end on first row of Middle Finger, 4 ch., a 2 tr. cluster into 4th ch. from hook, 1 d.c. into first 3-ch. loop on opp. side, (4 ch., a 2 tr. cluster into 4th ch. from hook, 1 d.c. between corresponding clusters on opp. side, 4 ch., a 2 tr. cluster into 4th ch. from hook, miss next 3-ch. loop, 1 d.c. into next loop) 8 times. Fasten off.

Joining. Place back and front of glove tog. wrong sides facing and join as follows: attach C. to first st. at wrist on Back, 1 d.c. into same place as join, 1 ch., 1 d.c. into corresponding st. on Palm, * 1 ch., 1 d.c. into next sp. on Back, 1 ch., 1 d.c. into next sp. on Palm; rep. from * 17 times more, 1 ch., miss next tr. on Back, 1 d.c. between next 2 tr., 1 ch., 1 d.c. into corresponding place on Palm, 1 ch., miss next row end on Back, (1 d.c. into next row end on Back, 1 ch., 1 d.c. into corresponding row end on Palm, 1 ch.) 3 times, miss next row end on Back, 1 d.c. between next 2 tr., 1 ch., 1 d.c. into corresponding place on Palm, 1 ch., 1 d.c. into next sp. on Back, cont. in this manner all round ending with 1 d.c. into base of last st. on Back, 1 ch., 1 d.c. into base of last st. on Palm. Do not fasten off.

Wrist. 1 d.c. into last 1-ch. sp. made, 4 ch., a 2 tr. cluster into 4th ch. from hook, miss next row end, (1 d.c. into next row end, 4 ch., a 2 tr. cluster into 4th ch. from hook) 6 times, 1 d.c. into next d.c. on Back Trimming, 4 ch., a 2 tr. cluster into 4th ch. from hook, 1 d.c. into next d.c. on Back Trimming, cont. in this manner all round ending with miss last row end, 1 s.s. into first d.c. Fasten off.

RIGHT HAND

Work as for Left Hand working Back Trimming and Joining to correspond.

Two-colour beret

(photographed in black and white on page 70)

MATERIALS

3 (3) oz. of Robin Vogue Double Knitting in a dark shade and 1 (1) oz. of Robin Vogue Double Knitting in a light shade (see note on wools and yarns, page 22); one crochet hook International Standard Size 4.00 (see page 9).

MEASUREMENTS

To fit 2–5 (5–8) years approx.

TENSION

4 d.c. to 1 in. with No. 4.00 hook (see note on tension, page 14).

ABBREVIATIONS

See page 20; D., dark shade; L., light shade.

MAIN PIECE

With D. make 5 ch. and join with a s.s. to form a ring.

1st round: 10 d.c. into ring.

2nd round: 2 d.c. into each d.c.: 20 sts.

3rd round: 1 d.c. into each d.c.

4th round: as 2nd round: 40 sts.

5th and 6th rounds: as 3rd round.

7th round: * 1 d.c. into each of next 3 d.c., 2 d.c. into next d.c.; rep. from * to end: 50 sts.

8th round: as 3rd round.

9th round: * 1 d.c. into each of next 3 d.c., 2 d.c. into next d.c.; rep. from * to end: 60 sts.

10th round: as 3rd round.

Cont. to inc. in this way on every alt. round until there are 120 d.c. in round, then cont. to inc. on every round until there are 160 (180) d.c.

Work 5 (7) rounds straight.

Next round: * 1 d.c. into next d.c., miss next d.c.; rep. from * to end: 80 (90) sts.

Cont. in rounds without shaping, working (2 rounds D., 2 rounds L.) twice, then 2 rounds D. Fasten off.

POMPON

Make pompon in L. following instructions in Pompon Helmet, below, but cut card circle 2½ in. in diameter with centre hole ⅝ in. in diameter.

TO COMPLETE

Press main piece lightly with a warm iron over a damp cloth.

Sew pompon on top.

Pompon helmet

(photographed in black and white on page 70)

MATERIALS

3 oz. of Robin Vogue Double Knitting in red and 1 oz. of Robin Vogue Double Knitting in navy (see note on wools and yarns, page 22); crochet hooks International Standard Sizes 4.00 and 3.50 (see page 9); cotton wool.

MEASUREMENTS

To fit approx. 5–8 years.

TENSION

4 d.c. to 1 in. with No. 4.00 hook (see note on tension, page 14).

ABBREVIATIONS

See page 20; R., red: N., navy.

MAIN PIECE

With No. 4.00 hook and R. make 6 ch. and join with a s.s. to form a ring.

1st round: 12 d.c. into ring.

2nd round: 1 d.c. into each d.c.

3rd round: 2 d.c. into each d.c.: 24 sts.

4th round: 1 d.c. into back loop only of each d.c. (thus making a ridge).

5th round: * 1 d.c. into next d.c., 2 d.c. into next d.c.; rep. from * to end: 36 sts.

6th round: 1 d.c. into each d.c.

7th round: as 6th round.

8th round: as 5th round.

Rep. last 3 rounds once: 81 sts; then rep. 6th round 3 times.

15th round: * 1 d.c. into each of next 2 d.c., 2 d.c. into next d.c.; rep. from * to end: 108 sts.

Rep. 6th round 10 times.

26th round: * 1 d.c. into each of next 8 d.c., miss next d.c.; rep. from * to end: 96 sts.

Rep. the 6th round once.

Shape Earpieces

1st row: 1 d.c. into each of next 30 d.c., s.s. into next d.c.; turn and cont. in rows.

2nd row: s.s. into first d.c., 1 d.c. into each of next 28 d.c., s.s. into next d.c.; turn.

3rd row: s.s. into first 2 d.c., 1 d.c. into each of next 24 d.c., s.s. into next d.c.; turn.

Cont. in this way, dec. 4 sts. on every row until 4 d.c. remain.

Next row: s.s. into first d.c., 1 d.c. into each of next d.c., s.s. into next d.c.; turn.

Next row: draw yarn through both d.c. (3 loops on hook), then draw yarn through all 3 loops and fasten off. With wrong side facing beg. at centre back and work second earpiece to match.

BORDER

With No. 3.50 hook and N. and right side facing, work 4 rounds of d.c. round edge of helmet, working 3 d.c. into point of each earpiece on every round.

BOBBLE

With No. 3.50 hook and R., work 1 d.c. into front loop of each d.c. on 4th round (where the ridge was made): 24 sts.

Work 2 rounds in d.c.

Next round: * 1 d.c. into next d.c., miss next d.c.; rep. from * to end: 12 sts.

Rep. the last round once: 6 sts.

Fasten off, leaving a long thread.

Press work on the wrong side with a warm iron over a damp cloth. Stuff bobble with a piece of cotton wool, thread end of wool through 6 d.c., pull up and fasten off securely.

TO COMPLETE

Pompons. Cut 2 circles of card each 1¼ in. in diameter. Cut a circle ¾ in. in diameter out of the centre of each card.

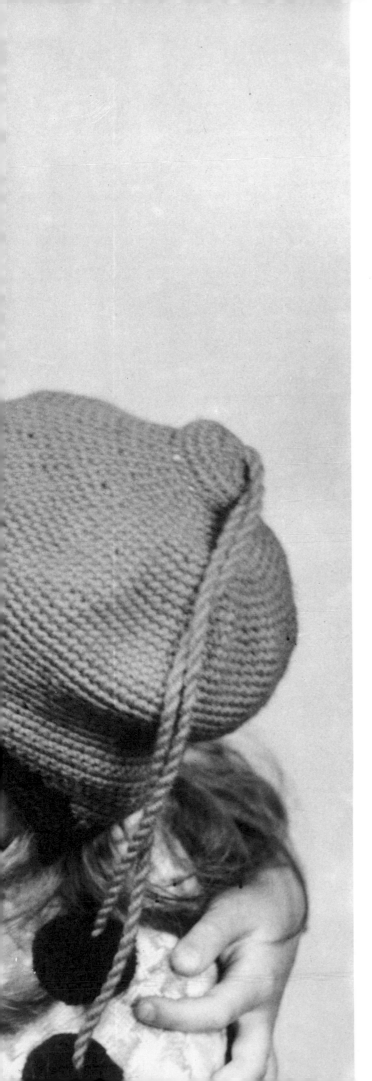

Put the 2 circles together and wind N. over card and out through centre hole, working round card until centre hole is full. Cut through strands round outside edge. Wind a strand of wool very tightly between cards and tie. Pull off cards and fluff out pompon. Make another pompon in the same way.

Cords. Twist 4 strands R. wool tog. to make 12-in. length. Rep., then twist 2 lengths tog. to make twisted cord. Make a second in same way. Sew one pompon to one end of each cord, then insert free ends of cords into bobble and stitch firmly.

Warm for chilly days—a two-colour beret for a boy (instructions on page 68), a pompon helmet for a girl (instructions start on page 69).

Chapter Four

Fashion outfits

Square-yoked sweater

MATERIALS
20 (21, 22) balls of Lister Lorette Double Crêpe (see note on wools and yarns, page 21); one crochet hook International Standard Size 3.00 (see page 9).

MEASUREMENTS
To fit bust size 34 (36, 38) in.

TENSION
2 rows to $\frac{3}{4}$ in. and 3 groups to $1\frac{1}{4}$ in. (see page 14).

ABBREVIATIONS
See page 20.

FRONT
Commence with 81 (85, 89) ch. loosely.
1st row: working into the 3rd ch. from hook, * (y.o.h., insert hook into ch., pull yarn through, y.o.h. and pull through 2 loops) 3 times, y.o.h. and pull through all loops on hook: 1 gr., 1 ch., miss 1 ch.; rep. from * ending with (y.o.h., pull yarn through, y.o.h. and pull through 2 loops) 3 times, y.o.h. and pull through all loops on hook.
2nd row: 1 ch., * 1 d.c. into top of group, 1 d.c. into ch.; rep. from * ending with 1 d.c. into starting ch.
3rd row: 3 ch., * 1 gr., 1 ch., miss 1 ch.; rep. from * ending with 1 gr. into last d.c.
Rep. last 2 rows until work measures $15\frac{1}{4}$ ($15\frac{1}{2}$, $15\frac{3}{4}$) in.
Shape Armholes. S.s. over 3 gr., patt. to within 3 grs. of other end.

Cont. straight until armholes measure 5 in.
Shape Neck. Starting on a gr. row work over 11 grs. from armhole edge; turn.
Next row: work 1 d.c. into first 1-ch. sp., d.c. to end; turn.
Next row: 3 ch., work over 9 grs., 1 tr. into next gr.; turn.
Next 2 rows: d.c. over first gr., d.c. to within 3 grs. of end; turn and s.s. over 3 grs., patt. to end and break yarn.
Rejoin yarn 11 grs. from other armhole edge and work to match the first side.

BACK
Work as for Front.

SLEEVES (make 2 alike)
Commence with 45 ch. and patt. until work measures 3 in.
Next row: 3 ch., 1 tr. into base of ch., * 1 ch., 1 gr., miss 1 ch.; rep. from * ending with 1 ch., 1 tr. into edge.
Next row: 1 d.c. over each ch.
Next row: 3 ch., work one 2-tr. gr. into base of starting ch., * 1 ch., 1 gr., miss 1 ch.; rep. from * ending with 1 ch., one 2-tr.gr. into edge.
Next row: 1 d.c. over each ch.
Next row: 3 ch., work 1 gr. into base of starting ch., * 1 ch., 1 gr., miss 1 ch.; rep. from * ending with 1 ch., 1 gr. into edge.

The sweater will team equally well with trousers, a skirt or a suit.

Next row: 1 d.c. over each ch.

Rep. these 6 rows until there are 67 (69, 71) grs. along row. Cont. straight until work measures 17¼ (17½, 17½) in. **Shape Top of Sleeve.** S.s. over 3 grs., work to within 3 grs. of end of row, then dec. 1 gr. at the beg. and end of each gr. row. When top of sleeve is 4 in. deep, break yarn.

TO COMPLETE

Sew the shoulder, side and sleeve seams using a flat seam (see page 19). Work 5 (5, 6) rounds of d.c. at bottom of sleeves and sweater. Work 5 (5, 6) rounds of d.c. round the neck, starting from right shoulder seam; break yarn.

Yoke. Starting from right shoulder seam, and working 2 grs. in from armhole edge, work 2 d.c. into side of gr. and 1 d.c. into the side of d.c.; cont. working down this line for 5 in.; turn and work along a row of d.c. working 1 d.c. into each d.c. along row, ending 2 grs. from armhole edge; turn and work up to shoulder seam. Work 5 rows of d.c. along these 3 lines, working 2 d.c. into the last d.c. on downwards line, 2 d.c. into the first and last d.c. on the line across the front and 2 d.c. into first d.c. on upwards line, thus inc. at the corners on each row.

Sew in sleeves. Stitch yoke shaping along shoulder seams. Using a very cool iron press the yoke shaping.

Sweater, scarf and socks set

(photographed in colour on page 134)

MATERIALS

22 (24, 26) balls of Lister Bel Air 4-ply (see note on wools and yarns, page 21); crochet hook International Standard Size 3.00 (see page 9); 2 ft. shirring elastic.

MEASUREMENTS

Sweater: to fit bust size 32 (34, 36) in.
Scarf: length 44 in.
Socks: to fit stocking size 9 (9½, 10) (Continental 37, 38, 39).

TENSION

1 patt. and 4 rows to 1 in. (see note on tension, page 14).

ABBREVIATIONS

See page 20.

SWEATER
FRONT

Commence with 99 (105, 111) ch.

Foundation row: leaving the last loop of each on hook work 2 tr. into the 3rd ch. from hook, y.o.h. and draw through all loops on hook, * 3 ch., miss 2 ch., 1 d.c. into next ch., 3 ch., miss 2 ch., leaving the last loop of each on hook work 3 tr. into the next ch., y.o.h. and draw through all loops on hook (3-tr. cl. made); rep. from * ending with 1 ch.; turn.

1st patt. row: * 1 d.c. into next cl., 1 d.c. into loop, 2 ch., 1 tr. into next d.c., 2 ch., 1 d.c. into next loop; rep. from * ending with 1 d.c. into last cl., 3 ch.; turn.

2nd patt. row: 3-tr. cl. into first d.c., * 3 ch., 1 d.c. into next tr., 3 ch., miss next d.c., 3-tr. cl. into next d.c.; rep. from * working the last cl. into last d.c., 1 ch.; turn.

Rep. 1st and 2nd patt. rows.

Cont. until work measures 14 (14¼, 14½) in., ending with a 1st patt. row.

Shape Armholes. Next row: s.s. over 1 patt., work to within 1 patt. of end of row; turn.

Cont. in patt. until armhole measures 4¾ (5, 5¼) in., ending with a 1st patt. row.

Shape Shoulders and Neck. Next row: s.s. to next cl., patt. next 5 cl.; turn and work over these sts. only.

Next row: s.s. over 1 patt., work to 3rd cl. from armhole edge, turn and s.s. to next cl.; turn, and work over half a patt. Break yarn.

Rejoin yarn 6 cls. from armhole edge.

Next row: work to within 1 patt. of end of row; turn.

Next row: s.s. over 1 patt., work over 3 patts.; turn. S.s. over half a patt.; break yarn.

BACK

Work as Front.

SLEEVES (make 2 alike)

Commence with 45 (51, 51) ch.

Patt. for 2 in. and then start inc. on a 2nd patt. row.

1st inc. row: 5 ch., 1 cl., cont. in patt., ending with 1 cl., 2 ch., 1 tr. into edge.

2nd inc. row: 3 ch., 3 d.c., 2 ch., 1 tr., cont. in patt., ending with 1 tr., 2 ch., 3 d.c., 2 ch., 1 tr.

3rd row: as 1st inc. row.

4th row: as 2nd inc. row.

5th row: 5 ch., 1 cl., 3 ch., 1 d.c., 3 ch.; cont. in patt., ending with 1 cl., 2 ch., 1 tr. into edge.

6th row: 3 ch., 1 tr. over tr., 2 ch., 3 d.c., cont. in patt.

continued on page 79

Opposite: black and white dress (see page 98).
Overleaf: flounced dress (see page 99).

ending with 3 d.c., 2 ch., 1 tr. into 3rd of ch., 2 ch., 1 tr. into edge.

7th row: 3 ch., 1 d.c. over first tr., 3 ch., 1 cl., cont. in patt., ending with 1 cl., 3 ch., 1 d.c. over tr., 3 ch., 1 tr. into edge.

8th row: 1 ch., 1 d.c. into loop, 2 ch., 1 tr. over d.c., 2 ch., 3 d.c., cont. in patt., ending with 3 d.c., 2 ch., 1 tr., 2 ch., 1 d.c. into loop.

9th row: 5 ch., 1 d.c. over tr., 3 ch., 1 cl., cont. in patt., ending with 1 cl., 3 ch., 1 d.c. over tr., 3 ch., 1 tr. into edge.

10th row: as 8th row.

11th row: 3 ch., 1 tr., (beg. of cl.) 3 ch., 1 d.c., 3 ch., 1 cl., cont. in patt. ending with 1 cl., 3 ch., 1 d.c., 3 ch., 2-tr. cl. into edge.

12th row: 1 ch., 1 d.c. over cl., 1 d.c. into loop, 2 ch., 1 tr., cont. in patt. ending with 3 d.c.

13th row: 1 cl., 3 ch., 1 d.c., 3 ch., cont. in patt., ending with 3 ch., 1 d.c., 3 ch., 1 cl.

14th row: 1 ch., 2 d.c., 2 ch., 1 tr., 2 ch., cont. in patt., ending with 3 d.c., 2 ch., 1 tr., 2 ch., 3 d.c.

15th row: as 13th row.

16th row: as 14th row.

Cont. inc. until there are 14 cls. (**size 34:** 14 cls. plus 2 more inc.; **size 36:** 14 cls. plus 4 more incs.) in row. Cont. straight until sleeve measures 14¾ (15¼, 15½) in., ending on a 2nd patt. row.

Shape Top. S.s. to centre of 2nd cl. from edge, and work to centre of 2nd cl. from other end.

Next row: 3 ch., 1 d.c. over tr., 3 ch., 1 cl., cont. in patt., ending with 1 cl., 3 ch., 1 d.c. over tr.

Next row: s.s. to next cl., d.c. over cl., d.c. into loop, cont. in patt., ending with 2 ch., d.c. into loop, d.c. over cl.

Next row: 3 ch., d.c. over tr., 3 ch., 1 cl., cont. in patt., ending with 1 cl., 3 ch., d.c. over tr.

Next row: 2 ch., d.c. in loop, d.c. over ch., d.c. in loop, 2 ch., 1 tr., cont. in patt. ending with 3 d.c., 2 ch., 1 tr.

Next row: 3 ch., 1 cl., cont. in patt., ending with 3 ch., 1 d.c., 3 ch., 1 cl.

Next row: 2 ch., 1 tr., 2 ch., 3 d.c., cont. in patt., ending with 3 d.c., 2 ch., 1 tr., 2 ch., 1 d.c.

Next row: s.s. to tr., 1 d.c. over last tr., 3 ch., 1 cl., cont. in patt., ending with 1 cl., 3 ch., 1 d.c. over tr.

Cont. dec. in this way until there are 4 cls. in row: 1 cl. at beg. and end and 2 in centre. Work 4 (4¼, 4½) in. straight for the saddle shoulder. Fasten off.

TO COMPLETE

Sew the saddle shoulders to shoulders of Front and Back, and sew the sleeves into the armholes at back and front. Sew the sleeve and side seams.

Work 5 rows of d.c. round the hemline of sweater and at the ends of sleeves.

Neck Border. Starting across a saddle shoulder, work 16 d.c., then 39 (42, 45) d.c. round Front neck edge, 16

Opposite: Chanel style suit (page 106). On previous page: floral-patterned dress (page 100).

d.c. across other shoulder, and 39 (42, 45) d.c. across Back neck edge. Work 5 rounds of d.c., dec. 1 st. at each side of shoulder seams (Back and Front) in each round: hook into next ch., y.o.h. and pull yarn through, hook into next ch., y.o.h. and pull yarn through, y.o.h. and pull through all loops on hook. Fasten off.

SCARF
MAIN PIECE
Commence with 51 ch., then work in patt. for 43 in.

EDGING FOR SHORT ENDS
Hook into ch. on corner of scarf and draw loop through, make 3 ch., leaving the last loop of each on hook work 2 tr. into 3rd ch. from hook and foundation ch., y.o.h. and draw through all loops on hook, s.s. into d.c. of edge of scarf, make another cl. in same way and s.s. into centre of next cl. on scarf, cont. to the end of scarf, s.s. cls. alt. into a d.c. and a cl. along row.

Rep. on other short edge. Fasten off.

SOCKS (make 2 alike)
Commence with 57 (63, 63) ch. and work 2 in. in patt. Dec. for calf and ankle, starting on a 2nd patt. row.

1st row: 3 ch., 1 tr., 2 ch., 1 d.c., 3 ch., cont. in patt., ending with 3 ch., 1 d.c., 2 ch., 2 tr.

2nd row: 2 d.c., 1 ch., 1 tr., 2 ch., 3 d.c., cont. in patt., ending with 3 d.c., 2 ch., 1 tr., 1 ch., 2 d.c. Work next 4 rows in patt.

7th row: 3 ch., 1 tr., 1 ch., 1 d.c., 3 ch., 1 cl., cont. in patt., ending with 1 cl., 3 ch., 1 d.c., 1 ch., 2 tr.

8th row: 2 d.c., 1 tr., 1 ch., 3 d.c., cont. in patt., ending with 3 d.c., 1 ch., 1 tr., 2 d.c.

9th row: 3 ch., 1 tr., 2 ch., 1 cl., cont. in patt. ending with 1 cl., 2 ch., 2 tr.

10th row: 5 d.c., 2 ch., 1 tr., 2 ch., cont. in patt., ending with 5 d.c.

11th row: 3 ch., 1 tr., 2 ch., 1 cl., cont. in patt., ending with 1 cl., 2 ch., 2 tr.

12th row: 4 d.c., 2 ch., 1 tr., 2 ch., cont. in patt., ending with 4 d.c.

13th row: 3 ch., 1 tr., 2 ch., 1 cl., cont. in patt., ending with 1 cl., 2 ch., 2 tr.

14th row: 4 d.c., 2 ch., 1 tr., cont. in patt., ending with 4 d.c.

15th row: 3 ch., 1 tr., 2 ch., 2-tr. cl., cont. in patt., ending with 2-tr. cl., 2 ch., 2 tr.

16th row: 4 d.c., 2 ch., 1 tr., 2 ch., 3 d.c., cont. in patt., ending with 1 tr., 2 ch., 4 d.c.

17th row: 3 ch., 1 tr., 1 ch., 1 tr., 3 ch., 1 d.c., 3 ch., 1 cl., cont. in patt., ending with 1 cl., 3 ch., 1 d.c., 3 ch., 1 tr., 1 ch., 2 tr.

18th row: 3 d.c., 2 ch., 1 tr., 2 ch., 3 d.c., cont. in patt., ending with 3 d.c., 2 ch., 1 tr., 2 ch., 3 d.c.

19th row: as 17th row.

20th row: as 18th row.

21st row: 3 ch., 1 tr., 3 ch., 1 d.c. over next tr., 3 ch., 1 cl., cont. in patt., ending with 1 d.c., 3 ch., 2 tr.

22nd row: 2 d.c., 2 ch., 1 tr., 2 ch., 3 d.c., cont. in patt. Work straight until leg measures 11¾ (12, 12¼) in. ending on a 1st patt. row.

Shape Half Heel. D.c. over 13 sts., turn and work 2¼ in. in d.c. on these sts.

Turn Half Heel. Start from centre back edge.

1st row: 3 d.c., hook into next d.c., y.o.h. and pull yarn through; hook into next d.c., y.o.h. and pull yarn through, y.o.h. and pull through all loops on hook: dec. made; turn.

2nd row: work 4 d.c.

3rd row: 4 d.c.; dec. in next 2 d.c.; turn.

4th row: 5 d.c. Cont. in this way until all sts. are worked off. Work to centre back; turn.

Next row: work 9 d.c. across heel and 14 d.c. along the side of heel, then work across the instep in patt., until 13 sts. remain, work last 13 sts. in d.c.

Cont. on these 13 d.c. only for the other half of heel until level with first half heel.

Next row: work across all sts., i.e. 23 sts. at each side in d.c. and instep sts. in patt.

Dec. 1 d.c. each side of instep every row in patt., until 10 d.c. each side remain. On these two groups of 10 sts., work 1 row tr. (on cl. row) and 1 row d.c., keeping middle sts. in patt., until foot measures 7 (7½, 8) in. from the beg. of heel d.c.

Shape the Toe. Next row: work across the 10 d.c., then work 28 (34, 34) d.c. across the patt., then 10 d.c. to end.

Next row: work 10 (12, 12) d.c., dec. in next 2 d.c., dec. in next 2 d.c., work 20 (22, 22) d.c., dec. in next 2 d.c., dec. in next 2 d.c., work to end.

Next row: work 9 d.c., dec. in next 2 d.c., dec. in next 2 d.c., work 18 (20, 20) d.c., dec. in next 2 d.c., dec. in next 2 d.c., work to end.

Cont. in this way dec. on each row until toe measures 1½ in. Fasten off.

TO COMPLETE

Work 5 rows of d.c. into starting ch. and thread in 2 rows of shirring elastic.

Sew the centre back seam, heel and under foot seam.

Frilled jumper

MATERIALS

9 (10, 11) oz. Coats Carefree Bri-Nylon 3-ply (see note on wools and yarns, page 20); one crochet hook International Standard Size 3.50 (see page 9).

MEASUREMENTS

To fit bust size 34 (36, 38) in.; length from shoulder 22½ (23½, 23½) in.; sleeve seam 1¾ in.

TENSION

2 patterns = 1 in. (see note on tension, page 14).

ABBREVIATIONS

See page 20.

BACK AND FRONT (both worked alike)

Commence with 112 (118, 124) ch. to measure 18 (19, 20) in.

1st row: into 5th ch. from hook work 1 tr., 1 ch. and 1 tr. (V st. made), * miss 2 ch., V st. into next ch.; rep. from * ending with 1 tr. into last ch., 3 ch.; turn: 36 (38, 40) V sts.

2nd row: miss first tr., 1 tr. into next tr., * 1 ch., 1 tr. into each of next 2 tr.; rep. from * ending with 1 ch., 1 tr. in

Close-up of stitch pattern.

The neck frill has a drawstring tie with bobble trimming.

next tr., 1 tr. in next st., 4 ch.; turn.

3rd row: miss first tr., * leaving last loop of each on hook work 1 tr. into each of next 2 tr., yarn over and draw through all loops on hook (a joint tr. made), 2 ch.; rep. from * ending with a joint tr., 1 ch., 1 tr. into 3rd of 3 ch., 3 ch.; turn.

4th row: 1 tr. into first sp., 1 tr. into next joint tr., * 2 tr. into next sp., 1 tr. into next joint tr.; rep. from * ending with 1 tr. into last sp., 1 tr. into 3rd of 4 ch., 3 ch.; turn.

5th row: miss first 2 tr., * V st. into next tr., miss 2 tr.; rep. from * ending with V st. into next tr., miss 1 tr., 1 tr. into 3rd of 3 ch., 3 ch.; turn.

2nd to 5th rows form patt.

Work in patt. for 35 rows more (or length required) ending with a 4th patt. row and omitting turning ch. at end of last row.

Armhole Shaping. 1st row: 1 s.s. into each of first 9 sts., 3 ch., patt. to within last 11 sts., miss 2 tr., 1 tr. into next tr., 3 ch.; turn.

Work in patt. for 14 (18, 18) rows more.

Neck Shaping. 1st row: 1 tr. into first sp., * 1 tr. into next joint tr., 2 tr. into next sp.; rep. from * 8 (9, 10) times, 1 tr. into next joint tr., 3 ch.; turn.

2nd row: miss first 3 tr., 1 tr. into next tr., miss 2 tr., V st. into next tr., patt. to end.

3rd row: work in patt. to within last tr., miss tr., 1 tr. into 3rd of 3 ch., 3 ch.; turn.

4th row: miss first tr., joint tr. over next 2 tr., patt. to end.

5th row: work in patt. to within last joint tr., miss joint tr., 1 tr. into next ch., 3 ch.; turn.

6th row: miss first 3 tr., V st. into next tr., work in patt., omitting turning ch. at end of row.

Shoulder Shaping. 1st row: 1 s.s. into each of first 7 sts., 3 ch., patt. to within last V st., 1 tr. into next tr., miss next tr., 1 tr. into next ch., 3 ch.; turn.

2nd row: miss first 2 tr., joint tr. over next 2 tr., patt. to last 4 sts., 1 tr. into next tr.

Fasten off.

Miss 10 joint tr. at centre, attach yarn to next joint tr., 3 ch. and complete to correspond with first side.

SLEEVES (make 2 alike)

Commence with 79 (85, 88) ch. to measure approx. 13 (14, 14½) in.

Work as Back for 4 rows, omitting turning ch. at end of 4th row: 25 (27, 28) sts.

Top Shaping. 1st row: 1 s.s. into each of first 4 sts., 3 ch., miss next tr., V st. into next tr., patt. to last 5 sts., miss next tr., 1 tr. in next tr., 3 ch.; turn.

2nd row: miss first 2 tr., 1 tr. into each of next 2 tr., patt. to last 3 sts., 1 tr. into 3rd of 3 ch.; turn.

3rd row: miss first 2 tr., joint tr. over next 2 tr., work in patt. to within last 5 sts., joint tr. over next 2 tr., 1 tr. into 3rd of 3 ch., 3 ch.; turn.

4th row: miss first joint tr., patt. to within last joint tr., 1 tr. into 3rd of 3 ch., 3 ch.; turn.

5th row: miss first 3 tr., V st. into next tr., patt. to within last 3 sts., 1 tr. into 3rd of 3 ch., 3 ch.; turn. Rep. 2nd to 5th rows 2 (3, 3) times, then rep. 2nd to 4th rows, omitting turning ch. at end of last row.

Fasten off.

TO COMPLETE

Do not press. Sew shoulder, side and sleeve seams. Sew in sleeves.

Frill. 1st row: with wrong side facing attach yarn at shoulder seam and work a row of d.c. evenly round neck edge having a multiple of 3 d.c., 1 s.s. into first d.c.

2nd row: working into back loop of each d.c., 3 ch., * 1 tr. into next d.c., 2 tr. into next d.c.; rep. from * ending 1 tr. into last d.c., 1 s.s. into 3rd of 3 ch.

3rd row: 3 ch., 1 tr. into each tr., 1 s.s. into 3rd of 3 ch. Rep. last row once more.

Fasten off.

Neck Edging. 1st row: with right side facing, attach yarn to any d.c. at shoulder seam, working into other loop of d.c., 3 ch., * a joint tr. over next 2 d.c., 1 tr. into next d.c.; rep. from * ending with a joint tr. over next 2 d.c., 1 s.s. into 3rd of 3 ch.

2nd row: 1 ch., 1 d.c. into next joint tr., 3 ch., 1 d.c. into same place as s.s., * miss next tr., 1 d.c. into next joint tr., 3 ch., 1 d.c. into tr. just missed; rep. from * ending with 1 s.s. into first ch.

Fasten off.

Lower Edging. 1st row: with right side facing, attach yarn at either side seam, 3 ch., * 2 tr. into next sp., 1 tr. into next ch.; rep. from * all round lower edge, 1 s.s. into 3rd of 3 ch.

2nd row: 1 ch., * miss 2 tr., 1 d.c. into next tr., 3 ch., 1 d.c. into last tr. missed; rep. from * all round, ending with 1 s.s. into first ch.

Fasten off.

Sleeve Edgings. With right side facing, attach yarn at the seam and work as for Lower Edging.

Neck Cord. With 3 thicknesses of yarn, work a length of ch. to measure 52 in. approx.

Fasten off.

Bobble (make 2). With 3 thicknesses of yarn, commence with 4 ch., join with s.s. to form a ring, 4 ch., 11 d.tr. into ring, 1 s.s. into 4th of 4 ch. Cut yarn, leaving an end, thread yarn through sts., draw up firmly and fasten off.

Thread cord through first row of Neck Edging. Sew a bobble to each end.

Lacy cotton blouse

MATERIALS

8 (9, 10) balls of Twilley's Lystra (see note on wools and yarns, page 22); one crochet hook International Standard Size 1.25 (see page 9).

MEASUREMENTS

To fit bust size 34 (36, 38) in.; length from shoulder 20½ (21, 21½) in.

TENSION

2 patt. to 2¼ in. (see note on tension, page 14).

Sweet and simple—a lacy top to partner a favourite summer skirt.

ABBREVIATIONS
See page 20.

BACK
Commence with 199 (211, 223) ch. to measure 18½ (19½, 20½) in.

Foundation row: 1 tr. into 10th ch. from hook, 1 tr. into each of next 6 tr., * 3 ch., miss 2 ch., 1 d.tr. into next ch., miss 2 ch., 1 tr. into each of next 7 ch.; rep. from * to within last 3 ch., miss 2 ch., 1 d.tr. into next ch.; turn: 16 (17, 18) 7-tr. grs.

1st patt. row: 1 d.c. into first d.tr., * 1 d.c. into next sp., 4 ch., miss 2 tr., 1 tr. into each of next 3 tr., 4 ch., 1 d.c. into next 3-ch. sp., 1 d.c. into next d.tr.; rep. from * ending with 1 d.c. into 4th of 7 ch.; turn.

2nd patt. row: 1 d.c. into first d.c.; 1 d.c. into next d.c., * 4 ch., 1 tr. into each of next 3 tr., 4 ch., 1 d.c. into each d.c.; rep. from * to end; turn.

3rd patt. row: 6 ch., * 2 tr. into next 4-ch. sp., 1 tr. into each of next 3 tr., 2 tr. into next 4-ch. sp., 2 ch., miss next d.c., 1 d.tr. into next d.c., 2 ch.; rep. from * to end, omitting 2 ch. at end of last rep.; turn.

4th patt. row: 3 ch., * 2 tr. into next 2-ch. sp., 1 tr. into each of next 3 tr., 1 ch., miss next tr., 1 tr. into each of next 3 tr., 2 tr. into next 2-ch. sp., 1 tr. into next d.tr.; rep. from * to end, working 1 tr. at end of last rep. into 4th of 6 ch.; turn.

5th patt. row: miss first tr., 7 ch., * miss next 2 tr., 1 tr. into each of next 3 tr., 1 tr. into next 1-ch. sp., 1 tr. into each of next 3 tr., 3 ch., miss 2 tr., 1 d.tr. into next tr., 3 ch.; rep. from * ending with 2 tr., 1 tr. into each of next 3 tr., 1 tr. into next 1-ch. sp., 1 tr. into each of next 3 tr., 3 ch., miss 2 tr., 1 d.tr. into 3rd of 3 ch.; turn.

These last 5 rows form patt. Rep. patt. until work measures 12½ in. from beg. ending with first patt. row.

Shape Armholes. 1st row: 1 s.s. into each of first 13 sts., 1 d.c. into each of next 2 d.c., then work rep. of 2nd patt. row to within last 15 sts., ending with 1 d.c. into next d.c.; turn.

2nd row: rep. 3rd patt. row.

3rd row: 1 s.s. into each of first 5 sts., 4 ch., miss next tr., 1 tr. into each of next 3 tr., 2 tr. into next 2-ch. sp., 1 tr. into next d.tr., then work rep. of 4th patt. row to within last 12 sts., ending with 2 tr. into next 2-ch. sp., 1 tr. into each of next 3 tr., 1 ch., miss next tr., 1 tr. into next tr.; turn.

4th row: 3 ch., 1 tr. into next 1-ch. sp., 1 tr. into each of next 3 tr., 3 ch., miss 2 tr., 1 d.tr. into next tr., 3 ch., then work rep. of 5th patt. row to within last 7 sts., miss 2 tr., 1 tr. into each of next 3 tr., 1 tr. into next 1-ch. sp., 1 tr. into 3rd of 4 ch.; turn.

5th row: 1 s.s. into each of first 7 sts., 1 d.c. into next d.tr., then work rep. of first patt. row to within last 8 sts.; turn.

Rep. patt. rows until armholes measure 5 (5½, 6) in. from beg., ending with 3rd patt. row, at right back edge.

Shape Neck. 1st row: patt. over first 37 sts.; turn
Rep. 5th patt. row once, then first to 3rd patt. rows once.

6th row: as 3rd row of armhole shaping but ending as 4th patt. row; turn.

7th row: as 5th patt. row but ending as 4th row of armhole shaping; turn.

8th row: as 5th row of armhole shaping but ending as first patt. row; turn.

Rep. patt. rows until armhole measures 7 (7½, 8) in. from beg., ending with either a 3rd or a first patt. row; fasten off.

2nd Side of Neck. 1st row: attach thread to 37th st., counting from opposite armhole edge, patt. to end; turn.

Rep. 5th patt. row once then rep. first to 3rd patt. rows once.

6th row: as 4th patt. row but ending as 3rd row of armhole shaping; turn.

7th row: as 4th row of armhole shaping, but ending as 5th patt. row; turn.

8th row: as first patt. row, but ending as 5th row of armhole shaping; turn.

Complete as for first side of neck. Fasten off.

FRONT
Work as Back until armholes measure 3 (3½, 4) in. approx. from beg., ending with 3rd patt. row, at front left edge.

Shape Neck. 1st to 8th rows: as 1st to 8th rows of first side of back neck shaping.

Rep. patt. rows until same number of rows are completed from beg. of armhole shaping as for Back. If Back ended with 3rd patt. row then work one more patt. row on Front. Fasten off.

2nd Side of Neck. 1st to 8th rows: as 1st to 8th rows of 2nd side of Back neck shaping.

Complete as for first side of neck. Fasten off.

TO COMPLETE
Join side and shoulder seams.

Neck and Lower Edging (alike). 1st round: with right side facing attach yarn to edge, then work d.c. evenly round, having a multiple of 3, 1 d.c. into first d.c.

2nd and 3rd rounds: working in continuous rounds make 1 d.c. into each d.c., s.s. into first d.c.

4th round: 5 ch., * miss 2 d.c., 1 tr. into next d.c., 2 ch.; rep. from * ending with s.s. into 3rd of 5 ch.

5th round: 3 d.c. into each 2-ch. sp., 1 d.c. into first d.c. Rep. 2nd and 3rd rounds once. Fasten off.

Armhole Edging. 1st to 3rd rounds: as 1st to 3rd rounds of neck and lower edging. Fasten off.

Starch, and press.

For all ages, all occasions—a longer length waistcoat. Instructions start on page 86.

Waistcoat

(photographed in black and white on page 85)

MATERIALS

12 (13, 14) balls of Patons Piccadilly (see note on wools and yarns, page 21); one crochet hook International Standard Size 3.50 (see page 9); four $\frac{5}{8}$-in. button moulds.

MEASUREMENTS

To fit bust size 34 (36, 38) in.; length, $24\frac{1}{2}$ in.

TENSION

4 patts. to $2\frac{1}{4}$ in., 3 rows to 2 in. (see note on tension, page 14).

ABBREVIATIONS

See page 20.

BACK

Make 104 (110, 116) ch.

Foundation row: 1 d.c. into 2nd ch. from hook, * 2 ch., miss 2 ch., 1 d.c. into next ch.; rep. from * to end.

1st patt. row: * 4 ch., 3 tr. into first of 4 ch., 1 d.c. into next sp.; rep. from * to end.

2nd patt. row: * 3 ch., 1 d.c. into top of 4th ch. of previous row; rep. from * to end: 34 (36, 38) patts. These 2 rows form patt. Cont. in patt. until Back measures 16 in., ending with a 2nd patt. row.

Shape Armholes. Next row: s.s. over first 4 patts. and into next d.c., * 4 ch., 3 tr. into first of 4 ch., 1 d.c. into 4th ch. of next patt.; rep. from * until 4 patts. remain; turn: 26 (28, 30) patts. Cont. straight until Back measures 24 in. from beg. Fasten off.

LEFT FRONT

Make 53 (56, 59) ch.

Work foundation row as for Back: 17 (18, 19) patts. Cont. in patt. until front measures 10 in., ending with a 2nd patt. row. * *

Shape Front Edge. 1st row: patt. until last patt. remains, 4 ch., 2 tr. into first of 4 ch., 1 d.c. into top of turning ch.; turn.

2nd row: as 2nd patt. row.

3rd row: patt. until last patt. remains, 4 ch., 1 tr. into first of 4 ch., 1 d.c. into top of turning ch.

4th row: as 2nd patt. row.

5th row: patt. until last patt. remains, 1 tr. into top of turning ch.; turn.

6th row: s.s. into first d.c., * 3 ch., 1 d.c. into top of the 4th ch., rep. from * to end: 1 patt. dec. Rep. last 6 rows until Front measures 16 in., ending with a 2nd patt. row.

Shape Armhole. Next row: s.s. over first 4 loops and into next d.c., patt. to end, *but still dec. at front edge as before.*

Cont. to dec. at Front Edge, repeating the 6 rows, until 7 (8, 9) patts. remain. Cont. straight until Front measures 24 in. Fasten off.

RIGHT FRONT

Work as for Left Front to * *.

Shape Front Edge. 1st row: 4 ch., 2 tr. into first of 4 ch., 1 d.c. into next sp., patt. to end.

2nd row: as 2nd patt. row.

3rd row: 4 ch., 1 tr. into first of 4 ch., 1 d.c. into next sp., patt. to end.

4th row: as 2nd patt. row.

5th row: 3 ch., miss first patt., 1 d.c. into next d.c., * 4 ch., 3 tr. into first of 4 ch., 1 d.c. into next sp., rep. from * to end.

6th row: as 2nd patt. row: 1 patt. dec.

Rep. last 6 rows until Front measures 16 in., ending with a 2nd patt. row.

Shape Armhole. Next row: patt. until 4 patts. remain *but still dec. at front edge as before;* turn.

Cont. to dec. at front edge, repeating the 6 rows, until 7 (8, 9) patts. remain. Cont. straight until Front measures 24 in. Fasten off.

TO COMPLETE

Press lightly with warm iron. Join shoulder and side seams.

Edging and Buttonhole Loops. 1st row: work 98 (104, 110) d.c. along lower edge of Back, 52 (55, 58) d.c. along lower edge of right front, 1 d.c. at corner, 56 d.c. up right front edge to first dec., 86 d.c. up right side of neck, 39 d.c. along back neck, 86 d.c. down left side of neck, 56 d.c. down left front edge, 1 d.c. at corner and 52 (55, 58) d.c. along lower edge of left front; turn with 1 ch.

2nd row: 1 d.c. into each of next 52 (55, 58) d.c., 3 d.c. into next d.c. (corner), 1 d.c. into each d.c. up left front, left side of neck, along back neck, then work 1 d.c. into each of next 88 d.c., (6 ch., miss 2 d.c., 1 d.c. into each of next 13 d.c.) 3 times, 6 ch., miss 2 d.c., 1 d.c. into each of next 7 d.c., 3 d.c. into next d.c. (corner), 1 d.c. into each d.c. to end of row; turn with 1 ch.

3rd row: 1 d.c. into each d.c. of previous row, working 3 d.c. into corner sts. and 7 d.c. into each buttonhole loop. Fasten off.

Buttons (make 4). Make 4 ch. and join into ring with s.s.

1st round: work 8 d.c. into ring.

2nd round: * 1 d.c. into next d.c., 2 d.c. into next d.c., rep. from * to end.

3rd and 4th rounds: work 1 d.c. into each d.c. of previous round. Fasten off.

Run a gathering thread round outer edge, insert button-mould, draw up gathering thread and secure.

Armhole Edging. Work 116 d.c. round armhole edge. Turn with 1 ch. and work another 2 rows of d.c. Fasten off. Join ends of edging. Make other armhole edging to match. Sew on buttons to correspond with buttonholes.

Long-sleeved jacket

MATERIALS

15 (16, 17) oz. of Sirdar 4-ply Fontein Crêpe (see note on wools and yarn, page 22); crochet hooks International Standard Sizes 3.50 and 4.00 (3.00, 4.00) (see page 9).

MEASUREMENTS

To fit bust size 34 (36, 38) in.; length from shoulder 29 (29½, 30) in.; length of sleeve 17 in.

TENSION

4 patt. to 5 in. (see note on tension, page 14).

ABBREVIATIONS

See page 20.

BACK

With No. 4.00 (3.50, 4.00) hook commence with 93 (105,

105) ch. to measure 21 (22, 23) in.

Foundation row: 6 tr. into 6th ch. from hook, * miss 2 ch., 1 tr. into next ch., miss 2 ch., 6 tr. into next ch.: sh. made; rep. from * ending with miss 2 ch., 1 tr. into last ch.; turn: 15 (17, 17) patts.

1st patt. row: 4 ch., * 4 tr. into next sh., 1 ch., 1 tr. into next single tr., 1 ch.; rep. from * ending with 4 tr. into next sh., 1 ch., 1 tr. into 3rd ch.; turn.

2nd patt. row: 3 ch., 2 tr. into first tr., * 1 tr. into next sh., 6 tr. into next single tr.; rep. from * ending with 1 tr. into next sh., 3 tr. into 3rd of 4 ch.; turn.

3rd patt. row: 3 ch., 1 tr. into first tr., * 1 tr. into next single tr., 1 ch., 4 tr. into next sh., 1 ch.; rep. from * ending with 1 tr. into next single tr., 1 ch., 2 tr. into 3rd of 3 ch.; turn.

4th patt. row: 3 ch., * 6 tr. into next single tr., 1 tr. into next sh.; rep. from * ending with 6 tr. into next single tr., 1 tr. into 3rd of 3 ch.; turn.

Rep. patt. rows until work measures 16 in. from beg. Change to No. 3.50 (3.00, 3.50) hook, cont. in patt. until Back measures 21 in. from beg., ending with first patt. row.

Shape Armholes. 1st row: miss first st., 1 s.s. into each of next 7 sts., 3 ch., then work rep. of 4th patt. row to within last sh.; turn.

Rep. last 4 rows once, then work patt. rows until armholes measure 7½ (8, 8½) in. from beg. Fasten off.

RIGHT FRONT

With No. 4.00 (3.50, 4.00) hook, commence with 51 (57, 57) ch. to measure 12 (12½, 13) in.

Foundation row: as Back foundation row: 8 (9, 9) patt. Work as Back to armhole shaping.

Shape Armhole. 1st row: as 2nd patt. row to within last sh.; turn.

Work 3 rows in patt. then rep. first row of armhole shaping once.

Rep. patt. rows until armhole measures 5 (5½, 6) in. from beg., ending with 2nd patt. row.

Shape Neck. 1st row: as 3rd patt. row, but working rep. 4 times only, 1 tr. into next tr., 1 ch., 2 tr. into next sh.; turn.

2nd row: 1 s.s. into next 8 sts., 4 ch., then work rep. of 4th patt. row ending with 1 tr. into 3rd of 3 ch.; turn.

Rep. patt. rows until one more row is completed from beg. of armhole shaping than for Back. Fasten off.

LEFT FRONT

Work as Right Front until armhole shaping is reached.

Shape Armhole. 1st row: miss first st., 1 s.s. into each of next 7 sts., then work as 2nd patt. row to end; turn. Work 3 rows in patt., then rep. first row of armhole shaping once. Cont. as Right Front to neck shaping.

Shape Neck. 1st row: miss first st., 1 s.s. into each of next 6 (13, 13) sts., 3 ch., 1 tr. into same place as last st., 1 ch., then work rep. and ending of first patt. row; turn.

2nd row: as 4th patt. row but working rep. 4 times only. Complete as Right Front. Fasten off.

SLEEVES (make 2 alike)

With No. 4.00 (3.50, 4.00) hook, commence with 45 (51, 51) ch. to measure 8 (9, 10) in.

Foundation row: as Back foundation row: 7 (8, 8) patt. Work 5 rows in patt.

* * Inc. row: 3 ch., 6 tr. into first tr., then work rep. of 2nd patt. row, ending with 1 tr. into next sh., 6 tr. into 3rd of 4 ch., 1 tr. into same place as last sh.; turn.

Rep. 1st to 4th patt. rows twice then 1st patt. row once. * * Rep. from * * to * * once, then cont. working patt. rows until sleeve measures 16½ in. from beg., ending with first patt. row.

Shape Top. 1st row: as first row of Back armhole shaping. Work 3 rows in patt. Rep. last 4 rows until top measures 3¾ (4, 4¼) in. from beg. Fasten off.

TO COMPLETE

Join side and shoulder seams. Join sleeve seams. Set in sleeves.

Edging. 1st round: with right side facing and No. 3.50 (3.00, 3.50) hook, attach yarn to edge, then work d.c. evenly round having a multiple of 6, s.s. into first d.c.

2nd round: * miss 2 d.c., 6 tr. into next d.c., miss 2 d.c., 1 d.c. into next d.c., 3 ch., 1 s.s. into last d.c. made; rep. from * all round, s.s. into first tr.; fasten off. Work cuff edgings in the same way. Fasten off.

Blue jumper and white dress

(photographed in colour on page 57)

MATERIALS

For jumper: 12 balls Lister Bel Air Starspun (see note on wools and yarns, page 21); crochet hooks International Standard Sizes 4.50 and 4.00 (see page 9).

For dress: 17 balls Lister Bel Air Starspun (see note on wools and yarns, page 21); crochet hooks International Standard Sizes 5.50, 5.00, 4.50 and 4.00 (see page 9).

MEASUREMENTS

Jumper: to fit bust size 34—36 in.; length from shoulder

20 in. **Dress:** to fit bust size 34—36 in.; hip size 36—38 in.; length from shoulder 33 in.

TENSION
4 sh. to 3 in. with No. 4.50 hook; 4 sh. to 3½ in. with No. 5.00 hook; 4 sh. to 4 in. with No. 5.50 hook (see note on tension, page 14).

ABBREVIATIONS
See page 20.

JUMPER
BACK
With No. 4.50 hook, commence with 96 ch.

1st row: 1 d.c. into 2nd ch. from hook, * 1 d.c. into each ch.; rep. from * to end, 2 ch.; turn.

2nd row: miss 1 d.c., * 1 d.c. into next d.c.; rep. from * to end, 2 ch.; turn.

3rd row: 1 d.c into 2nd d.c. from hook, 5 tr. into same d.c.; * miss 3 d.c., 1 sh. into next d.c.; rep. from * to last 4 d.c., miss 3 d.c., 1 d.c. into end d.c., 3 ch.; turn.

4th row: 3 tr. into first sp. on previous row, miss next sh., * 1 sh. into sp. between sh.; rep. from * to end, miss last sh., 1 d.c. into turning ch., 3 ch.; turn.
The 4th row forms patt. **

Cont. in patt. until work measures 13 in. from beg., ending with right side facing.

Shape Armholes. Next row: s.s. across first d.c. and 5 tr., 3 tr. into next sp., miss next sh., * 1 sh. into sp. between shs.; rep. from * to last complete sh., 1 d.c. into 2nd tr., 3 ch.; turn.

Next row: patt. to last 3 tr., 1 d.c. into 3rd tr.
Rep. last 2 rows twice. ***
Cont. straight until work measures 20 in. Fasten off.

FRONT
Work as Back as far as ***.
Cont. straight until work measures 17 in. from beg., ending with right side facing.

Shape Neck. Next row: patt. half a sh., (3 tr. into first sp.), then 6 shs., then half a sh., (1 d.c., 3 tr.) into next sp., 3 ch.; turn.

Next row: work in patt.

Next row: patt. half a sh., then 5 sh., then half a sh. into next sp., 3 ch.; turn.

Next row: work in patt.
Cont. thus, taking one sh. fewer on each alt. row until half a sh., 3 sh., then half a sh. into next sp. has been worked. Cont. straight until work measures 20 in. from beg. Fasten off.
Return to rem. sts., miss 3 shs., rejoin yarn and work to correspond with first side.

TO COMPLETE
Armbands. Join shoulder seams. With No. 4.00 hook and right side of work facing, rejoin yarn and work 2 rows of d.c. evenly round armholes; fasten off.

To Make Up. Pin out and press each piece on wrong side under a dry cloth. Join side seams. Press all seams.

DRESS
BACK
With No. 5.50 hook, commence with 96 ch.
Work as Jumper Back as far as **. Cont. in patt. until work measures 8 in. from beg. Change to No. 5.00 hook and cont. in patt. until work measures 16 in. from beg. Change to No. 4.50 hook and cont. in patt. until work measures 26 in. from beg. ending with right side facing. ****

Shape Armholes. Work as Jumper Back, but cont. straight until work measures 33 in.
Fasten off.

FRONT
Work as Dress Back as far as ****
Shape Armholes. Work as Jumper Back until work measures 30 in. from beg.
Shape Neck. Work as Jumper Front. Fasten off.

TO COMPLETE
Work armbands and make up as for Jumper.

White shift dress
(photographed in black and white on page 90)

MATERIAL
16 (17, 18) balls Emu Scotch 4-ply, Emu Super Crêpe, Emu Bri-Nylon 4-ply or Emu Diadem (see note on wools and yarns, page 21); crochet hooks International Standard Sizes 3.50 and 3.00 (see page 9).

MEASUREMENTS
To fit bust size 34 (36, 38) in.; length 35 (35½, 36) in.

TENSION
10 tr. and 5 rows to 2 in. (see note on tension, page 14).

ABBREVIATIONS
See page 20.

BACK
With No. 3.50 hook, commence with 126 (131, 136) ch.

to measure $24\frac{1}{2}$ ($25\frac{1}{2}$, $26\frac{1}{2}$) in.

Foundation row: 1 tr. into 4th ch. from hook, 1 tr. into each ch. to end; turn.

Patt. row: 3 ch., miss first tr., 1 tr. into each tr., 1 tr. into 3rd of 3 ch.; turn.

Rep. last row 8 times.

1st dec. row: 3 ch., miss first tr., 1 tr. into each of next 12 (13, 13) tr., * leaving last loop of each hook, make 1 tr. into each of next 2 tr., y.o.h. and draw through all loops on hook: a dec. made; 1 tr. into each of next 22 (23, 24) tr.; rep. from * 3 times, ending with 1 dec. over next 2 tr., 1 tr. into each tr., 1 tr. into 3rd of 3 ch.; turn.

Work patt. row 9 times.

2nd dec. row: 3 ch., miss first tr., 1 tr. into each of next 12 (13, 13) tr., * 1 dec. over next 2 tr., 1 tr. into each of next 21 (22, 23) tr.; rep. from * 3 times, ending with 1 dec. over next 2 tr., 1 tr. into each tr., 1 tr. into 3rd of 3 ch.; turn.

Work patt. row 9 times.

3rd dec. row: 3 ch., miss first tr., 1 tr. into each of next 11 (12, 12) tr., * 1 dec. over next 2 tr., 1 tr. into each of next 20 (21, 22) tr.; rep. from * 3 times, ending with 1 dec. over next 2 tr., 1 tr. into each tr., 1 tr. into 3rd of 3 ch.; turn.

Work patt. row 9 times.

4th dec. row: 3 ch., miss first tr., 1 tr. into each of next 11 (12, 12) tr., * 1 dec. over next 2 tr., 1 tr. into each of next 19 (20, 21) tr.; rep. from * 3 times, ending with 1 dec. over next 2 tr., 1 tr. into each tr., 1 tr. into 3rd of 3 ch.; turn.

Work patt. row 9 times.

5th dec. row: 3 ch., miss first tr., 1 tr. into each of next 10 (11, 11) tr., * 1 dec. over next 2 tr., 1 tr. into each of next 18 (19, 20) tr.; rep. from * 3 times, ending with 1 dec. over next 2 tr., 1 tr. into each tr., 1 tr. into 3rd of 3 ch.; turn.

Work patt. row 9 times.

6th dec. row: 3 ch., miss first tr., 1 tr. into each of next 10 (11, 11) tr., * 1 dec. over next 2 tr., 1 tr. into each of next 17 (18, 19) tr.; rep. from * 3 times, ending with 1 dec. over next tr., 1 tr. into each tr., 1 tr. into 3rd of 3 ch.; turn.

Rep. patt. row until work measures $27\frac{1}{2}$ in. from beg.

Shape Armholes. 1st row: s.s. into each of first 8 sts., 3 ch., 1 dec. over next 2 tr., 1 tr. into each tr. to within last 11 sts., 1 dec. over next 2 tr., 1 tr. into next tr.; turn.

2nd row: s.s. into first st., 3 ch., 1 dec. over next 2 sts., 1 tr. into each st. to within last 4 sts., 1 dec. over next 2 sts., 1 tr. into next st.; turn.

3rd row: 3 ch., 1 dec. over next 2 sts., 1 tr. into each st. to within last 3 sts., 1 dec. over next 2 sts., 1 tr. into last st.; turn.

Rep. 2nd and 3rd rows 1 (2, 2) times.

For 1st and 3rd sizes only: work 2nd row once; turn.

For all sizes: work patt. rows until armhole measures 5 ($5\frac{1}{2}$, 6) in. from beg.

Shape Neck. * * **1st row:** 3 ch., miss first tr., 1 tr. into each of next 12 (13, 13) tr., 1 dec. over next 2 tr., 1 tr. into next tr.; turn.

2nd row: s.s. into first st., 3 ch., 1 dec. over next 2 sts., 1 tr. into each st., 1 tr. into 3rd of 3 ch.; turn.

3rd row: 3 ch., miss first tr., 1 tr. into each tr. to within last 4 sts., 1 dec. over next 2 sts., 1 tr. into next st.; turn.

Rep. last 2 rows once, then rep. patt. row until work measures 7 ($7\frac{1}{2}$, 8) in. Fasten off.

2nd Side of Neck. 1st row: attach wool to 16th (17th, 17th) st. counting from other armhole edge, 3 ch., 1 dec. over next 2 tr., 1 tr. into each tr., 1 tr. into 3rd of 3 ch.; turn.

Rep. 3rd and 2nd rows of first side of neck shaping twice. Complete as for first side of neck. Fasten off. * *

FRONT

Work as for Back until armhole shaping is completed, then work as for Back from * * to * *. Fasten off.

TO COMPLETE

Join seam down each side of garment to run between 2nd and 3rd tr. on each side. Sew shoulder seams.

Edgings. With No. 3.50 hook and right side facing, attach yarn to lower edge at one seam.

1st round: 6 ch., s.s. into 3rd ch. from hook, * miss 1 tr., 1 tr. into next tr., 3 ch., s.s. into 3rd ch. from hook; rep. from * evenly round, s.s. into 3rd of 6 ch.; fasten off.

With No. 3.50 hook and right side facing, attach yarn to neck edge at one shoulder seam.

1st round: 4 ch., * 1 tr. into edge, 1 ch., miss 1 tr.; rep. from * evenly round, s.s. into 3rd of 4 ch.

2nd round: change to No. 3.00 hook, 3 ch., 1 tr. into each sp. and each tr., s.s. into 3rd of 3 ch.

3rd round: 6 ch., s.s. into 3rd ch. from hook, * miss 1 tr., 1 tr. into next tr., 3 ch., s.s. into 3rd ch. from hook; rep. from * ending with s.s. into 3rd of 3 ch.; fasten off.

Press lightly.

Lacy dress

(photographed in black and white on page 93)

MATERIALS

8 balls Coats Mercer-Crochet No. 20 (20 grm.) (see note

White shift dress is easy enough for a beginner to make (instructions start page 89).

on wools and yarns, page 20); one crochet hook International Standard Size 1.75 (see page 9).

MEASUREMENTS

To fit bust size 34 in.; length from shoulder 32 in.

TENSION
2 blks. and sps. to 1 in., 4 rows of blks. and sps. to 1 in. (see note on tension, page 14).

ABBREVIATIONS
See page 20.

BODICE BACK AND FRONT (make 2 alike)
This dress is worked from the shoulders.

Make 3 lengths of 7 ch. for neck shaping on first side; make 1 length of 13 ch. for shoulder shaping on second side; make 2 lengths of 4 ch. and 3 lengths of 7 ch. for armhole shaping.

Shoulder and Neck Shaping (first side). Commence with 11 ch.

1st row: 1 tr. into 4th ch. from hook, 1 tr. into next ch., 3 ch., miss 3 ch., 1 tr. into next ch., 1 h.tr. into next ch., 1 d.c. into next ch., 18 ch.; turn.

2nd row (right side): 1 tr. into 10th ch. from hook, 1 tr. into each of next 2 ch., 3 ch., miss 3 ch., 1 tr. into each of next 3 ch., 3 ch., 3 tr. into next sp.: a blk. made; 3 ch., attach 1 length of 7 ch. (already worked) to last foundation ch., 1 tr. into each of next 3 ch., 3 ch., miss 3 ch., 1 d.c. into next ch., 1 ch.; turn.

3rd row: 1 d.c. into first d.c., into next sp. work 1 h.tr. and 2 tr., * 3 ch., a blk. into next sp.; rep. from * ending with 3 ch., a blk. over next 3 turning ch., 1 tr. into next ch., 6 ch.; turn.

4th row: * a blk into next sp., 3 ch.; rep. from * to end, attach another length of 7 ch. to last d.c. on previous row, 1 tr. into each of next 3 ch., 3 ch., miss 3 ch., 1 d.c. into next ch., 1 ch.; turn.

Rep. 3rd and 4th rows once more omitting turning ch. at end of last row. Fasten off.

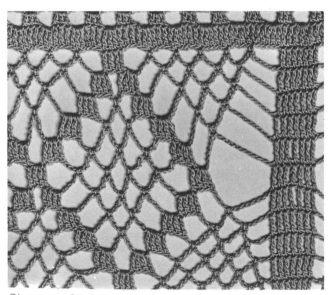

Close-up of stitch pattern of lacy dress — the dress may be lined, if wished.

92

Shoulder and Neck Shaping (second side). Commence with 10 ch.

1st row: 1 d.c. into 2nd ch. from hook, 1 h.tr. into next ch., 1 tr. into next ch., 3 ch., miss 3 ch., 1 tr. into each of next 3 ch., 8 ch.; turn.

2nd row: 1 d.c. into 2nd ch. from hook, 3 ch., miss 3 ch., 1 tr. into each of next 3 ch., 3 ch., a blk. into next sp., 3 ch., attach length of 13 ch. to last d.c. on previous row, (1 tr. into each of next 3 ch., 3 ch., miss 3 ch.) twice, 1 tr. into next ch., 3 ch.; turn.

3rd row: * a blk. into next sp., 3 ch.; rep. from * to within last sp., into last sp. work 2 tr. and 1 h.tr., 1 d.c. into next d.c., 8 ch.; turn.

4th row: 1 d.c. into 2nd ch. from hook, 3 ch., miss 3 ch., 1 tr. into each of next 3 ch., * 3 ch., a blk. into next sp.; rep. from * to within last blk., 3 ch., miss 3 tr., 1 tr. into 3rd of 3 ch., 3 ch.; turn.

Rep. 3rd and 4th rows once more then 3rd row again working 69 ch. at end of last row, 1 d.c. into first d.c. on first side, into next sp. work 1 h.tr. and 2 tr., * 3 ch., a blk. into next sp.; rep. from * ending with a blk. into last sp., 1 tr. into 3rd of 6 ch., 6 ch.; turn.

Next row: (a blk. into next sp., 3 ch.) 6 times, * 1 tr. into each of next 3 ch., 3 ch., miss 3 ch.; rep. from * 10 times, 1 tr. into each of next 3 ch., (3 ch., a blk. into next sp.) 6 times, 3 ch., 1 tr. into 3rd of 3 ch., 3 ch.; turn.

1st patt. row: a blk. into first sp., * 3 ch., a blk. into next sp.; rep. from * ending with 1 tr. into 3rd of 6 ch., 6 ch.; turn.

2nd patt. row: * a blk. into next sp., 3 ch.; rep. from * ending with 1 tr. into 3rd of 3 ch., 3 ch.; turn. Work in patt. for 14 rows, or length required, ending with a 2nd patt. row and turning with 5 ch. at end of last row.

Armhole Shaping. 1st row: 1 d.c. into 2nd ch. from hook, 3 ch., miss 3 ch., a blk. into next sp., work in patt. ending with a blk. into last sp., attach 1 length of 4 ch. to 3rd of 6 ch. on previous row, 3 ch., miss 3 ch. of 4 ch. attached, 1 d.c. into next ch., 1 ch.; turn.

2nd row: 1 d.c. into first d.c., into next sp. work 1 h.tr. and 2 tr., 3 ch., work in patt. to within last sp., into last sp. work 2 tr. and 1 h.tr., 1 d.c. into next d.c., 5 ch.; turn.

3rd row: 1 d.c. into 2nd ch. from hook, 1 h.tr. into next ch., 1 tr. into each of next 2 ch., 3 ch., work in patt. to within last sp., a blk. into last sp., 3 ch., attach second length of 4 ch. to last d.c. on previous row, 1 tr. into each of next 2 ch., 1 h.tr. into next ch., 1 d.c. into next ch., 8 ch.; turn.

4th row: 1 d.c. into 2nd ch. from hook, 3 ch., miss 3 ch., 1 tr. into each of next 3 ch., 3 ch., work in patt. to within last sp., a blk. into last sp., 3 ch., attach 1 length of 7 ch. to last d.c. on previous row, 1 tr. into each of next 3 ch., 3 ch., miss 3 ch., 1 d.c. into next ch., 8 ch.; turn.

5th row: 1 d.c. into 2nd ch. from hook, 1 h.tr. into next ch., 1 tr. into each of next 2 ch., 3 ch., a blk. into next sp., work in patt. to within last sp., a blk. into last sp., 3 ch., attach another length of 7 ch. to last d.c. on previous row, miss 3 ch., 1 tr. into each of next 2 ch., 1 h.tr. into next ch., 1 d.c. into next ch., 8 ch.; turn.

6th row: as 4th row, turning with 3 ch. at end of row.

Work in patt. for 12 rows omitting turning ch. at end of last row. Fasten off.

Sew shoulder and side seams neatly.

SKIRT FRONT AND BACK (made together)

1st round: with right side facing attach yarn to first sp. to left of any seam, 4 ch., 2 d.tr. into same sp., * 1 d.tr. into each of next 3 tr., 3 d.tr. into next sp.; rep. from * 31 times, 3 d.tr. into next sp.; rep. from * again, omitting 3 d.tr. at end of rep., 1 s.s. into 4th of 4 ch.

2nd round: 4 ch., 1 d.tr. into each of next 2 d.tr., * (6 ch., miss 4 d.tr., 1 d.c. into next d.tr.) 5 times, 6 ch., miss 4 d.tr., 1 d.tr. into each of next 4 d.tr., (6 ch., miss 4 d.tr., 1 d.c. into next d.tr.) 4 times, 6 ch., miss 4 d.tr., 1 d.tr. into each of next 4 d.tr., (6 ch., miss 4 d.tr., 1 d.c. into next d.tr.) 5 times, 7 ch., miss 5 d.tr., 1 d.tr. into each of next 7 d.tr., 7 ch., miss 5 d.tr., 1 d.c. into next d.tr., (6 ch., miss 4 d.tr., 1 d.c. into next d.tr.) 4 times, 6 ch., miss 4 d.tr., 1 d.tr. into each of next 4 d.tr., (6 c.h., miss 4 d.tr., 1 d.c. into next d.tr.) 4 times, 6 ch., miss 4 d.tr., 1 d.tr. into each of next 4 d.tr., (6 ch., miss 4 d.tr., 1 d.c. into next d.tr.) 5 times, 6 ch., miss 4 d.tr., 1 d.tr. into each of next 6 d.tr.; rep. from * once omitting 3 d.tr. at end of last rep., 1 s.s. into 4th of 4 ch.

3rd round: 4 ch., 1 d.tr. in each of next 2 d.tr., 7 ch., miss next sp., * (1 d.c. into next loop, 7 ch.) 4 times, 3 d.tr. into next sp., 1 d.tr. into next d.tr., 2 ch., miss 2 d.tr., 1 d.tr. into next d.tr., 3 d.tr. into next sp., (7 ch., 1 d.c. into next loop) 3 times, 7 ch., 3 d.tr. into next sp., 1 d.tr. into next d.tr., 2 ch., miss 2 d.tr., 1 d.tr. into next d.tr., 3 d.tr. into next sp., (7 ch., 1 d.c. into next loop) 4 times, * 8 ch., 1 d.tr. into each of next 7 d.tr., 8 ch.; rep. from * to * once, 7 ch., 1 d.tr. into each of next 6 d.tr., 7 ch., miss next sp.; rep. from first * once omitting 3 d.tr. and 7 ch. at end of rep., 1 s.s. into 4th of 4 ch.

4th round: 4 ch., 1 d.tr. in each of next 2 d.tr., 8 ch., miss next sp., * (1 d.c. into next loop, 8 ch.) 3 times, 3 d.tr. into next sp., 1 d.tr. into next d.tr., 5 ch., 1 d.c. into next sp., 5 ch., miss 3 d.tr., 1 d.tr. into next d.tr., 3 d.tr. into next sp., (8 ch., 1 d.c. into next loop) twice, 8 ch., 3 d.tr. into next sp., 1 d.tr. into next d.tr., 5 ch., 1 d.c. into next sp., 5 ch., miss 3 d.tr., 1 d.tr. into next d.tr., 3 d.tr. into next sp., (8 ch., 1 d.c. into next loop) 3 times, * 9 ch., 1 d.tr. into each of next 7 d.tr., 9 ch., miss next sp.; rep. from * to * once, 8 ch., 1 d.tr. into each of next 6 d.tr., 8 ch., miss next sp.; rep. from first * once omitting 3 d.tr. and 8 ch. at end of rep., 1 s.s. into 4th of 4 ch.

5th round: 4 ch., 1 d.tr. into each of next 2 d.tr., 10 ch., miss next sp., * (1 d.c. into next loop, 8 ch.) twice, 3 d.tr. into next sp., 1 d.tr. into next d.tr., (6 ch., 1 d.c. into next sp.) twice, 6 ch., miss 3 d.tr., 1 d.tr. into next d.tr., 3 d.tr. into next sp., 8 ch., 1 d.c. into next loop, 8 ch., 3 d.tr. into next sp., 1 d.tr. into next d.tr., (6 ch., 1 d.c. into next sp.) twice, 6 ch., miss 3 d.tr., 1 d.tr. into next d.tr., 3 d.tr. into next sp., (8 ch., 1 d.c. into next loop) twice, * 10 ch., 1

Coat with fashion flair, made in double knitting yarn. Instructions on page 108.

d.tr. into each of next 7 d.tr., 10 ch., miss next sp.; rep. from * to * once, 10 ch., 1 d.tr. into each of next 6 d.tr., 10 ch.; rep. from first * once omitting 3 d.tr. and 10 ch. at end of rep., 1 s.s. into 4th of 4 ch.

6th round: 4 ch., 1 d.tr. into each of next 2 d.tr., 10 ch., miss next sp., * 1 d.c. into next loop, 8 ch., 3 d.tr. into next sp., 1 d.tr. into next d.tr., (7 ch., 1 d.c. into next loop) 3 times, 7 ch., miss 3 d.tr., 1 d.tr. into next d.tr., 3 d.tr. into next sp., 2 ch., 3 d.tr. into next sp., 1 d.tr. into next d.tr., (7 ch., 1 d.c. into next loop) 3 times, 7 ch., miss 3 d.tr., 1 d.tr. into next d.tr., 3 d.tr. into next sp., 8 ch., 1 d.c. into next loop, * 11 ch., 1 d.tr. into each of next 7 d.tr., 11 ch., miss next loop; rep. from * to * once, 10 ch., 1 d.tr. into each of next 6 d.tr., 10 ch.; rep. from first * once omitting 3 d.tr. and 10 ch. at end of rep., 1 s.s. into 4th of 4 ch.

7th round: 4 ch., 1 d.tr. into each of next 2 d.tr., 11 ch., miss next sp., * 3 d.tr. into next sp., 1 d.tr. into next d.tr., (8 ch., 1 d.c. into next loop) 4 times, 8 ch., miss 3 d.tr., 1 d.tr. into next d.tr., 2 d.tr. into next sp., 1 d.tr. into next d.tr., (8 ch., 1 d.c. into next loop) 4 times, 8 ch., miss 3 d.tr., 1 d.tr. into next d.tr., 3 d.tr. into next sp., 11 ch., * 1 d.tr. into each of next 7 d.tr., 11 ch., miss next sp.; rep. from * to * once, 1 d.tr. into each of next 6 d.tr., 11 ch.; rep. from first * once more omitting 3 d.tr. and 11 ch. at end of rep., 1 s.s. into 4th of 4 ch.

8th round: 4 ch., 1 d.tr. into each of next 2 d.tr., * 7 ch., 1 d.c. into next sp., 7 ch., miss 3 d.tr., 1 d.tr. into next d.tr., 3 d.tr. into next sp., (7 ch., 1 d.c. into next loop) 3 times, 7 ch., 3 d.tr. into next sp., 1 d.tr. into next d.tr., 2 ch., miss 2 d.tr., 1 d.tr. into next d.tr., 3 d.tr. into next sp., (7 ch., 1 d.c. into next loop) 3 times, 7 ch., 3 d.tr. into next sp., 1 d.tr. into next d.tr., 7 ch., 1 d.c. into next sp., 7 ch., * 1 d.tr. into each of next 7 d.tr.; rep. from * to * once, 1 d.tr. into each of next 6 d.tr.; rep. from * once omitting 3 d.tr. at end of rep., 1 s.s. into 4th of 4 ch.

9th round: 4 ch., 1 d.tr. into each of next 2 d.tr., * (6 ch., 1 d.c. into next sp.) twice, 6 ch., miss 3 d.tr., 1 d.tr. into next d.tr., 3 d.tr. into next sp., (6 ch., 1 d.c. into next loop) twice, 6 ch., 3 d.tr. into next sp., 1 d.tr. into next d.tr., 5 ch., 1 d.c. into next sp., 5 ch., miss 3 d.tr., 1 d.tr. into next d.tr., 3 d.tr. into next sp., (6 ch., 1 d.c. into next loop) twice, 6 ch., 3 d.tr. into next sp., 1 d.tr. into next d.tr., (6 ch., 1 d.c. into next sp.) twice, 6 ch., * 1 d.tr. into each of next 7 d.tr.; rep. from * to * once, 1 d.tr. into each of next 6 d.tr.; rep. from first * once omitting 3 d.tr. at end of rep., 1 s.s. into 4th of 4 ch.

10th round: 4 ch., 1 d.tr. into each of next 2 d.tr., * (5 ch., 1 d.c. into next loop) 3 times, 5 ch., miss 3 d.tr., 1 d.tr. into next d.tr., 3 d.tr. into next sp., 5 ch., 1 d.c. into next loop, 5 ch., 3 d.tr. into next sp., 1 d.tr. into next d.tr., (6 ch., 1 d.c. into next sp.) twice, 6 ch., miss 3 d.tr., 1 d.tr. into next d.tr., 3 d.tr. into next sp., 5 ch., 1 d.c. into next loop, 5 ch., 3 d.tr. into next sp., 1 d.tr. into next d.tr., (5 ch., 1 d.c. into next loop) 3 times, 5 ch., * 1 d.tr. into each of next 7 d.tr.; rep. from * to * once, 1 d.tr. into each of next 6 d.tr.; rep. from first * once omitting 3 d.tr. at end of rep., 1 s.s. into 4th of 4 ch.

11th round: 4 ch., 1 d.tr. into each of next 2 d.tr., * (5 ch., 1 d.c. into next loop) 4 times, 5 ch., miss 3 d.tr., 1 d.tr. into next d.tr., 3 d.tr. into next sp., 2 ch., 3 d.tr. into next sp., 1 d.tr. into next d.tr., (7 ch., 1 d.c. into next loop) 3 times, 7 ch., miss 3 d.tr., 1 d.tr. into next d.tr., 3 d.tr. into next sp., 2 ch., 3 d.tr. into next sp., 1 d.tr. into next d.tr., (5 ch., 1 d.c. into next loop) 4 times, 5 ch., * 1 d.tr. into each of next 7 d.tr.; rep. from * to * once more, 1 d.tr. into each of next 6 d.tr.; rep. from first * once more omitting 3 d.tr. at end of rep., 1 s.s. into 4th of 4 ch.

12th round: 4 ch., 1 d.tr. into each of next 2 d.tr., * (5 ch., 1 d.c. into next loop) 5 times, 5 ch., miss 3 d.tr., 1 d.tr. into next d.tr., 2 d.tr. into next sp., 1 d.tr. into next d.tr., (8 ch., 1 d.c. into next loop) 4 times, 8 ch., miss 3 d.tr., 1 d.tr. into next d.tr., 2 d.tr. into next sp., 1 d.tr. into next d.tr., (5 ch., 1 d.c. into next loop) 5 times, 5 ch., * 1 d.tr. into each of next 7 d.tr.; rep. from * to * once, 1 d.tr. into each of next 6 d.tr.; rep. from first * once omitting 3 d.tr. at end of rep., 1 s.s. into 4th of 4 ch.

Rep. 3rd to 12th rounds once more.

Rep. 3rd to 12th rounds twice but having 1 ch. more on each ch. loop inside diamonds only.

Rep. 3rd to 12th rounds twice but having 2 ch. more on each ch. throughout and ending last rep. with 11th round.

Next round: 1 d.c. into same place as last s.s., 1 d.c. into each of next 2 d.tr., * 1 d.c. into next sp., (7 ch., 1 d.c. into next loop) 4 times, 8 ch., miss 3 d.tr., 1 d.tr. into next d.tr., 2 d.tr. into next sp., 1 d.tr. into next d.tr., (10 ch., 1 d.c. into next loop) 4 times, 10 ch., miss 3 d.tr., 1 d.tr. into next d.tr., 2 d.tr. into next sp., 1 d.tr. into next d.tr., (8 ch., 1 d.c. into next loop) 5 times, * 1 d.c. into each of next 7 d.tr.; rep. from * to * once, 1 d.c. into each of next 6 d.tr.; rep. from first * once omitting 3 d.c. at end of rep., 1 s.s. into first d.c.

Next round: 4 ch., 1 d.tr. into each of next 3 d.c., * (7 d.tr. into next loop, 1 d.tr. into next d.c.) 4 times, 7 d.tr. into next loop, 1 d.tr. into each of next 4 d.tr., 10 d.tr. into next loop, (1 d.tr. into next d.c., 10 d.tr. into next loop) 4 times, 1 d.tr. into each of next 4 d.tr., 7 d.tr. into next loop, (1 d.tr. into next d.c., 7 d.tr. into next loop) 4 times, * 1 d.tr. into each of next 9 d.c.; rep. from * to * once, 1 d.tr. into each of next 8 d.c.; rep. from first * once more, omitting 4 d.tr. at end of rep., 1 s.s. into 4th of 4 ch. Fasten off.

TO COMPLETE

Neck Edging. 1st round: with right side facing attach yarn to any shoulder seam, 1 d.c. into same place as join, work a round of d.c. evenly all round, 1 s.s. into first d.c.

2nd round: 3 ch., 1 tr. into each d.c., 1 s.s. into 3rd of 3 ch.; fasten off.

Armhole Edgings. With right side facing attach yarn to underarm seam, 1 d.c. into same place as join and complete as neck edging.

Damp and pin out to measurements. If wished dress may be lined in a matching or contrasting coloured fabric.

As good as gold—party dress made in a special glittering yarn (see page 100)

Black and white dress

(photographed in colour on page 75)

MATERIALS

5 balls (2-oz.) Twilley's Stalite in black and 5 balls (2-oz.) in white (see note on wools and yarns, page 22); one crochet hook International Standard Size 3.50 (see page 9); 16-in. black zip fastener; 1 black hook and eye.

MEASUREMENTS

To fit bust size 32 (34, 36) in.; length 31 in.

TENSION

2 patt. to $2\frac{1}{4}$ in. and 4 rows to $1\frac{1}{2}$ in. over bodice patt. (see note on tension, page 14).

ABBREVIATIONS

See page 20; B., Black; W., white.

BODICE

With B., commence with 122 (130, 138) ch.

Foundation row: 1 d.c. into 2nd ch. from hook, * miss 1 ch., 3 d.tr. into next ch., miss 1 ch., 1 d.c. into next ch.; rep. from * to end.

1st patt. row: 4 ch., 1 d.tr. into fitst d.c., * 1 d.c. into centre d.tr. of d.tr.gr., 3 d.tr. into next d.c.; rep. from * ending with 2 d.tr. into last d.c.

2nd patt. row: 1 ch., 1 d.c. into first d.tr., * 3 d.tr. into next d.c., 1 d.c. into centre d.tr. of next d.tr.gr.; rep. from * ending with 1 d.c. into last d.tr.

These 2 rows form patt. Cont. in patt. until work measures 6 in. from beg., ending with 2nd patt. row.

Divide for Armholes. 1st row: 1 ch., 1 d.c. into first d.tr., (3 d.tr. into next d.c., 1 d.c. into centre d.tr. of next d.tr.gr.) 6 (7, 7) times, s.s. across next 11 sts., 1 d.c. into next d.tr., (3 d.tr. into next d.c., 1 d.c. into centre d.tr. of next d.tr.gr.) 12 (12, 14) times, s.s. across next 11 sts., 1 d.c. into next d.tr., (3 d.tr. into next d.c., 1 d.c. into centre d.tr. of next d.tr.gr.) 6 (7, 7) times, but work last d.c. of last rep. into last d.tr.

Work on last set of sts. for right side of back. Cont. in patt. until work measures $13\frac{1}{2}$ in. from beg. Fasten off. Rejoin B. to set of sts. on other side edge and work left side of back to match right. Rejoin B. to centre set of sts. for Front. Work in patt. until work measures 11 in. from beg., ending with a 1st patt. row.

Shape Neck. 1st row: 1 ch., 1 d.c. into first d.tr., (3 d.tr. into next d.c., 1 d.c. into centre d.tr. of next gr.) 4 (4, 5) times, s.s. across centre 15 sts., 1 d.c. into next d.tr., patt. to end.

Work on last set of sts. only.

Next row: patt. to last st.; turn.

Next row: s.s. across first st., patt. to end.

Rep. last 2 rows once: 1 complete patt. dec. Cont. straight in patt. until work measures $13\frac{1}{2}$ in. from beg. Fasten off. Rejoin B. to inner edge of other side.

Next row: s.s. across first st., patt. to end.

Next row: patt. to last st.; turn.

Rep. last 2 rows once. Complete as other side.

Edgings. With B., work p. border along lower edge of Bodice: 1 d.c. into first ch., * miss 1 ch., 2 d.tr. into next ch., 3 ch., s.s. into first of 3 ch., 1 d.tr. into same ch. as 2 d.tr., miss 1 ch., 1 d.c. into next ch.; rep. from * to end; fasten off.

Join shoulders. With B., work 2 rows of d.c. around neck and down back openings; fasten off.

SLEEVES (make 2 alike)

With B., commence with 42 ch. Work foundation row as for Bodice, then work 1st and 2nd patt. rows.

Dec. row: s.s. across first 4 sts. (1 patt.), patt. to last 4 sts.; turn.

Work 5 rows straight. Rep. last 6 rows 3 times then dec. row again. Fasten off.

Edgings. With B., work p. border along ch. edge as given for Bodice lower edge.

SKIRT

Join B. to first ch. at lower edge of bodice, then work underneath p. border.

1st row: 3 ch., * 1 ch., miss 1 ch., 1 tr. into next ch.; rep. from * to end.

Break off B. and join W. at other end of row.

2nd row (right side): 4 ch., (1 d.tr. into next 1-ch. sp., 1 ch., 1 d.tr. in same ch.sp., 5 d.tr. into next 1-ch.sp.) 30 (32, 34) times, 1 d.tr. into last tr.

1st patt. row: 5 ch., * 1 d.tr. into centre d.tr. of next 5-d.tr.gr., 1 ch., 1 d.tr. into same d.tr., 1 d.tr. into next 1-ch.sp., 1 ch., 1 d.tr. into same ch.sp.; rep. from * to end, 1 d.tr. into 4th of 4 ch.

2nd patt. row: 4 ch., * 1 d.tr. into next 1-ch.sp., 1 ch., 1 d.tr. into same ch.sp., 5 d.tr. into next 1-ch.sp.; rep. from * to end, 1 d.tr. into 4th of 5 ch. Rep. last 2 rows 3 times, then first patt. row again, omitting last d.tr. into 4th of 4 ch.

Now join work in a ring and placing edges tog. work in rounds.

1st round: * 1 d.tr. into next 1-ch.sp., 1 ch., 1 d.tr. in same ch.sp., 5 d.tr. into next 1-ch.sp.; rep. from * all round, s.s. into first d.tr.

2nd round: 5 ch., 1 d.tr. into next 1-ch.sp., 1 d.tr. into centre d.tr. of next 5-d.tr.gr., 1 ch., 1 d.tr. into same d.tr., * 1 d.tr. into next 1-ch.sp., 1 ch., 1 d.tr. into same ch.sp., 1 d.tr. into centre d.tr. of next 5-d.tr.gr., 1 ch., 1 d.tr. into same d.tr.; rep. from * to end, s.s. into 4th of 5 ch.

3rd round: 5 ch., 1 d.tr. into next 1-ch.sp., 6 d.tr. into next 1-ch.sp., * 1 d.tr. into next 1-ch.sp., 1 ch., 1 d.tr. into same sp., 6 d.tr. into next 1-ch.sp.; rep. from * to end, s.s. into 4th of 5 ch.

1st patt. round: 5 ch., 1 d.tr. into next 1-ch.sp., 1 d.tr. between 3rd and 4th d.tr. of next 6-d.tr.gr., 2 ch., 1 d.tr. into same sp., * 1 d.tr. into next 1-ch.sp., 1 ch., 1 d.tr. into same sp., 1 d.tr. between 3rd and 4th d.tr. of next 6-d.tr.gr., 2 ch., 1 d.tr. into same d.tr.; rep. from * to end, s.s. into 4th of 5 ch.

2nd patt. round: 5 ch., 1 d.tr. into next 1-ch.sp., 6 d.tr. into next 2-ch.sp., * 1 d.tr. into next 1-ch.sp., 1 ch., 1 d.tr. into same sp., 6 d.tr. into next 2-ch.sp.; rep. from * to end, s.s. into 4th of 5 ch.

Rep. last 2 rounds until work measures 30½ in. from shoulders, ending with a first patt. round.

Next round: 5 ch., 1 d.tr. into next 1-ch.sp., 3 d.tr. into next 2-ch.sp., 3 ch., s.s. into first ch., 3 d.tr. into same sp., * 1 d.tr. into next 1-ch.sp., 1 ch., 1 d.tr. into same sp., 3 d.tr. into next 2-ch.sp., 3 ch., s.s. into first ch., 3 d.tr. into same sp.; rep. from * to end, s.s. into 4th of 5 ch.; fasten off.

Edging. With W., work 2 rows d.c. around opening at top

of skirt.

Flowers (make 7): with B., make 4 ch. and s.s. into first ch. to form a ring.

1st round: work 8 d.c. into ring, s.s. into first d.c.

2nd round: (8 ch., miss 1 d.c., 1 d.c. into next d.c.) 4 times.

3rd round: (3 d.c., 9 tr. and 3 d.c. into next 8-ch.sp.) 4 times, s.s. into first d.c.; fasten off.

TO COMPLETE
Do not press. Join sleeve seams. Set in sleeves. Join Bodice and Skirt back-opening borders. Sew in zip fastener. Sew hook and eye at top of opening. Sew flowers around top of skirt as shown in photograph on page 75. Press seams.

Flounced dress
(photographed in colour on page 76)

MATERIALS
11 (11, 12, 12) balls (2-oz.) Twilley's Stalite (see note on wools and yarns, page 22); crochet hooks International Standard Sizes 3.50 and 3.00 (see page 9).

MEASUREMENTS
To fit bust size 32 (34, 36, 38) in.; length from shoulder 33 in.

TENSION
1 patt. to 1 in. with No. 3.50 hook (see note on tension, page 14).

ABBREVIATIONS
See page 20.

BACK
With No. 3.50 hook, commence with 103 (108, 113, 118) ch. to measure 20½ (21½, 22½, 23½) in.

Foundation row: 1 tr. into 3rd ch. from hook, * miss 4 ch., 1 ch., 4 tr. into next ch.: a sh. made; rep. from * to within last 5 ch., 1 ch., miss 4 ch., 2 tr. into last ch.; turn: 19 (20, 21, 22) 4-tr. shs.

Patt. row: 3 ch., 1 tr. into first tr., * 1 ch., 4 tr. into centre sp. of next sh.; rep. from * ending with 1 ch., 2 tr. into 3rd of 3 ch.; turn.

Rep. last row until work measures 5 in. from beg.

Dec. row: 3 ch., 1 tr. into first tr., (1 ch., 4 tr. into centre sp. of next sh.) 4 times, 2 tr. into centre sp. of next 2 shs., * 1 ch., 4 tr. into centre sp. of next sh.; rep. from * to within last 6 shs., 2 tr. into centre sp. of next 2 shs., (1 ch., 4 tr. into centre sp. of next sh.) 4 times, 2 tr. into 3rd of 3 ch.; turn.

Rep. patt. row until Back measures 14½ in. from beg.,

change to No. 3.00 hook and cont. working patt. row until Back measures 20½ in. from beg.

Shape Armholes. 1st row: 1 s.s. into each of first 5 sts., patt. to within last 5 sts.; turn.

Work 1 row in patt.

Rep. last 2 rows once, then work patt. rows until armholes measure 6½ (7, 7½, 8) in. from beg. Fasten off.

FRONT
Work as Back until 6 (6, 7, 7) rows less than Back are completed.

Shape Neck. 1st row: patt. until 4 (4, 5, 5) whole shs. are completed, 1 ch., 2 tr. into centre sp. of next sh.; turn.

2nd row: 1 s.s. into each of first 5 sts., patt. to end; turn.

3rd row: patt. to within last 5 sts.; turn.

Work 3 (3, 4, 4) rows in patt. Fasten off.

2nd Side of Neck. 1st row: attach yarn to centre sp. of 5th (5th, 6th, 6th) whole sh. from opposite armhole edge, patt. to end; turn.

Work 3rd and 2nd rows of neck shaping once each then work 3 (3, 4, 4) rows in patt. Fasten off.

TO COMPLETE
Join side and shoulder seams.

Lower Frill. 1st round: with right side facing and with No. 3.50 hook attach yarn to same place as a sh. on lower edge, 1 d.c. into same place as join, 4 ch., 3 d.tr. into same place, 1 ch., * 8 d.tr. into same place as next sh., 1 ch.; rep. from * all round ending with 4 d.tr. into same place as join, s.s. into 4th of 4 ch.; turn.

2nd round: 1 s.s. into next sp., 4 ch., 3 d.tr. into same place as s.s., * 1 ch., 8 d.tr. into centre sp. of next sh.; rep. from * ending with 1 ch., 4 d.tr. into same sp. as s.s., s.s. into 4th of 4 ch.; turn.

Rep. last round 5 times. Fasten off.

2nd Frill. Measure $3\frac{1}{2}$ in. up from beg. of lower frill on main section and attach yarn to a 1-ch. sp. on next row.

1st round: 1 d.c. into same place as join, 4 ch., 3 d.tr. into same place, * 1 ch., 8 d.tr. into next 1-ch. sp.; rep. from * all round ending with 1 ch., 4 d.tr. into same place as join, s.s.

into 4th of 4 ch.; turn.

Rep. 2nd round of lower frill 6 times. Fasten off.

Edgings for Neck and Armholes. 1st round: with right side facing and with No. 3.00 hook, attach yarn to edge and work d.c. evenly round, 1 d.c. into first d.c.

2nd round: 1 d.c. into each d.c., s.s. into first d.c.; fasten off. Press lightly.

Floral-patterned dress

(photographed in colour on the front cover and on page 77)

MATERIALS

12 balls (2-oz) of Twilley's Stalite in white, 1 ball (2-oz.) Twilley's Stalite in yellow and 1 ball (2-oz.) Twilley's Stalite in green (see note on wools and yarns, page 22); crochet hooks International Standard Sizes 3.00 and 3.50 (see page 9); 22-in. white zip fastener.

MEASUREMENTS

To fit bust size 32 (34, 36) in.; length 33 in.

TENSION

2 patts. to $2\frac{1}{4}$ in. and 4 rows to $1\frac{1}{2}$ in. with No. 3.50 hook over bodice patt. (see note on tension, page 14).

ABBREVIATIONS

See page 20; W., white; Y., yellow; G., green.

BODICE

With No. 3.00 hook and W., commence with 106 (113, 120) ch. for waistband.

1st row: 1 d.c. into 2nd ch. from hook, 1 d.c. into each ch. to end.

2nd row: 1 ch., 1 d.c. into each d.c. to end.

Rep. 2nd row 6 times.

Next row: 1 ch., 1 d.c. into first d.c., * 2 d.c. into next d.c., 1 d.c. into each of next 6 d.c.; rep. from * 14 (15, 16) times: 121 (129, 137) sts.

Patt. foundation row: 1 ch., 1 d.c. into first d.c., * miss 1 d.c., 3 d.tr. into next d.c., miss 1 d.c., 1 d.c. into next d.c.; rep. from * to end.

1st patt. row (wrong side): 4 ch., 1 d.tr. into first d.c., * 1 d.c. into centre d.tr. of 3-d.tr.gr., 3 d.tr. into next d.c.; rep. from * ending with 2 d.tr. into last d.c.

2nd patt. row: 1 ch., 1 d.c. into first d.tr., * 3 d.tr. into next d.c., 1 d.c. into centre d.tr. of next gr.; rep. from * ending with 1 d.c. into last d.tr.

These last 2 rows form patt. Work 8 more rows in patt. Change to No. 3.50 hook. Cont. in patt. until work measures 9 in. from beg. of waistband, ending with a first patt. row.

Divide for Armholes. 1st row: 1 ch., 1 d.c. into first d.tr., (3 d.tr. into next d.c., 1 d.c. into centre d.tr. of next gr.) 6 (7, 7) times, s.s. across next 11 sts., 1 d.c. into next d.tr., (3 d.tr. into next d.c., 1 d.c. into centre d.tr. of next gr.) 12 (12, 14) times, s.s. across next 11 sts., 1 d.c. into next d.tr., (3 d.tr. into next d.c., 1 d.c. into centre d.tr. of next gr.) 6 (7, 7) times, but work last d.c. of last rep. into last d.tr.

Work on last set of sts. for right side of back.

Cont. in patt. until work measures $16\frac{1}{2}$ in. from beg. of waistband. Fasten off.

Rejoin W. to centre set of sts. for front. Cont. in patt. until work measures $14\frac{1}{2}$ in. from beg. of waistband, ending with a first patt. row.

Shape Neck. Next row: 1 ch., 1 d.c. into first d.tr., (3 d.tr. into next d.c., 1 d.c. into centre d.tr. of next gr.) 4 (4, 5) times, s.s. across centre 15 sts., 1 d.c. into next d.tr., patt. to end.

Work on last set of sts. only.

Next row: s.s. across first st., patt. to end.

Rep. last 2 rows once: 1 complete patt. dec. Work 1 row straight. Fasten off.

Rejoin W. to inner edge of other side.

Next row: s.s. across first st., patt. to end.

Next row: patt. to last st.; turn.

Rep. last 2 rows once. Work 1 row straight. Fasten off. Rejoin W. to remaining set of sts. for left side of back and complete as right side.

SLEEVES (make 2 alike)

With No. 3.50 hook and W., commence with 42 ch. Work patt. foundation row as Bodice, then work 1st and 2nd patt. rows.

Dec. row: s.s. across first 4 sts. (1 patt.), patt. to last 4 sts.; turn.

Work 5 rows straight in patt. Rep. last 6 rows 3 times then work dec. row again. Fasten off.

Edging. Work p. border along lower edge of sleeve:

1st row: with W., work 1 d.c. into first ch., * miss 1 ch.,

2 d.tr. into next ch., 3 ch., s.s. into first of 3 ch., 1 d.tr. into same ch. as 2 d.tr., miss 1 ch., 1 d.c. into next ch.; rep. from * to end; fasten off.

SKIRT WHITE MOTIF (make 20)
With No. 3.50 hook and W., commence with 4 ch. and join with s.s. to form a ring.
1st round: 3 ch., 2 tr. into ring, 1 ch., * 3 tr. into ring, 1 ch.; rep. from * twice, s.s. into top of 3 ch.
2nd round: s.s. across next 2 tr. and into 1-ch.sp., 3 ch., into same 1-ch.sp. work 2 tr., 1 ch. and 3 tr., 1 ch., * into next 1-ch.sp. work 3 tr., 1 ch. and 3 tr., 1 ch.; rep. from * twice, s.s. into top of 3 ch.
3rd round: s.s. across next 2 tr. and into next 1-ch.sp., 3 ch., into same ch.sp. work 2 tr., 1 ch. and 3 tr., 1 ch., 3 tr. into next 1-ch.sp., 1 ch., * into next 1-ch.sp. work 3 tr., 1 ch. and 3 tr., 1 ch., 3 tr. into next 1-ch.sp., 1 ch.; rep. from * twice, s.s. into top of 3 ch.
4th round: s.s. across next 2 tr. and into next 1-ch.sp., into same ch.sp. work 2 tr., 1 ch. and 3 tr., 1 ch., (3 tr. into next 1-ch.sp., 1 ch.) twice, * into next 1-ch.sp. work 3 tr., 1 ch. and 3 tr., 1 ch., (3 tr. into next 1-ch. sp., 1 ch.) twice; rep. from * twice, s.s. into top of 3 ch.
5th round: s.s. across next 2 tr. and into next 1-ch.sp., into same 1-ch.sp. work 2 tr., 1 ch. and 3 tr., 1 ch., (3 tr. into next 1-ch.sp., 1 ch.) 3 times, * into next 1-ch.sp. work 3 tr., 1 ch. and 3 tr., (3 tr. into next 1-ch.sp., 1 ch.) 3 times; rep. from *twice, s.s. into top of 3 ch.; fasten off.

SKIRT FLOWER MOTIF (make 20)
With No. 3.50 hook and G., commence with 6 ch., s.s. into first ch. to form a ring.
1st round: work 16 d.c. into ring, s.s. into first d.c.
2nd round: 5 ch., * miss next d.c., 1 h.tr. into next d.c., 3 ch.; rep. from * 6 times, s.s. into 2nd of 5 ch. Break off G.
3rd round: join Y. to next 3-ch.sp. with a s.s., 2 ch., 3 h.tr. into same sp., * 10 ch., 4 h.tr. into next 3-ch.sp.; rep. from * 6 times, 10 ch., s.s. into top of 2 ch.

4th round: 1 d.c. into sp. between next 2 h.tr., into next 10-ch. loop work 7 tr., 3 ch., 7 tr., * 1 d.c. into sp. between 2nd and 3rd h.tr. of next h.tr.gr., into next 10-ch. loop work 7 tr., 3 ch. and 7 tr.; rep. from * 6 times, s.s. into first d.c. Break off Y.
5th round: join W. to next 3-ch.sp. at top of petal with a s.s., 1 d.c. into same 3-ch.sp., 5 ch., 1 t.tr. into next d.c. between petals, 5 ch., * 1 d.c. into next 3-ch.sp., 5 ch., 1 t.tr. into next d.c., 5 ch.; rep. from * 6 times, s.s. into first d.c.
6th round: * 4 d.c. into next 5-ch. loop, 1 d.c. into t.tr., 4 d.c. into next 5-ch. loop, 1 d.c. into next d.c.; rep. from * 7 times.
7th round: * 7 ch., leaving last loop of each d.tr. on hook, work 1 d.tr. into each of next 9 d.c., y.o.h. and draw through all loops on hook firmly, 7 ch., 1 d.c. into each of next 11 d.c.; rep. from * 3 times.
Next round: work d.c. along one edge of motif, working 1 d.c. into each st., * work d.c. along next edge also working through edge of one white motif to join; rep. from * twice, joining with a new W. motif each time, s.s. into first d.c.; fasten off.
Work 19 more flower motifs, joining to W. motifs on last d.c. round so that you have a circle 4 motifs deep and 10 motifs across, but do not join 2 motifs on top line at back opening. With No. 3.00 hook and W., work 1 row d.c. around lower edge of waistband working through top edge of skirt at same time and easing skirt into waistband.

TO COMPLETE
Edgings. With No. 3.00 hook and W., work border around lower edge of skirt: * 1 d.c. into each of next 4 d.c., 3 ch., s.s. to first ch.; rep. from * all round, s.s. into first d.c.; fasten off.
Join shoulders. With No. 3.00 hook and W., work 3 rows d.c. around neck and back opening.
Do not press. Join sleeve seams. Set in sleeves. Sew in zip fastener.
Press seams.

Blouse-topped dress
(photographed in colour on page 17)

MATERIALS
25 (26, 27) oz. of Twilley's Cortina crochet wool (see note on wools and yarns, page 22); crochet hooks International Standard Sizes 2.00 and 3.50 (see page 9); a 9-in. zip fastener; 6 hooks and bars.

MEASUREMENTS
To fit bust size 34 (36, 38) in.; length 34 in. (adjustable);

sleeve seam 18 in.

TENSION
5 gr. and 5 rows to 2 in. over bodice patt. (see note on tension, page 14).

ABBREVIATIONS
See page 20.

BODICE

Front. With No. 2.00 hook make 93 (97, 101) ch. loosely.

1st row: miss 1 ch., 1 d.c. into each ch. to end.

Now patt. thus:

Foundation row: 3 ch., miss 1 d.c., * (1 tr., 2 ch., 1 tr.) into next d.c., miss 1 d.c.; rep. from * to last d.c., 1 tr. into last d.c.

Patt. row: 3 ch., * (1 tr., 2 ch., 1 tr.) into next 2-ch.sp.: gr. worked; rep. from * ending with 1 tr. into 3-ch. sp.: 45 (47, 49) gr. * *

Rep. patt. row until work measures 10½ in.

Armhole Shaping. 1st row: s.s. to centre of 4th gr., 3 ch., patt. to within last 4 gr., 1 tr. into centre of next gr.; turn.

2nd row: s.s. to centre of first gr., 3 ch., patt. to within last gr., 1 tr. into centre of last gr.; turn.

Rep. 2nd row 3 times: 29 (31, 33) gr.

Cont. until work measures 16¼ in.

Neck Shaping. 1st row: 3 ch., (1 gr. into next 2-ch. sp.) 8 (8, 9) times, 1 tr. into next 2-ch. sp.; turn.

2nd row: s.s. to centre of first gr., 3 ch., patt. to end.

3rd row: 3 ch., patt. to within last gr., 1 tr. into centre of last gr.; turn.

Work 1 row straight. Fasten off. Rejoin wool to centre of 9th (9th, 10th) gr. from other end.

1st row: 3 ch., (1 gr. in next 2-ch. sp.) 8 (8, 9) times, 1 tr. into 3-ch. sp.

2nd row: 3 ch., patt. to within last gr., 1 tr. into centre of last gr.; turn.

3rd row: s.s. to centre of first gr., 3 ch., patt. to end.

Work 1 row straight. Fasten off.

Back. As Front to * *.

Rep. patt. row until work measures 7¾ in.

Back opening row: 3 ch., (1 gr. in next 2-ch. sp.) 22 (23, 24) times, 1 tr. into centre of next gr.; turn.

Cont. on these sts. only until work measures 10½ in. ending at side.

Armhole Shaping. 1st row: s.s. to centre of 4th gr., 3 ch., patt. to end.

2nd row: 3 ch., patt. to within last gr., 1 tr. into centre of last gr.; turn.

3rd row: s.s. to centre of first gr., 3 ch., patt. to end.

Rep. 2nd and 3rd rows once.

Cont. straight until work measures 16¾ in. ending at inner edge.

Neck Shaping. 1st row: s.s. to centre of 8th (8th, 9th) gr., 3 ch., patt. to end. Work 1 row straight. Fasten off.

Rejoin yarn to centre 2-ch. sp. at base of back opening (already worked into).

Next row: 3 ch., patt. to end.

Cont. on these sts. until work measures 10½ in., ending at inner edge.

Armhole Shaping. 1st row: 3 ch., patt. to within last 4 gr., 1 tr. into centre of next gr.; turn.

2nd row: s.s. to centre of first gr., 3 ch., patt. to end.

3rd row: 3 ch., patt. to within last gr., 1 tr. into centre of last gr.; turn.

Rep. 2nd and 3rd rows once.

Cont. straight until work measures 16¾ in. ending at arm-hole.

Neck Shaping. 1st row: 3 ch., (1 gr. in next 2-ch. sp.) 6 (6, 7) times, 1 tr. into centre of next gr.; turn. Work 1 row straight. Fasten off.

SKIRT

Join side and shoulder seams of bodice. Using yarn double for skirt, join yarn to one side seam and with No. 3.50 hook, work thus.

1st round: 1 ch., work 187 (195, 203) d.c. around lower edge of bodice, s.s. to 1 ch.

2nd round: 3 ch., (1 tr., 2 ch., 2 tr.) into same sp., * miss 3 d.c., (2 tr., 2 ch., 2 tr.) into next d.c.; rep. from * to end, finishing miss 3 d.c., s.s. to 3rd ch.

3rd round: s.s. to first 2-ch. sp., 3 ch., (1 tr., 2 ch., 2 tr.) into same sp., * (2 tr., 2 ch., 2 tr.) into next 2-ch. sp.; rep. from * to end, finishing s.s. to 3rd ch.

Rep. 3rd round until work measures 34 in. from shoulder (adjust length here if required).

Last round: 1 ch., 1 d.c. into each tr. and 2 d.c. into each ch. sp. to end, s.s. to 1 ch., fasten off.

SLEEVES (make 2 alike)

With No. 2.00 hook make 36 ch. loosely. Work first row as for Bodice Front. Now patt. thus:

Foundation row: 3 ch., (1 tr., 2 ch., 1 tr.) into each ch. to end, finishing 1 tr. into last ch.

Rep. patt. row as for Bodice Front (34 gr.) until sleeve measures 16 in.

Top Shaping. 1st row: as first armhole shaping row of Bodice Front.

2nd row: as 2nd armhole shaping row of Bodice Front.

3rd row: 3 ch., patt. to end. Rep. last 3 rows once, then rep. 2nd row 7 times. Fasten off.

TO COMPLETE

Press work.

Neckband. With No. 2.00 hook join wool to left side of back opening.

1st row: 1 ch., work 76 (82, 82) d.c. around neck.

2nd row: 1 ch., 1 d.c. into each d.c. to end. Rep. 2nd row for 1½ in. then work 2 rows d.c. along side edges of neck-band around back opening. Fasten off. Sew in zip, setting top of zip to base of neckband. Join sleeve seams, leaving 1 in. open at lower edge.

Cuffs. With No. 2.00 hook, join wool to foundation ch. of sleeve.

1st row: 1 ch., work 35 d.c. along base of sleeve.

2nd row: 1 ch., 1 d.c. into each d.c. to end. Rep. 2nd row for 1½ in. then work 2 rows d.c. along side edges of cuffs and around sleeve openings.

Waist Tie. Using 4 strands of yarn and No. 3.50 hook make a 66-in. length of ch.

Thread ch. through patt. at top of skirt for waist tie. Finish each end of tie with a small pompon (follow pompon instructions on page 69). Sew on 2 hooks and bars to back neck and 2 to each cuff.

Motif skirt and bolero

(photographed in black and white on page 105)

MATERIALS

For bolero: 4 (5, 5) oz. of Sirdar 4-ply Fontein Crêpe in 1st colour and 5 (6, 7) oz. of Sirdar 4-ply Fontein Crêpe in 2nd colour (see note on wools and yarns, page 22); one crochet hook International Standard Size 3.00 (3.00, 3.50) (see page 9).

For skirt: 6 (7, 7) oz. of Sirdar 4-ply Fontein Crêpe in 1st colour and 8 (9, 10) oz. of Sirdar 4-ply Fontein Crêpe in 2nd colour (see note on wools and yarns, page 22); one crochet hook International Standard Size 2.50 (3.00, 3.50) (see page 9); waist length of elastic $\frac{3}{4}$ in. wide.

MEASUREMENTS

Bolero: to fit bust size 34 (36, 38) in.; length down centre back, including borders $16\frac{3}{4}$ ($17\frac{1}{4}$, 18) in. **Skirt:** to fit hip size 36 (38, 40) in.; length 22 ($22\frac{3}{4}$, $23\frac{1}{2}$) in. (this can be lengthened or shortened by adding or omitting rows of motifs as required).

TENSION

Diagonal length of 1 motif $2\frac{7}{8}$ (3, $3\frac{1}{8}$) in. (see note on tension, page 14).

ABBREVIATIONS

See page 20.

MOTIF

Commence with 4 ch. and join with s.s. to form a ring.
1st round: 3 ch., 15 tr. into ring, join to 3rd of 3 ch. with a s.s.
2nd round: 3 ch., 2 d.tr. and 1 tr. into same st. as last s.s., * miss 1 tr., 1 tr., 2 d.tr. and 1 tr. into next tr.; rep. from * 6 times, s.s. into 3rd of 3 ch. at beg. of round.
3rd round: s.s. into next d.tr., then s.s. into sp. between this d.tr. and next d.tr., 3 ch., 1 d.tr. and 1 tr. into same sp., * 3 ch., 1 d.c. between next 2 tr., 3 ch., 1 d.c. between next 2 d.tr., 3 ch., 1 d.c. between next 2 tr., 3 ch., * * 1 tr., 1 d.tr. and 1 tr. between next 2 d.tr.; rep. from * twice, then rep. from * to * * once, s.s. into 3rd of 3 ch. at beg. of round. Fasten off.

HALF MOTIF

Commence with 3 ch. and join with s.s. to form a ring.
1st row: 3 ch., then work 8 tr. into one half of ring, 4 ch.; turn.
2nd row: 1 tr. into first tr., * miss next tr., 1 tr., 2 d.tr. and 1 tr. into next tr.; rep. from * twice, 1 tr. and 1 d.tr. into 3rd of 3 ch., 4 ch.; turn.
3rd row: 1 tr. into d.tr., * 3 ch., 1 d.c. between next 2 tr., 3 ch., 1 d.c. between next 2 d.tr., 3 ch., 1 d.c. between next 2 tr., * 3 ch., 1 tr., 1 d.tr. and 1 tr. between next 2 d.tr.; rep. from * to * once, 3 ch., 1 tr. and 1 d.tr. into 4th of 4 ch.; fasten off.

QUARTER MOTIF

Commence with 3 ch. and join with s.s. to form a ring.
1st row: 3 ch., then work 4 tr. into quarter of ring, 4 ch.; turn.
2nd row: 1 tr. into first tr., miss 1 tr., 1 tr., 2 d.tr. and 1 tr. into next tr., miss 1 tr., 1 tr. and 1 d.tr. into 3rd of 3 ch., 4 ch.; turn.
3rd row: 1 tr. into d.tr., 3 ch., 1 d.c. between next 2 tr., 3 ch., 1 tr., 1 d.tr. and 1 tr. between next 2 d.tr., 3 ch., 1 d.c. between next 2 tr., 3 ch., 1 tr. and 1 d.tr. into 4th of 4 ch.; fasten off.

DECREASED MOTIF

Commence with 3 ch. and join with s.s. to form a ring.
1st row: 2 ch., 7 tr. into ring, 1 d.c.; turn.
2nd row: 2 ch., 1 tr. into first tr., * 1 tr., 2 d.tr. and 1 tr. into next tr., miss 1 tr.; rep. from * twice, 1 tr. and 1 d.c. into last tr.; turn.
3rd row: 2 ch., 1 tr., 1 d.tr. and 1 tr. between 2 d.tr., 3 ch., 1 d.c. between next 2 tr., 3 ch., 1 d.c between next 2 d.tr., 3 ch., 1 d.c. between next 2 tr., 3 ch., 1 tr., 1 d.tr. and 1 tr. between next 2 d.tr., 1 tr. in last st.; fasten off.

TO JOIN MOTIFS

The motifs may be joined by sewing them together or by crocheting them together as you work the last round. The motifs are placed as diamonds and are joined by the d.tr. at corners.

1st-row motifs: work a s.s. into corner d.tr. of first motif as you work 2nd motif.
Subsequent motifs: join with s.s. into corner d.tr. and s.s. at centre of sides.

BOLERO

1st row: make 6 motifs in 1st colour for lower edge and leave aside. Then make 6 motifs in 2 colours: work from beg. to end of 1st round with 2nd colour, join 1st colour and work 2nd and 3rd rounds with 1st colour. Join these motifs alt. with the 1st-colour motifs already worked at the d.tr. at corners. This makes the base of the Bolero, with half motifs filled in later.
2nd row: work 6 motifs in 2nd colour then 5 motifs with 1st-colour centre and 2nd-colour outside. Place first 2nd-colour motif between 1st and 2nd motifs of 1st row, then work alt. the 5 motifs with 1st-colour centre and 2nd-colour motifs, this time joining at corners and sides.
3rd row: as 1st row, but with 1st-colour motif above motif with 2nd-colour centre of 1st row.
4th row: as 2nd row, but make 5 motifs in 2nd colour and 6 motifs with 1st-colour centre. Place 2nd-colour motifs above motifs with 1st-colour centre of 2nd row.
5th row: as 1st row.
Right Front. 6th row: work a 2nd colour motif and join

in same position as on 2nd row. Work 1 motif with 1st-colour centre and join.

7th row: work a 1st-colour motif and join in same position as on 3rd row, work 1 motif with 2nd-colour centre and join.

8th row: work 1 motif with 1st-colour centre and a 2nd-colour motif and join as on 4th row.

9th row: work a 1st-colour motif and join between 2 motifs of previous row.

Back. 6th row: miss 1 motif each side for armhole, then work and join rest of row to match 2nd row.

Leaving 2 motifs each side for armholes on 7th and 9th rows and 1 motif each side on 8th row, work and join 3 more rows to match 3rd, 4th and 1st rows.

Left Front. 6th, 7th and 8th rows: work as Right Front but join to match previous rows on Left Front.

9th row: work 1 motif with 2nd-colour centre and join between 2 motifs of 8th row.

Edges. Make 6 half motifs with 1st-colour centres and 5 half motifs in 2nd colour and join alt. along lower edge, starting with half motif with 1st-colour centre between 1st and 2nd motifs of 1st row. Make 2 half motifs with 1st-colour centres and 1 half motif in 2nd colour for *each* front edge. Join alt. starting with 1 half motif with 1st-colour centre between 1st and 2nd rows. Work 3 half motifs with 1st-colour centres and 2 half motifs in 2nd colour for top of Back. Join alt., starting with half motif with 1st-colour centre at edge. Work 1 half motif with 1st-colour centre for *each* Front top edge; join above 2nd-colour motif of 8th row.

Armholes. Make 1 half motif in 2nd colour, 2 half motifs in 1st colour and 2 half motifs with 2nd-colour centres for *each* armhole. Join 2nd-colour half motif under arm, to straighten, then remaining half motifs round armhole to match rows.

To Make Up. Work 4 quarter motifs in 2nd colour. Insert 1 at lower edge of each front, and 1 at neck edge of each front shoulder. Press work slightly on wrong side. Join shoulder seams, matching the motifs. Fill in space at neck edge of front shaping on 9th row: with 1st colour join with a d.c. into ch.sp. between d.c. of 8th-row motif, 3 ch., 1 tr. into ch.sp. between d.c. and tr.-d.tr.-tr.gr., 3 d.tr. at join of motifs, 1 tr. in ch.sp. of next quarter motif, 3 ch., 1 d.c. in next tr.; fasten off. Work a similar fill-in on opposite side, but beg. with d.c. in 2nd row of quarter motif.

With right side of work facing and 2nd colour, commence at corner of right front, and work 1 row d.c. all round bolero edge, join with a s.s. to first d.c., 3 ch., 1 d.tr., 1 ch., 1 d.tr. and 1 tr. into same d.c. as s.s., * miss 2 d.c., 1 tr., 1 d.tr., 1 ch., 1 d.tr. and 1 tr. into next d.c.; rep. from * all round, join with a s.s.

Rep. last round once placing the grs. in the 1-ch. sp. between the d.trs. of previous round; join with a s.s. to 3rd of 3 ch. at beg. of round; fasten off.

Starting at underarm of armholes, work the same edging round each armhole. Fasten off. Press lightly on wrong side.

The individual motifs for this skirt and bolero can be sewn or crocheted together.

SKIRT

The skirt is made in the same way as lower edge of Bolero, but 2 extra motifs are required in width.

For the entire skirt you will need: 49 motifs in 1st colour; 42 motifs in 2nd colour; 49 motifs with 2nd-colour centres; 42 motifs with 1st-colour centres. Start with 1st-colour motifs and motifs with 2nd-colour centres. Join 7 of each alt. in a circle (no side seam). Then work 12 more rows on top. If a longer or shorter skirt is required add or omit 1 row of motifs (or as required). The lower edge is filled in with half motifs as lower edge of Bolero. Insert decreased motifs at waist edge. Making 7 in 2nd colour and 7 with 1st-colour centres. If an odd number of rows has been added, or omitted, make 7 motifs in 1st colour and 7 with 2nd-colour centres. Join alternately along waist edge, keeping patt. correct.

Waistband. With 2nd colour, work 1 row d.c. all round top of skirt; turn. Work 7 more rounds. Fasten off and join. Press work on wrong side, then herringbone-stitch the elastic into back of band, joining elastic to fit waist.

Lower Edge. Work edging as given for Bolero all round lower edge of skirt. Press on wrong side.

Chanel-style suit

(photographed in colour on page 78)

MATERIALS

26 (28, 30) balls of Patons Piccadilly (see note on wools and yarns, page 21); crochet hooks International Standard Sizes 3.50 and 3.00 (see page 9); waist length of elastic, 1 in. wide.

MEASUREMENTS

Jacket: to fit bust size 34 (36, 38) in.; length from shoulder to lower edge $21\frac{1}{2}$ ($21\frac{1}{2}$, $22\frac{1}{4}$) in.; length of sleeve seam 16 in.

Skirt: to fit hip size 36, (38, 40) in.; length $20\frac{1}{2}$ in.

TENSION

4 joint tr. to $1\frac{1}{2}$ in. in width, with No. 3.50 hook (see note on tension, page 14).

ABBREVIATIONS

See page 20.

JACKET
BACK

With No. 3.50 hook make 100 (106, 112) ch.

1st row: 1 d.c. into 4th ch. from hook, * 1 ch., miss 1 ch., 1 d.c. into next ch.; rep. from * to end.

2nd row: 4 ch., y.o.h., insert hook into first ch. sp. and draw yarn through, y.o.h. and draw through 2 loops, y.o.h., insert hook into 2nd ch. sp., and draw yarn through, y.o.h. and draw through 2 loops, y.o.h. and draw through all loops on hook: 1 joint tr. made in first and 2nd ch. sp.; * 1 ch., 1 joint tr. in ch. sp. just worked into and next ch. sp.; rep. from * to end, working 1 ch., 1 tr. in 3rd of 4 ch. at end: 48 (51, 54) joint tr.

3rd row: 4 ch., 1 joint tr. in ch. sp. each side of first joint tr., * 1 ch., 1 joint tr. in ch. sp. just worked into and next ch. sp.; rep. from * to end, 1 tr. in 3rd of 4 ch. at end. Rep. last row 32 times * *.

Shape Armholes. 1st row: 1 ch., s.s. across 3 joint tr. and into next ch. sp., 4 ch., leaving last loop of each on hook, work 1 tr. into sp. just worked into, 1 tr. into each of next 2 sps., y.o.h. and draw through all loops on hook: 3 tr. drawn tog., patt. until 5 joint tr. rem., 1 ch., 3 tr. drawn tog. in sp. just worked into and next 2 sps., 1 ch., 1 tr. in sp. just worked into; turn.

2nd row: 4 ch., 3 tr. drawn tog. in first 3 sps., patt. until 2 sps. rem., 1 ch., 3 tr. drawn tog. starting in sp. just worked into, 1 ch., 1 tr. in 3rd of 4 ch.

Rep. last row 1 (1, 2) times.

Work 14 (14, 15) rows straight.

Shape Shoulders. 1 ch., s.s. over 5 (6, 6) joint tr. and into next ch.sp., 2 ch., y.o.h., insert hook into next sp. and draw yarn through, y.o.h., insert hook into next sp. and draw yarn through, y.o.h., and draw yarn through all loops on hook: a joint h.tr. made, (1 ch., 1 joint h.tr.) 4 times, patt. over 14 (14, 15) joint tr., (1 ch., 1 joint h.tr.) 5 times, 2 ch., 1 s.s. into next sp., s.s. to end; fasten off.

RIGHT FRONT

With No. 3.50 hook make 52 (56, 60) ch. and work as for Back as far as * *; 24 (26, 28) joint tr.

Shape Armholes. 1st row (right side facing): patt. until 5 joint tr. remain, 3 tr. drawn tog., 1 tr. in sp. just worked into; turn.

2nd row: 4 ch., 3 tr. drawn tog., patt. to end.

3rd row: patt. until 1 joint tr. and 3 tr. drawn tog. rem., 1 tr. in ch.

Rep. 2nd row once for largest size only.

Patt. 8 (8, 9) rows straight.

Shape Neck. 1st row: patt. until 6 joint tr. rem., 3 tr. drawn tog., 1 tr.; turn.

2nd row: 4 ch., 3 tr. drawn tog., patt. to end.

3rd row: patt. until 1 joint tr. and 3 tr. drawn tog. rem., 3 tr. drawn tog., 1 tr.

4th row: as 2nd row.

Work 2 rows straight.

Shape Shoulder. 1 ch., s.s. over 5 (5, 6) joint tr. and into next sp., 2 ch., then starting in next sp. patt. to end; fasten off.

LEFT FRONT

Work as Right Front as far as armhole shaping.

Shape Armhole. 1st row (right side facing): 1 ch., s.s. across 3 joint tr. and into next sp., 4 ch., 3 tr. drawn tog., patt. to end.

2nd row: patt. until 2 sps. rem., 1 ch., 3 tr. drawn tog., 1 tr. in ch.

3rd row: 4 ch., 3 tr. drawn tog., patt. to end.

Rep. 2nd row once for largest size only.

Patt. 8 (8, 9) rows straight.

Shape Neck. 1st row: 1 ch., s.s. over 4 joint tr. and into next sp., 4 ch., 3 tr. drawn tog., patt. to end.

Rep. 3rd, 2nd and 3rd rows of Right Front neck shaping.

Work 2 rows straight.

Shape Shoulder. Patt. until 6 (6, 7) joint tr. rem., 2 ch., s.s. to end starting in next sp.; fasten off.

SLEEVES (make 2 alike)

With No. 3.50 hook make 48 (52, 56) ch. and work as for Back until 4 patt. rows have been worked: 22 (24, 26) joint tr.

Shape Sides. 1st row: 4 ch., 1 tr. in first sp., 1 ch., then, starting in first sp., patt. to last sp., 1 ch., 1 tr. in last sp., 1 ch., 1 tr. in ch. at end.

2nd row: 4 ch., 1 joint tr. in sp. each side of first tr., patt. to end, working last joint tr. in ps. each side of last tr., 1 tr. in ch.

Work 4 rows straight.

Rep. last 6 rows 4 times.

Patt. 1 row or until required length is reached.

Shape Top. 1st and 2nd rows: as 1st and 2nd rows of Back armhole shaping.

3rd row: patt.

Repeat 2nd and 3rd rows twice, then rep. 2nd row 4 (5, 6) times.

Next row: 2 ch., starting in 2nd sp., 3 tr. drawn tog., (1 ch., 1 joint tr.) 4 times, 1 ch., 3 tr. drawn tog., 2 ch., s.s. into ch.; fasten off.

POCKETS (make 2 alike)

With No. 3.50 hook make 26 ch. and work as Back until 8 patt. rows have been worked.

Edging. Change to No. 3.00 hook.

1st row: 2 ch. (for first d.c.), 1 d.c. into sp., * 1 d.c. into top of joint tr., 1 d.c. into sp.; rep. from * working last d.c. into ch.; 25 d.c.

2nd row: with No. 3.50 hook work 5 ch., miss 1 d.c., leaving last 2 loops of each on hook into next d.c. work 5 d.tr., y.o.h. and draw through all loops on hook, 1 ch. to secure: 1 cl. made, * 2 ch., miss 3 d.c., 1 cl. in next d.c.; rep. from * 4 times, 1 ch., miss 1 d.c., 1 d.tr. in ch. at end.

3rd row: with No. 3.00 hook make 2 ch. (for first d.c.),

1 d.c. into ch., * 1 d.c. into ch. at top of cl., 1 d.c. in top of cl., 1 d.c. in each of next 2 ch.; rep. from * to end; do not turn.

4th row: 2 ch., then work reversed d.c. (d.c. worked from left to right) all along; fasten off.

SKIRT

BACK AND FRONT (make 2 pieces alike)

With No. 3.50 hook make 106 (112, 118) ch. and work as for Back of Jacket until 32 patt. rows have been worked.

Decrease for Top. 1st row: 4 ch., 3 tr. drawn tog., patt. until 2 joint tr. remain, 1 ch., 3 tr. drawn tog., 1 ch., 1 tr. in ch. at end.

Work 2 rows in patt.

Now work 14 more rows, decreasing in same way on next and each foll. alt. row.

Waistband. Change to No. 3.00 hook.

1st row: 3 ch., * 1 tr. in ch.sp., 1 tr. in joint tr.; rep. from * to last sp., 1 tr. in ch. at end.

2nd and 3rd rows: 3 ch., then 1 tr. in each tr. to end; fasten off.

TO COMPLETE

Using a cool iron and dry cloth, press lightly on wrong side. Join side, shoulder and sleeve seams of jacket and side seams of skirt.

Jacket Border. 1st round: with right side facing and No. 3.00 hook and starting at lower end of right side seam, work all round thus: 1 d.c. in each foundation ch., 3 d.c. in corner, 2 d.c. in end of each row up right front, 3 d.c. in corner 69 (69, 73) d.c. round neck, 3 d.c. in corner, 2 d.c. in end of each row down left front, 3 d.c. in corner, 1 d.c. in each foundation ch.; join with s.s. and turn.

2nd round: with No. 3.50 hook, 4 ch., 1 cl. in first d.c., * 2 ch., miss 3 d.c., 1 cl. in next d.c.; rep. from * all round, but each side of corner cls. work 4 ch. instead of 2 and miss 2 d.c. instead of 3; join with s.s. and turn.

3rd round: with No. 3.00 hook, 2 ch., * 1 d.c. in each of next 2 ch., 1 d.c. in ch. at top of cl., 1 d.c. in top of cl.; rep. from * all round, working 3 d.c. at top of corner cls. and 1 d.c. in each ch. each side of corner cls., and missing every 4th stitch round neck edge; join with s.s. but do not turn.

4th round: 2 ch., then work reversed d.c. all round: join with s.s. and fasten off.

Sleeve Border. 1st round: with right side facing and No. 3.00 hook, work 1 d.c. in each foundation ch.; join with s.s. and turn.

Complete as for Jacket border, ignoring instructions for corners.

Skirt Border. With right side facing and No. 3.00 hook, work a row of d.c. all round lower edge; join with s.s. but do not turn, then 2 ch., and work a row of reversed d.c. all round; join and fasten off.

Sew sleeves into armholes, then sew on pockets just above border and 3 in. from side seams.

Join ends of waist elastic and secure to wrong side of waistband with a herringbone casing.

Press seams and skirt border lightly, but do not press clusters at all.

Pink coat

(photographed in colour on page 95)

MATERIALS

26 (27, 28) oz. of Sirdar Double Knitting (see note on wools and yarns, page 22); one crochet hook International Standard Size 4.50 (4.00, 4.50) (see page 9); 5 button moulds each 1 in. in diameter; 5 press studs.

MEASUREMENTS

To fit bust size 34 (36, 38) in., hip size 36 (38, 40) in., length from shoulder 33 (33½, 34) in.

TENSION

9 d.c. to 2 in. with No. 4.50 hook; 12 d.c. to 2½ in. with No. 4.00 hook (see note on tension, page 14).

ABBREVIATIONS

See page 20.

BACK

Commence with 110 (118, 118) ch. to measure 25 (26, 27) in.

Foundation row: 1 d.c. into 2nd ch. from hook, 1 d.c. into each ch. to end; turn: 109 (117, 117) d.c.

1st patt. row: 3 ch., miss first 2 d.c., y.o.h., insert hook into next d.c. and draw through a loop, (y.o.h., insert hook into same place and draw though a loop) twice, y.o.h. and draw through all loops on hook: a puff st. formed, 2 ch., a puff st. into same place, * miss 3 d.c., into next d.c. work a puff st., 2 ch. and a puff st.; rep. from * ending with miss next d.c., 1 tr. into last d.c.; turn.

2nd patt. row: 1 d.c. into first tr., * d.c. into next puff st., 2 d.c. into next sp., 1 d.c. into next puff st.; rep. from * ending with 1 d.c. into last puff st., 1 d.c. into 3rd of 3 ch.; turn.

3rd patt. row: 1 d.c. into first d.c., 1 d.c. into each d.c. to end; turn.

Rep. last row an odd number of times until Back measures 5½ in. from beg. then rep. 1st and 2nd patt. rows once.

Dec. row: 1 d.c. into first d.c., 1 d.c. into each of next 6 d.c., miss next d.c., 1 d.c. into each of next 12 d.c., miss next d.c., 1 d.c. into each d.c. to within last 21 d.c.; end with miss next d.c., 1 d.c. into each of next 12 d.c., miss next d.c., 1 d.c. into each of last 7 d.c.; turn: 4 dec.

Rep. 3rd patt. row 7 times, then rep. dec. row once. Rep. 3rd patt. row an odd number of times until Back measures 10 in. from beg.

Work 1st and 2nd patt. rows once, rep. dec. row once, 3rd patt. row 7 times, dec. row once, then 3rd patt. row an odd number of times until Back measures 14 in. from beg.

Work 1st and 2nd patt. rows once, dec. row once, 3rd patt. row 7 times, dec. row once, 3rd patt. row an odd number of times until Back measures 17½ in. from beg.

Work 1st and 2nd patt. rows once, rep. dec. row once, 3rd patt. row 7 times, dec. row once, 3rd patt. row an odd number of times until Back measures 21 in. from beg.

Inc row: 1 d.c. into first d.c., 1 d.c. into each of next 6 d.c., 2 d.c. into next d.c., 1 d.c. into each of next 12 d.c., 2 d.c. into next d.c., 1 d.c. into each d.c. to within last 21 d.c., end with 2 d.c. into next d.c., 1 d.c. into each of next 12 d.c., 2 d.c. into next d.c., 1 d.c. into each of last 7 d.c.; turn: 4 inc.

Rep. 3rd patt. row 3 times, inc. row once, 3rd patt. row an odd number of times until Back measures 26 in. from beg.

Shape Armholes. 1st row: miss first d.c., 1 s.s. into each of next 5 sts., 1 d.c. into each d.c. to within last 6 sts.; turn.

2nd row: as 3rd patt. row; turn.

3rd row: miss first d.c., 1 s.s. into next d.c., 1 d.c. into each d.c. to within last 2 d.c.; turn.

Rep. last 2 rows 2 (2, 3) times, then rep. 3rd patt. row until armholes measure 7½ (8, 8½) in. from beg. Fasten off.

RIGHT FRONT

Commence with 66 (70, 70) ch. to measure 14½ (15, 15½) in. Work as for Back until armhole shaping but replacing each dec. row and each inc. row with the foll.:

Dec. row: 1 d.c. into first d.c., 1 d.c. into each of next 6 d.c., miss next d.c., 1 d.c. into each of next 12 d.c., miss next d.c., 1 d.c. into each d.c. to end; turn: 2 dec.

Inc. row: 1 d.c. into first d.c., 1 d.c. into each of next 6 d.c., 2 d.c. into next d.c., 1 d.c. into each of next 12 d.c., 2 d.c. into next d.c., 1 d.c. into each d.c. to end; turn: 2 inc.

Shape Armhole. 1st row: working into front loops only miss first d.c., 1 s.s. into each of next 5 sts., 1 d.c. into each d.c. to end; turn.

2nd row: as 3rd patt. row; turn.

3rd row: miss first d.c., 1 s.s. into next d.c., 1 d.c. into each d.c. to end; turn.

4th row : as 3rd patt. row; turn.

Rep. last 2 rows 2 (3, 3) times, then cont. working 3rd patt. row until armhole measures 6 (6½, 7) in. from beg. ending at armhole edge.

Shape Neck. 1st row : make 1 d.c. into first d.c., 1 d.c. into each of next 20 (24, 24) d.c.; turn.

Rep. 3rd, 4th and 3rd rows of armhole shaping, then rep. 3rd patt. row until one more row is completed from beg. of armhole shaping than for Back. Fasten off.

LEFT FRONT

Commence with 65 (69, 69) ch. to measure 14½ (15, 15½) in. Cont. as for Back to armhole shaping but replace dec. rows and inc. rows with the foll.:

Dec. row : 1 d.c. into first d.c., 1 d.c. into each d.c. to within last 21 d.c., end with miss next d.c., 1 d.c. into each of next 12 d.c., miss next d.c., 1 d.c. into each of last 7 d.c.; turn: 2 dec.

Inc row : 1 d.c. into first d.c., 1 d.c. into each d.c. to within last 21 d.c., end with 2 d.c. into next d.c., 1 d.c. into each of next 12 d.c., 2 d.c. into next d.c., 1 d.c. into each of last 7 d.c.; turn: 2 inc.

Shape Armhole. 1st row : make 1 d.c. into first d.c., 1 d.c. into each d.c. to within last 6 sts.; turn.

2nd row : as 3rd patt. row; turn.

3rd row : make 1 d.c. into first d.c., 1 d.c. into each d.c. to within last 2 d.c.; turn.

Rep. last 2 rows 2 (3, 3) times, then rep. 3rd patt. row as for Right Front to neck shaping ending at neck edge.

Shape Neck. 1st row : miss first d.c., 1 s.s. into each d.c. to within last 21 (25, 25) d.c., 1 d.c. into each d.c. to end; turn.

Rep. 3rd, 2nd and 3rd rows of armhole shaping once, then complete as for Right Front. Fasten off.

SLEEVES (make 2 alike)

Commence with 58 (67, 67) ch. to measure 12½ (13½, 14½) in.

Foundation row : 1 d.c. into 2nd ch. from hook, 1 d.c. into each ch. to end; turn. Rep. 3rd patt. row until sleeve measures 16½ in. from beg.

Shape Top. 1st row : as first row of Back armhole shaping; turn. * * Rep. 2nd and 3rd rows of Back armhole shaping once then rep. 3rd patt. row once. Rep. from * * until sleeve measures 3¾ (4, 4½) in. from beg. of shaping.

Fasten off.

COLLAR

Commence with 62 (70, 70) ch. to measure 13½ (14½, 15½) in.

Foundation row : 1 d.c. into 2nd ch. from hook, 1 d.c. into each d.c. to end; turn.

Rep. 3rd patt. row 3 times then Back inc. row once.

Rep. last 4 rows until collar measures 4 in. from beg. Fasten off.

TO COMPLETE

Collar Edging. 1st row : with wrong side facing attach yarn to neck corner, 4 ch., (a puff st., 2 ch., a puff st.) 3 times along side edge, into corner work a puff st., 2 ch., a puff st., 2 ch. and a puff st., * miss 3 d.c., into next d.c. work a puff st., 2 ch. and a puff st.; rep. from * to within last 4 d.c., miss 3 d.c., into next d.c. work a puff st., 2 ch., a puff st., 2 ch. and a puff st., complete to correspond with other side, ending with 1 tr.; turn.

2nd row : 1 d.c. into tr., then work 1 d.c. into each puff st., and 2 d.c. into each 2-ch. sp. all round, 1 d.c. into 3rd of 4 ch.; fasten off.

Cuffs (2 alike). 1st round : with right side facing attach yarn to edge, draw loop through, into same place as join work a puff st., 2 ch. and a puff st., * miss 3 d.c., into next d.c. work a puff st., 2 ch. and a puff st.; rep. from * ending with s.s. into first puff st.

2nd round : * 1 d.c. into next puff st., 2 d.c. into next 2-ch. sp., 1 d.c. into next puff st.; rep. from *, s.s. into first d.c.; fasten off.

Front Edgings. With right side facing attach yarn to lower corner of Right Front, then work d.c. evenly up to neck corner; fasten off.

Work Left Front edging in the same way but attach yarn to neck corner.

Buttons. 1st round : yarn round finger to form a ring.

2nd round : 8 d.c. into ring; draw commencing ring tight.

Next rounds : * 1 d.c. into next d.c., 2 d.c. into next d.c.; rep. from * until work is large enough to cover button mould. Fasten off.

Attach cover to mould. Make 4 more buttons in same way. Overlap fronts 1½ in. Set collar. Sew buttons evenly down Right Front and sew press studs behind buttons and down Left Front.

Gold party dress

(photographed in colour on page 96)

MATERIALS

20 (22, 23, 25, 26, 28) oz. of Twilley's Goldfingering (see note on wools and yarns, page 22); one crochet hook International Standard Size 2.50 (see page 9).

MEASUREMENTS

To fit bust size 32 (34, 36, 38, 40, 42) in.; length from shoulder 33 in. (adjustable).

TENSION

6 d.c. to 1 in. (see note on tension, page 14).

ABBREVIATIONS

See page 20.

BODICE BACK

Begin with 109 (115, 121, 127, 133, 139) ch. to measure 18 (19, 20, 21, 22, 23) in.

Foundation row: 1 d.c. into 2nd ch. from hook, 1 d.c. into each ch. to end; turn.

Patt. row: 1 d.c. into first d.c., 1 d.c. into each d.c. to end; turn.

Dec. row: work in patt. until 10 sts. have been formed, (insert hook into next st. and draw a loop through) twice, y.o.h. and draw through all loops on hook: a dec. formed; 1 d.c. into each d.c. to within last 12 sts., a dec. over next 2 sts., complete as patt. row; turn.

Work 20 rows in patt.

Work last 21 rows twice more, then cont. working patt. row until work measures 13 in. from beg.

Shape Armholes. 1st row: 1 s.s. into each of first 5 sts., patt. to within last 5 sts.; turn.

2nd row: 1 s.s. into first st., patt. to within last d.c.; turn. Rep. last row 5 (6, 8, 9, 11, 12) times more, then work patt. row until armholes measure 6 (6½, 7, 7½ 8, 8½) in. from beg. Fasten off.

BODICE FRONT

Work as for Bodice Back until armholes measure 2½ (3, 3½, 3½, 4, 4½) in. from beg.

Shape Neck. 1st row: patt. until 30 (31, 32, 34, 35, 36) d.c. have been formed; turn.

2nd row: 1 s.s. into first st., patt. to end; turn.

3rd row: 1 d.c. into each d.c. to within last d.c.; turn. Rep. last 2 rows 5 times more, then work patt. row until same number of rows have been completed from beg. of armholes as for Back. Fasten off.

Rejoin yarn at armhole edge of other side and complete to correspond.

SKIRT BACK AND FRONT (both alike)

Foundation row: working along lower edge of bodice attach yarn to first ch., 1 d.c. into first ch., 1 d.c. into each of next 2 ch., * 3 ch., 1 d.c. into each of next 6 ch.; rep. from * to within last 3 ch., 3 ch., 1 d.c. into each ch. to end; turn.

1st row: 1 d.c. into first d.c., 1 d.c. into next d.c., * 5 ch., miss 2 d.c., 1 d.c. into each of next 2 d.c., 1 ch., 1 d.c. into each of next 2 d.c.; rep. from * omitting last d.c. at end of last rep.; turn.

2nd row: 1 d.c. into first d.c., * 2 ch., 9 tr. into next 5-ch. loop, 2 ch., 1 d.c. into next 1-ch. sp.; rep. from * making last d.c. at end of last rep. into first d.c.; turn.

3rd row: 3 ch., * 1 tr. into each tr., 1 tr. into next d.c.; rep. from * to end; turn.

4th row: 1 d.c. into first tr., * miss next sp., 1 d.c. into next sp., * * (1 d.c. into next tr., 1 d.c. into next sp.) * * 3 times, 3 ch., 1 d.c. into next sp., work * * to * * 3 times more, miss next tr., 1 d.c. into next tr.; rep. from * to end, working last d.c. of last rep. into 3rd of 3 ch.; turn.

5th row: 5 ch., miss first 3 d.c., * 1 d.c. into each of next 3 d.c., 5 ch., miss 4 d.c., 1 d.c. into each of next 3 d.c., 2 ch., miss 2 d.c., 1 tr. into next d.c., 2 ch., miss 2 d.c.; rep. from * ending with 1 d.c. into each of next 3 d.c., 5 ch., miss 4 d.c., 1 d.c. into each of next 3 d.c., 2 ch., 1 tr. into last d.c.; turn.

6th row: 1 d.c. into first tr., * 2 ch., 9 tr. into next 5-ch. loop, 2 ch., 1 d.c. into next tr.; rep. from * to end working last d.c. of last rep. into 3rd of 5 ch.; turn.

Rep. 3rd to 6th rows until work measures 33 in. from shoulder, ending with 4th patt. row.

Fasten off.

TO COMPLETE

Join side and shoulder seams, taking in 1½ in. at side seams if a tighter fit is required.

Neck and Armhole Edging. With right side facing attach yarn to a seam, 1 d.c., * a 6-tr.gr. into edge, 1 d.c. into edge; rep. from * ending with a 6-tr.gr. into edge, s.s. into first d.c. Fasten off. Press lightly.

Evening dress

(photographed in colour on page 113)

MATERIALS

21 (22, 22, 23) balls (2-oz.) of Twilley's Stalite in apricot and 2 (3, 3, 3) oz. of Twilley's Goldfingering in bronze (see note on wools and yarns, page 22); crochet hooks International Standard Sizes 3.50 and 4.00 (see page 9);

9 buttons ½ in. in diameter.

MEASUREMENTS

To fit bust size 32, (34, 36, 38) in.; length 50 (50, 51, 51) in.; length of sleeve 5 (5, 5½, 5½) in.

TENSION

6 sts. and 5 rows to 1 in. with No. 3.50 hook over bodice patt. (see note on tension, page 14).

ABBREVIATIONS

See page 20; A., apricot; B., bronze.

BODICE FRONT

With No. 3.50 hook and A., commence with 87 (93, 99, 105) ch. worked loosely.

1st row: 1 d.c. into 2nd ch. from hook, 1 d.c. into each ch. to end.

2nd row: with B., hook through last loop of last row, 2 ch., 1 h.tr. into each d.c. of previous row.

3rd row: with A., and working from other end, 1 d.c. over each h.tr., 2 ch.; turn.

4th row: * miss first d.c., 1 tr. into next d.c., then pull hook behind tr. just worked and work 1 tr. in st. missed; rep. from * ending with 1 tr. into last st.

5th row: with B., make a long loop to reach row just worked and s.s. into top of first tr., then work as 2nd row.

6th row: with A., 1 d.c. into each h.tr., 2 ch.; turn.

7th row: as 4th row.

The last 6 rows form patt.; rep. these 6 rows 3 (4, 4, 4) times, then rep. 2nd, 3rd and 4th rows 1 (0, 1, 1) time.

Shape Armholes. 1st row: s.s. over 7 (8, 9, 10) sts., work to within 7 (8, 9, 10) sts. from other end.

Cont. in patt. until work measures 5 (5, 5¼ 5¼) in. from armholes (8 rows of B. worked).

Shape Neck. 1st row: work over 20 (21, 22, 23) sts.; turn and work on these sts. only. Work straight until armhole measures 7 (7, 7¼. 7½) in. Fasten off.

Rejoin yarn 20 (21, 22, 23) sts. from other armhole edge and complete to match first side. Fasten off.

BODICE HALF BACKS

With No. 3.50 hook and A., commence with 44 (47, 50, 53) ch. worked loosely.

1st row: 1 d.c. into 2nd ch. from hook, 1 d.c. into each ch. to end.

Cont. in patt. as given for Bodice Front until armhole is reached.

Shape Armhole. 1st row: s.s. over 7 (8, 9, 10) sts., work to end of row.

Work straight until armhole measures 6½ (6½, 6¾, 7) in.

Shape Neck. Leave 13 (14, 15, 16) sts. at opposite edge from armhole, then work 3 rows in patt. on remaining sts. Fasten off. Work other Half Back in similar way, but reverse shaping.

SLEEVES (make 2 alike)

With No. 3.50 hook and A., commence with 54 (57, 60, 64) ch.

Work in patt. as given for Bodice Front, but inc. 1 st. at beg. and end of each d.c. row and each h.tr. row until 6 incs. have been made at each side. Cont. straight until 8 (8, 9, 9) rows of B. have been worked.

Shape Top. 1st row: s.s. over 7 (7, 8, 8) sts., then work to within 7 (7, 8, 8) sts. of other end; turn.

Cont. in patt., dec. 1 st. at beg. and end of each d.c. and h.tr. row until top is 20 (22, 22, 24) rows in depth. Fasten off.

SKIRT (worked from waist to hem)

Join side and shoulder seams of bodice.

1st round: with No. 3.50 hook and A., and starting from centre back, work d.c. evenly around bottom edge of Bodice, s.s. into top of first d.c.; turn: 160 (172, 184, 196) d.c.

Next round: 1 d.c., * 4 ch., miss 1 d.c., 1 d.c. into next d.c.; rep. from * ending with 4 ch., s.s. into top of first d.c., s.s. into centre of next 4-ch.sp.; turn.

Next round: * 4 ch., 1 d.c. into centre of next 4-ch.sp.; rep. from * ending with 4 ch., s.s. into top at start of round; turn.

Next round: as last round; turn.

** **Next round:** 3 ch. (standing as 1 tr.), into first 4-ch.sp. work 1 tr., 3 ch. and 2 tr., * into next 4-ch.sp. work 2 tr., 3 ch. and 2 tr.; rep. from * to end of round, s.s. into top of starting ch. at beg. of round, then s.s. into centre of 3 ch. between tr., 4 ch.; turn.

Next round: * 1 d.c. into next 3-ch.sp. between tr., 4 ch.; rep. from * to end of round, s.s. into beg. of round; turn.

Next round: 3 ch. (standing as 1 tr.), into first sp. work 1 tr., 3 ch. and 2 tr., * into next sp. work 2 tr., 3 ch. and 2 tr.; rep. from * to end of round, s.s. into top of starting ch., then s.s. into centre of 3 ch. between trs., 4 ch.; turn.

Work 3 rounds of 4-ch. loops. * *

The last 6 rounds between * * and * * form basis of patt. Cont. rep. patt. rows, but after first rep. inc. by working 3 tr., 3 ch. and 3 tr. into each 4-ch.sp. and on foll. 3 rows of loops work 5 ch. between each d.c.

Work one more rep. of patt. as last, then cont. working this patt., but work d.tr. in place of tr. on tr. rows. On 8th rep. of patt. rows, change to No. 4.00 hook, and cont. until skirt measures 40 (40, 41, 41) in., ending with a loop row. Leave work to hang for about 48 hours in case it drops.

To Finish Skirt. With A., work 3 d.c., 3 ch. and 3 d.c. into each 5-ch. loop along edge of skirt, ending with s.s. into beg. of round. Fasten off.

TO COMPLETE

Sew sleeves into armholes.

Edgings. With No. 3.50 hook and A., work 3 rows of d.c. around neck. Work 6 rows d.c. along edge of left side of centre back opening, then mark positions for 9 buttons, evenly spaced.

Work 2 rows of d.c. along right edge of centre back opening, then on 3rd row make buttonholes to match positions marked on left side by working 3 ch., miss 3 d.c., for each buttonhole.

Work 2 more rows of d.c. along right edge. Sew on buttons at positions marked.

Cord for Waist. With No. 4.00 hook and 4 thicknesses of A., make a ch. about 2 yd. long. Knot each end and thread through first row of loops at waist line. Press work lightly on wrong side with warm iron over damp cloth.

Chapter Five

Leisure wear

Blue bathing costume

(photographed in colour on page 114)

MATERIALS

5 (5, 6) oz. Emu 4-ply Tricel with Nylon in main colour, 1 oz. in contrast colour (see note on wools and yarns, page 21); one crochet hook International Standard Size 4.00 (see page 9); shirring elastic; 2 press studs. (N.B. We used blue for main shade, white for contrast.)

MEASUREMENTS

To fit bust size 34 (36, 38) in.; hip size 36 (38, 40) in.

TENSION

5 d.c. to 1 in. (see note on tension, page 14).

ABBREVIATIONS

See page 20; M., main colour; C., contrast colour.

PANTS
BACK

* With M. make 91 (96, 101) ch. to measure $18\frac{1}{4}$ ($19\frac{1}{4}$, $20\frac{1}{2}$) in.

Foundation row: 1 d.c. into 2nd ch. from hook, 1 d.c. into each ch. to end; turn.

Patt. row: 1 d.c. into first d.c., 1 d.c. into each d.c. to end; turn.

Rep. last row until back measures $3\frac{1}{2}$ in. from beg. * *

Shape Legs. 1st row: miss first st., 1 s.s. into each of next 8 (9, 10) sts.; turn.

2nd row: miss first d.c., 1 d.c. into each d.c. to within last d.c.; turn.

Rep. last row until 10 (11, 12) d.c. remain, then rep. patt. row 10 (12, 14) times. Fasten off.

FRONT

Work as for Back from * to * *

Shape Legs. 1st row: miss first st., 1 s.s. into each of next 18 (20, 22) d.c., 1 d.c. into each d.c. to within last 18 (20, 22) d.c.; turn.

Rep. 2nd row of back leg shaping until 10 (11, 12) d.c. rem., then work patt. row until same number of rows are completed from beg. as for back. Fasten off.

BATHING COSTUME
MAIN SECTION

With M. make 10 (11, 12) ch. to measure 2 ($2\frac{1}{2}$, 2) in.

Foundation row: as foundation row of Back of Pants. Rep. patt. row 6 times.

* * **8th row:** 2 ch., 1 h.tr. into first d.c., 1 d.c. into each d.c., 2 h.tr. into last d.c.; turn.

9th row: as patt. row. * *

Rep. from * * to * * until there are 49 (54, 59) d.c., then rep. 8th row until there are 65 (70, 75) d.c.

Next row: attach a second M. yarn to beg. of last row and make 50 (53, 55) ch. Fasten off.

Evening elegance in apricot laced with bronze. Instructions on page 110.

With original thread make 51 (54, 56) ch., 1 d.c. into 2nd ch. from hook, 1 d.c. into each ch., 1 d.c. into each of next 15 d.c., 3 d.c. into next d.c., 1 d.c. into each d.c. to within last 16 d.c., 3 d.c. into next d.c., 1 d.c. into each d.c., 1 d.c. into each ch.; turn.

Next row: 1 d.c. into first d.c., * 1 d.c. into each d.c. to centre d.c. of next 3 d.c. group, 3 d.c. into next d.c., rep. from * once more, 1 d.c. into each d.c. to end; turn. Rep. last row once more, then rep. patt. row for 2¾ in. Fasten off.

Shape Armholes. 1st row: miss first 55 (57, 60) d.c. and attach yarn to next d.c., 1 d.c. into each d.c. to within last 55 (57, 60) d.c.; turn.

2nd row: 1 s.s. into each of first 2 d.c., 1 d.c. into each d.c. to within last 2 d.c.; turn.

Rep. last row 3 (4, 5) times.

Shape Neck. 1st row: 1 d.c. into first d.c., 1 d.c. into each of next 9 (11, 11) d.c.; turn.

2nd row: miss first d.c., 1 d.c. into each d.c. to end; turn.

3rd row: 1 d.c. into first d.c., 1 d.c. into each d.c. to end; turn.

Rep. last 2 rows 2 (3, 3) times more, then work patt. row until armhole measures 13 (13½, 14) in. from beg. Fasten off.

2nd Side of Neck. 1st row: miss first 9 (11, 11) d.c., continuing from opposite edge and attach yarn to next d.c., 1 d.c. into each d.c. to end; turn.

Rep. 3rd and 2nd rows of first side of neck 3 (4, 4) times, then work patt. row same number of times as for first side of neck. Fasten off.

TO COMPLETE

Join side and crutch seam of pants. Join back of top; join shoulder straps to back of top.

Pants Leg Edgings (both alike). 1st round: with right side facing attach C. to edge, 1 d.c. into same place as join then work * 1 d.c. ½-in. deep into edge, 3 d.c. into edge; rep. from * all round omitting 1 d.c. at end of last rep., s.s. into first d.c.

2nd round: 1 d.c. into first d.c., * 3 ch., 1 s.s. into last d.c. formed, miss next d.c., 1 d.c. into each of next 3 d.c., rep. from * omitting 1 d.c. at end of last repeat, s.s. into first d.c. Fasten off.

Waistband. 1st round: with right side facing attach M. to edge then work d.c. evenly round, 1 d.c. into first d.c.

2nd round: * 3 ch., 1 s.s. into last d.c. formed, 1 d.c. into each of next 3 d.c., rep. from * ending with s.s. into first d.c. Fasten off.

Lower Edging for Top. With right side facing attach C. to centre back lower edge, then work as for leg edging all round. Fasten off.

Armhole Edgings. Work as for waistband edging.

Neck Edging. 1st row: with right side facing attach C. to last row of shoulder strap, 1 d.c. into same place as join, then work * 1 d.c. ½-in. deep into edge, 3 d.c. into edge; rep. from * to last row of 2nd shoulder strap. Fasten off.

2nd row: with right side facing attach C. to first d.c., 1 d.c. into first d.c., * 3 d.c., 1 s.s. into last d.c. formed, miss next d.c., 1 d.c. into each of next 3 d.c., rep. from * omitting 1 d.c. at end of last repeat, s.s. into first d.c. Fasten off.

Thread elastic through top band of pants and round lower edge of top. Sew a press stud to each end of top foundation row to join to pants.

Matching beach set

(photographed in colour opposite and black and white on page 117)

MATERIALS

18 oz. of Emu 4-ply in white and 3 oz. of Emu 4-ply in yellow (see note on wools and yarns, page 21); one crochet hook International Standard Size 4.00 (see page 9); approx. 2½ yd. shirring elastic; 3 rings, each 1½ in. in diameter.

MEASUREMENTS

To fit bust size 34 (36, 38) in.; hip size 36 (38, 40) in.

TENSION

5 d.c. to 1 in. (see note on tension, page 14).

For sun and sea—blue bathing costume (page 112) and yellow and white costume (see matching beach set, above).

ABBREVIATIONS

See page 20; W., white; Y., yellow.

BATHING COSTUME

PANTS BACK

With W., commence with 91 (96, 101) ch. to measure 81¼ (19¼, 20¼) in.

Foundation row: 1 d.c. into 2nd ch. from hook, 1 d.c. into each d.c. to end; turn.

Patt. row: 1 d.c. into each d.c. to end; turn.

Rep. last row until back measures 1 in. from beg.

Shape Legs. 1st row: 1 s.s. into each of first 8 (9, 10) sts., 1 d.c. into each d.c. to within last 8 (9, 10) sts.; turn.

2nd row: miss first d.c., 1 d.c. into each d.c. to within last d.c.; turn.

Rep. last row until 12 (13, 14) d.c. remain, then rep. patt. row 12 (14, 16) times. Fasten off.

PANTS FRONT

Work as for Pants Back until leg shaping is reached.
Shape Legs. 1st row: 1 s.s. into each of first 18 (20, 22) d.c., 1 d.c. into each d.c. to within last 18 (20, 22) d.c.; turn.
Rep. 2nd row of Back leg shaping until 12 (13, 14) d.c. remain, then work patt. row until same number of rows are completed from beg. as for Back. Fasten off.

WAIST EDGING

Join side and crutch seams.
1st round: with right side facing attach W. to waist centre back of Pants, then work 1 d.c. into each loop all round, s.s. into first d.c.; fasten off and turn.
2nd round: mark d.c. at centre front of Pants, attach Y. to first d.c., 1 d.c. into each d.c. to within 1 d.c. of marked d.c., 2 tr. into next d.c., into next d.c. work 1 d.tr., 1 t.tr. and 1 d.tr., 2 tr. into next d.c., 1 d.c. into each d.c., s.s. into first d.c.; turn.
3rd round: 1 d.c. into each d.c. to 1 d.c. before first tr., miss next d.c., 1 d.c. into each of next 3 sts., 5 d.c. into next st., 1 d.c. into each of next 3 sts., miss next d.c., 1 d.c. into each d.c., s.s. into first d.c.; fasten off and turn.
4th round: attach W. to first d.c., 1 d.c. into each d.c. to within 1 d.c. before dec., miss next d.c., 1 d.c. into each d.c. to centre d.c., 3 d.c. into next d.c., 1 d.c. into each d.c. to next dec., miss next d.c., 1 d.c. into each d.c., s.s. into first d.c.; turn.
Rep. last row 7 times working 1 more row in W. then 2 rows of each colour alternately. Fasten off.

TOP

Cups (make 2 alike). Work in continuous rounds. With W., wind yarn round finger to form a ring.
1st round: 9 d.c. into ring; draw commencing ring tight.
2nd round: * 1 d.c. into each of next 2 d.c., 3 d.c. into next d.c.; rep. from * twice.
3rd round: * 1 d.c. into each d.c. until centre d.c. of next 3-d.c. group is reached, 3 d.c. into next d.c.; rep. from * twice.
Rep. last round until work measures 3½ (3¾, 4) in. from commencing ring to a corner. Fasten off.
Edging Band. With W., make 150 (160, 170) ch. to measure 30 (32, 34) in., s.s. into first ch. to form a ring.
Foundation round: 1 d.c. into each ch., s.s. into first d.c.; fasten off.
Complete as Pants waist edging from 2nd round to end.

PONCHO
MAIN PIECE

Commence with 100 ch. to measure 20 in., s.s. into first ch. to form a ring.
Foundation round: 1 d.c. into each ch., 1 d.c. into first d.c.
1st round: * 1 d.c. into each of next 3 d.c., 2 d.c. into next

Cover up with the matching poncho when the sun goes down.

d.c.; rep. from * ending with 1 d.c. into first d.c.
2nd to 5th rounds: working in continuous rounds, make 1 d.c. into each d.c., 1 d.c. into first d.c.
6th round: * 1 d.c. into each of next 4 d.c., 2 d.c. into next d.c.; rep. from * ending with 1 d.c. into next d.c.
Cont. to inc. 25 d.c. on every 5th round, each time having 1 more d.c. between inc. sts., until work measures 20 in. from beg. ending with an inc. round. Fasten off.

LOWER EDGING
1st round: mark first d.c. of each 2-d.c. group, then work 2nd round of Pants waist edging from attaching Y. yarn, making the start of 25 points round lower edge.
2nd round: 1 d.c. into each d.c. to 1 d.c. before first tr., miss next d.c., * 1 d.c. into each of next 3 sts., 5 d.c. into next st., 1 d.c. into each of next 3 sts., miss next d.c., 1 d.c. into each d.c. to within 1 d.c. before next tr., miss next d.c.; rep. from * all round, s.s. into first d.c.; fasten off and turn.
3rd round: attach W. to first d.c., * 1 d.c. into each d.c. to within 1 d.c. before dec., miss next d.c., 1 d.c. into each d.c. to centre d.c., 3 d.c. into next d.c., 1 d.c. into each d.c. to dec., miss next d.c.; rep. from * ending with s.s. into first d.c.; turn.

Rep. last round 7 times working 1 more row of W. then 2 rows of each colour alternately. Fasten off.

TO COMPLETE
Pants Leg Edging. 1st round: with right side facing attach Y. to leg edge of Pants, then work d.c. evenly round, 1 d.c. into first d.c.
2nd round: make 1 d.c. into each d.c., s.s. into first d.c.; fasten off.
Work edging round other leg. Thread shirring elastic through top and legs of Pants.
Top Edging. Sew cups to edging band already made.
1st row: with right side facing attach Y. to lower outside corner of a cup, then work d.c. evenly along both sides of each cup; turn.
2nd row: make 1 d.c. into first d.c., 1 d.c. into each d.c. to end; fasten off.
Strings (make 2 alike). Attach Y. to top corner of cup and make a length of chain 15 in. long; fasten off.
Thread shirring elastic through lower edge of Top.
Rings. Cover the 3 rings with d.c. worked in Y. and sew these together and to the 2 points on Top and Pants.
Poncho Neck Edging. As for Pants leg edging.

○range trouser suit
(photographed in colour on page 131)

MATERIALS
17 (18, 19) oz. of Sirdar 4-ply Crêpe (see note on wools and yarns, page 22); one crochet hook International Standard Size 4.50 (see page 9); 1½ yd. narrow elastic.

MEASUREMENTS
Trousers: to fit hip size 36 (38, 40) in.; inside leg measurement 30 in.
Top: to fit bust size 34 (36, 38) in.

TENSION
5 tr. to 1 in. (see note on tension, page 14).

ABBREVIATIONS
See page 20.

TROUSERS
LEGS (make 2 alike)
Commence with 77 (83, 89) ch. to measure 15½ (16¾, 17¾) in.
Foundation row: 1 tr. into 4th ch. from hook, 1 tr. into each ch. to end; turn.
1st patt. row: 3 ch., miss first 2 tr., * 1 h.tr. into next tr., 1 ch., miss next tr.; rep. from * ending with 1 h.tr. into 3rd

of 3 ch.; turn.
2nd patt. row: 3 ch., 1 tr. into first sp., 2 tr. into each sp., 1 tr. into 2nd of 3 ch.; turn.
* * Rep. first patt. row once.
Inc. row: mark 1 (2, 1) sp. at centre of row; 3 ch., 1 tr. into first sp., 2 tr. into next sp., 3 tr. into next sp., 2 tr. into each sp. to within 3 sp. before marked sp., 3 tr. into next sp., 2 tr. into each of next 5 sp., 3 tr. into next sp., 2 tr. into each sp. to within last 3 sp., 3 tr. into next sp., 2 tr. into each of last 2 sp., 1 tr. into 2nd of 3 ch. * *
Rep. from * * to * * 4 times more, then work patt. rows until leg measures 10 in. from beg. ending with first patt. row.
Shape Crutch. Using a 2nd thread attach yarn to beg. of last row and make 8 ch. Fasten off.
1st row: using original thread make 10 ch., 1 tr. into 4th ch. from hook, 1 tr. into each ch., 1 tr. into first tr., 1 tr. into first sp., 2 tr. into each sp., 1 tr. into 2nd of 3 ch., 1 tr. into each of next 8 ch.; turn: 111 (117, 123) sts.
Rep. patt. rows for 3 in., ending with first patt. row.
* * * **Dec. row:** mark 1 (2, 1) sp. at centre of row, 3 ch., 1 tr. into first sp., 2 tr. into next sp., 1 tr. into next sp., 2 tr. into each sp. to within 3 sp. before marked sp., 1 tr. into next sp., 2 tr. into each of next 5 sp., 1 tr. into next sp., 2 tr. into each sp. to within last 3 sp., 1 tr. into next sp., 2 tr. into

each of last 2 sp., 1 tr. into 2nd of 3 ch.; turn. Work first and 2nd patt. rows twice, then work first patt. row once. * * *

Rep. from * * * to * * * 5 times more, then work first and 2nd patt. rows until leg measures 19 in. from crutch shaping ending with first patt. row.

* * * * Rep. inc. row once then rep. first and 2nd patt. rows 3 times then first patt. row once. * * * *

Rep. from * * * * to * * * * until leg measures 30 in. from crutch shaping ending with 2nd patt. row.

Fasten off.

TOP
BACK
Commence with 87 (93, 99) ch. to measure 17½ (18½, 19½) in.

Foundation row: work as for foundation row of Legs.
Rep. first and 2nd patt. rows until work measures 4 in. from beginning ending with first patt. row.

Shape Armholes. 1st row: 1 s.s. into each of first 6 sts., 3 ch., 1 tr. into next sp., 2 tr. into each sp. to within last 3 sp., 1 tr. into next h.tr.; turn.

2nd row: 1 s.s. into each of first 2 sts., then work as for first patt. row working rep. to within last 3 sts., end with 1 h.tr. into next tr.; turn.

Rep. last row 2 (2, 3) times more, then rep. patt. rows until armholes measure 6½ (7, 7½) in. from beg. Fasten off.

FRONT
Commence with 71 (77, 83) ch. to measure 14 (15¼, 16½) in.

Foundation row: work as for foundation row of Legs.
Rep. first patt. row once.

Inc. row: 3 ch., 1 tr. into first sp., 2 tr. into each of next 8 sp., 4 tr. into next sp., 2 tr. into each sp. to within last 10 sp., end with 4 tr. into next sp., 2 tr. into each sp. to end, 1 tr. into 2nd of 3 ch.; turn.

Rep. last 2 rows once more then rep. patt. rows until same

number of patts. are completed up to armhole shaping as for Back.

Shape Neck and Armhole. 1st row: 1 s.s. into each of first 6 sts., 3 ch., 1 tr. into next sp., 2 tr. into each of next 10 (11, 12) sp., 1 tr. into next h.tr.; turn.

Rep. 2nd row of back armhole shaping 3 (3, 4) times, then rep. patt. row until one more row is completed from beg. of armhole shaping than for Back. Fasten off.

2nd Side of Neck. 1st row: attach yarn to 14 (15, 16) sp. counting from other edge, 3 ch., 1 tr. into same place as join, 2 tr. into each sp. to within last 4 sp., 3 tr. into next sp.; turn.

Rep. 2nd row of Back armhole shaping 3 (3, 4) times, then complete as for first side of neck. Fasten off.

TO COMPLETE
Join side and shoulder seams of top. Join crutch and leg seams of trousers.

Leg Edgings (both alike). With right side of work towards you, attach yarn to edge, 1 d.c. into same place, * 3 ch., 1 s.s. into last d.c. formed, 1 d.c. into each of next 3 sts.; rep. from * to end omitting 1 d.c. at end of last rep., s.s. into first d.c. Fasten off.

Trouser Waist Edging. With right side of work towards you, attach yarn to edge, 1 d.c. into same place, * 3 ch., 1 s.s. into last d.c. formed, miss next st., 1 d.c. into each of next 3 sts.; rep. from * to end omitting 1 d.c. at end of last rep., s.s. into first d.c. Fasten off.

Neck and Armhole Edgings (both alike). 1st row: with right side of work towards you attach yarn to edge, then work d.c. evenly round having a multiple of 3, 1 d.c. into first d.c.

2nd round: 1 d.c. into each d.c., 1 d.c. into first d.c.

3rd round: * 3 ch., 1 s.s. into last d.c. formed, 1 d.c. into each of next 3 sts.; rep. from * to end omitting 1 d.c. at end of last rep., s.s. into first d.c. Fasten off.

Lower Edging for Top. Work as for Leg Edgings.

White trouser suit
(photographed in colour on page 131)

MATERIALS
28 balls Lister Bel Air Double Crepe (see note on wools and yarns, page 21); one crochet hook International Standard Size 4.00 (see page 9); 4-in. zip fastener; 1 hook and eye; shirring elastic; 4 small buttons.

MEASUREMENTS
Trousers: to fit hip size 36 in.; inside leg measurement 24 in. (adjustable).
Top: to fit bust size 34 in.

TENSION
5 patt. and 8 rows to 3 in. with No. 4.00 hook (see note on tension, page 14).

ABBREVIATIONS
See page 20.

TROUSERS
LEFT LEG
With No. 4.00 hook make 77 ch.

1st row: 1 d.c. into 2nd ch. from hook, * 1 d.c. into each ch., rep. from * to end, 2 ch.; turn.

2nd row: miss 1 d.c., * 1 d.c. into each d.c., rep. from * to end, 2 ch.; turn.

Rep. 2nd row 8 times more, ending with 3 ch.

Commence Pattern. 1st row: miss 1 d.c., * 3 tr. into next d.c., miss 2 d.c., rep. from * to last 2 d.c., miss 1 d.c., 1 tr. into end d.c., 3 ch.; turn.

2nd row: * miss 2 tr., 3 tr. into next tr., rep. from * to last tr., miss 1 tr., 1 tr. into 3rd of 3 turning ch., 3 ch.; turn. * *

3rd row: * miss 2 tr., 3 tr. into next tr., rep. from * to last tr., miss 1 tr., 3 tr. into 3rd of 3 turning ch., 3 ch.; turn.

4th row: miss 1 tr., 3 tr. into next tr., * miss 2 tr., 3 tr. into next tr., rep. from * to last tr., miss 1 tr., 1 tr. into 3rd of 3 turning ch., 3 ch.; turn.

Rep. 3rd and 4th rows once more. Rep. 2nd row twice more. Rep. 3rd and 4th rows once more.

11th row: 3 tr. into 1st tr., miss 1 tr., * 3 tr. into next tr., miss 2 tr., rep. from * to last tr., miss 1 tr., 3 tr. into 3rd of 3 turning ch., 3 ch.; turn.

12th row: as 4th row.

Rep. 2nd row twice more.

Now rep. 11th and 12th rows once, then 2nd row 6 times with no ch. to turn on last row.

* * * **Next row:** s.s. across first 2 tr., 3 ch., 1 tr. into next tr., * miss 2 tr., 3 tr. into next tr., rep. from * to last 4 tr., miss 2 tr., 2 tr. into next tr.; turn.

Next row: s.s. across 1 tr., 3 ch., * miss 2 tr., 3 tr. into next tr., rep. from * to last 2 tr., miss 1 tr., 1 tr. into next tr., 3 ch.; turn.

Rep. 2nd row of patt. 6 times more, then rep. 2 dec. rows once, then rep. 2nd row of patt. twice more.

Work 8 rows straight.

Join leg seam from 16th row of patt.

1st round: 4 ch., * 4 d.tr. into centre of 3 tr., 1 ch., rep. from * to end, s.s. into 3rd ch., 4 ch.

2nd round: * 4 d.tr. into centre of 4 d.tr., 2 ch., rep. from * to end omitting final 2 ch., s.s. into 3rd ch., 4 ch.

Rep. last row until leg measures 24 in. (or required length).

RIGHT LEG

Work as Left Leg as far as * *.

3rd row: 3 tr. into first tr., miss 1 tr., * 3 tr. into next tr., miss 2 tr., rep. from * to last 3 tr., 3 tr. into next tr., 1 tr. into 3rd of 3 turning ch., 3 ch.; turn.

4th row: * miss 2 tr., 3 tr. into next tr., rep. from * to last 2 tr., miss 1 tr., 1 tr. into end tr., 3 ch.; turn. Rep. 3rd and 4th rows once, 2nd row twice more, then rep. 3rd and 4th rows once more.

11th row: 3 tr. into 1st tr., miss 1 tr., * 3 tr. into next tr., miss 2 tr., rep. from * to last tr., miss 1 tr., 3 tr. into 3rd of 3 turning ch., 3 ch.; turn.

12th row: miss 1 tr., 3 tr. into next tr., * miss 2 tr., 3 tr. into next tr., rep. from * to last tr., miss 1 tr., 1 tr. into 3rd of 3 turning ch., 3 ch.; turn.

Rep. 2nd row twice more, 11th and 12th rows once, then 2nd row 6 times.

Now work as Left Leg from * * * to end.

TOP
MAIN SECTION

With No. 4.00 hook make 118 ch.

1st row: 1 d.c. into 2nd ch. from hook, * 1 d.c. into next ch., rep. from * to end, 2 ch.; turn: 117 d.c.

2nd row: miss 1 d.c., * 1 d.c. into next d.c., rep. from * to end, 2 ch.; turn. Rep. 2nd row 3 times more.

Next row: miss 1 d.c., 1 d.c. into next 7 d.c., * 2 d.c. into next d.c., 1 d.c. into next d.c., rep. from * to last 9 d.c., 1 d.c. into each d.c., 3 ch.; turn: 167 d.c.

Work 1st and 2nd patt. rows as Left Leg: 55 shells.

Rep. 2nd row 6 times more with no ch. to turn on last row.

Left Back Strap. Next row (right side facing): s.s. across first 16 tr., 3 ch., patt. across next 7 shells, miss 1 tr., 1 tr. into next tr.; turn.

Next row: s.s. across first 2 tr., 3 ch., 1 tr. into next tr., patt. to last 4 tr., miss 2 tr., 2 tr. into next tr.; turn.

Next row: s.s. across 1 tr., 3 ch., patt. to last 2 tr., miss 1 tr., 1 tr. into next tr.; turn.

Rep. last 2 rows once more then work in patt. for 11 rows. Fasten off.

With wrong side of work facing rejoin yarn at beg. of row and work to correspond with first side to make Right Back Strap.

With right side of work facing miss 5 shells from left armhole shaping, rejoin yarn, into next space, 3 ch., patt. across 9 shells, miss 1 tr., 1 tr. into next tr.; turn.

Next row: s.s. across first 2 tr., 3 ch., 1 tr. into next tr., patt. to last 4 tr., miss 2 tr., 2 tr. into next tr.; turn.

Next row: s.s. across 1 tr., 3 ch., patt. to last 2 tr., miss 1 tr., 1 tr. into next tr.; turn.

Rep. last 2 rows once more.

Keeping armhole edge straight cont. to shape neck edge as before until 3 shells remain.

With wrong side of work facing miss 5 shells at right underarm, rejoin yarn and work to correspond with other side.

SLEEVES (make 2 alike)

Join shoulder seams.

Rejoin yarn at centre of underarm, 4 ch., work 4 d.tr. (all into same st.) 25 times evenly round armhole, join with s.s. into 3rd of 4 ch.

Next row: 4 ch., * d.tr. into centre of 4 d.tr. of previous round, 1 ch., rep. from * to end, join with s.s. into 3rd of 4 ch.

Next row: 4 ch., * 4 d.tr. into centre of 4 d.tr. of previous round, 2 ch., rep. from * to end, omitting 2 ch., s.s. into 3rd of 4 ch.

Rep. last row 9 times more. Fasten off.

LEFT BACK BAND

With right side facing, rejoin yarn and with No. 4.00 hook work 3 rows of d.c. along left back edge. Fasten off.

RIGHT BACK BAND

Work first 2 rows as Left Back Band.

Last row (buttonhole row): 1 d.c., 2 ch., miss 2 d.c.

(buttonhole made), cont. in d.c. placing buttonholes at 1-in. intervals: 4 buttonholes. Fasten off.

TO COMPLETE
Work 3 rows of d.c. round neck edge.
Top. Add buttons to correspond to buttonholes.

Trousers. Join back seam. Join front seam to within 4 in. of top and insert zip fastener here. Sew hook and eye at top of front opening. Thread double shirring elastic through alternate rows of d.c. at hipline starting with 2nd row from top.
Press work lightly on the wrong side.

☺range beach dress and pants
(photographed in colour on page 133)

MATERIALS
13 (14, 15) balls of Lister Bel Air 4-ply (see note on wools and yarns, page 21); crochet hooks International Standard Sizes 2.50 (3.00, 3.00) and 3.00 (3.50, 3.50) (see page 9); 4-in. zip fastener; 1½ yd. elastic, ½ in. wide.

MEASUREMENTS
To fit bust size 32 (34, 36) in.

TENSION
13 tr. to 2 in. and 3 rows to 1 in. with No. 2.50 hook; 6 tr. to 1 in. and 3 rows to 1⅛ in. with No. 3.00 hook (see note on tension, page 14).

ABBREVIATIONS
See page 20.

DRESS

BRA TOP (make 2 pieces alike)
With No. 2.50 (3.00, 3.50) hook, make 4 ch., and join into a ring with s.s.

1st round: work 10 d.c. into ring, s.s. into top of first d.c.
2nd round: 1 ch. (this stands as 1 d.c.), work 2 d.c. into each d.c. of the last round, s.s. into the top of ch.
3rd round: 1 ch., work 2 d.c. into next d.c., * 1 d.c. into the next d.c., 2 d.c. into next d.c., rep. from * ending with s.s. into top of 1 ch.
4th round: 1 ch., 1 d.c., 2 d.c. in next d.c., * 1 d.c. in each of next 2 d.c., 2 d.c. into next d.c., rep. from * ending with a s.s. into top of 1 ch.: 40 d.c.
5th round: 2 ch. (standing always as 1 tr.), 1 tr. into each of the next 11 d.c., (2 tr., 1 ch., 2 tr.) into the next d.c., miss 1 d.c., 1 tr. into each of the next 12 d.c., (2 tr., 1 ch., 2 tr.) into next d.c., 1 tr. into each of the next 12 d.c., (2 tr.,

1 ch., 2 tr.) into next d.c., s.s. into the top of 2 ch.
6th round: 2 ch., 1 tr. into each of the next 4 tr., dec. in next 2 sts., (y.o.h., hook into next tr., y.o.h. and pull through, y.o.h. and pull through 2 loops, y.o.h., hook into next tr., y.o.h. and pull through, y.o.h. and pull through rem. loops: 1 dec. made), work 5 tr., (3 tr., 1 ch., 3 tr.) into 1-ch.sp. between trs., * work 5 tr., dec. in next 2 sts., work 5 tr., (3 tr., 1 ch., 3 tr.) into 1-ch.sp. between trs., rep. from * once missing rem. trs. immediately before final corner, end with a s.s. into top of 2 ch.
7th round: 2 ch., work 4 tr., work 2 tr. into the next tr., 5 tr., (3 tr., 1 ch., 3 tr.) in 1-ch.sp., * 5 tr., 2 tr. in next tr., 5 tr., (3 tr., 1 ch., 3 tr.) in 1-ch.sp., rep. from * once, end with a s.s. into top of turning ch.
8th round: 2 ch., 1 tr. into the base of ch., 10 tr., 2 tr. in the next tr., (4 tr., 2 ch., 4 tr.) into 1-ch.sp., * 2 tr. in first tr., 10 tr., 2 tr. in the last tr., (4 tr., 2 ch., 4 tr.) into 1-ch.sp., rep. from * once, ending with s.s. into 2 ch.
9th round: 2 ch., 1 tr. into the base of ch., 12 tr., 2 tr. in the last tr., 1 ch., (4 tr., 2 ch., 4 tr.) in 2-ch.sp., 1 ch., * 2 tr. in first tr., 12 tr., 2 tr. in last tr., 1 ch., (4 tr., 2 ch., 4 tr.) in 2-ch.sp., 1 ch., rep. from * once, end with s.s. into the 2 ch. Break yarn. Rejoin yarn in the centre of last 2 cl.
10th round: make 2 ch., 3 tr. into the 2-ch.sp., 1 ch., 2 tr. in first tr., work in tr. to last tr. and work 2 tr. into it, 2 ch., (4 tr., 2 ch., 4 tr.) in 2-ch.sp., 2 ch., 2 tr. in next tr., work in tr. to last tr. and work 2 tr. into it, 1 ch., 4 tr. in sp.; turn.
11th round: 2 ch., 3 tr. in top of first tr. of cl., 1 ch., 2 tr. in next tr., 7 tr., 2 tr. in next tr., work to last tr. and work 2 tr. into it, 2 ch., (4 tr., 2 ch., 4 tr.) into 2-ch.sp., 2 ch., 2 tr. in next tr., 7 tr., 2 tr. in next tr., work to the last tr., and work 2 tr. into it, 1 ch., 4 tr. in last tr. of cl., 2 ch.; turn.
12th round: rep. the last row, working the central inc. over the inc. in the last row. Break yarn.

SHOULDER STRAP (make 2 alike)

1st row: rejoin yarn at far side of centre line of cls., hook into last tr. of tr. block, 4 ch., (4 tr., 2 ch., 4 tr.) into 2-ch.sp., 2 ch., 1 tr. over first tr. of block; turn.

2nd row: 4 ch., (4 tr., 2 ch., 4 tr.), 1 tr. in 2nd of 4 ch.

3rd row: 4 ch., (3 tr., 2 ch., 3 tr.), 2 ch., 1 tr. into 2nd of ch.

4th row: 3 ch., (3 tr., 2 ch., 3 tr.), 1 ch., 1 tr. into 2nd of ch.

5th row: as 4th row.

6th row: 3 ch., (2 tr., 2 ch., 2 tr.), 1 ch., 1 tr. into ch.

7th row: as 6th row.

8th row: as 6th row.

9th row: 2 ch., (2 tr., 1 ch., 2 tr.), 1 tr. into last tr. of cl.
Rep. the last row until the shoulder strap measures 18 in. or length required.

SKIRT

Join the 2 cups at centre front. Join yarn at side corner and made a ch. of 32 (32, 38). Break yarn. Rejoin at the opposite corner and make another ch. of 32 (32, 38). With the right side of the work facing you and so that you will be working away from the cups, using No. 2.50 (3.00, 3.00) hook join in yarn at the end of right hand ch., 2 ch., work 1 tr. into each ch. (not the 2 ch. just made), 13 tr. across cl., 17 tr. across the tr. block, 27 tr. across the centre front cls., 17 across the next tr. block, 13 tr. across the clusters, and 1 tr. into each ch. to end; turn.

Work 3 rows of tr.

Patt. as follows using No. 3.00 hook for all sizes:

1st row: 3 ch., * (2 tr., 1 ch., 2 tr.) into next tr., 1 ch., miss 2 tr., 1 tr. in next tr., 1 ch., miss 2 tr., rep. from * ending with 1 tr. in the last tr., 5 ch.; turn.

2nd row: * (2 tr., 1 ch., 2 tr.) into 1-ch.sp., 1 ch., 1 tr. over the 1 tr., 1 ch., rep. from * ending with 1 tr. into 3rd of turning ch., 5 ch.; turn.

3rd row: * (3 tr., 1 ch., 3 tr.) into 1-ch.sp., 1 ch., 1 tr. over 1 tr., 1 ch., rep. from * ending with 1 tr. into 3rd of turning ch.

Work 4 rows more, and at the end of the 4th join the 2 sides tog. with s.s. into 2nd turning ch.

1st round: 4 ch., * (4 tr., 1 ch., 4 tr.) into 1-ch.sp., 1 ch., 1 tr. over 1 tr., 1 ch., rep. from * ending with 1 ch., then s.s. into 3rd of turning ch.

Rep. the last round 4 times.

Next round: 5 ch., * (5 tr., 1 ch., 5 tr.), 2 ch., 1 tr. over 1 tr., 2 ch., rep. from * ending with s.s. into 3rd of turning ch.
Rep. the last round 4 times.

For sizes 34 and 36 only: change to No. 3.50 hook.

For all sizes. Next round: 5 ch., * (5 tr., 2 ch., 5 tr.), 3 ch., 1 tr., 3 ch., rep. from * end with a s.s. into 3rd of turning ch.

Rep. this last row until the skirt measures 19 (20, 21) in. from the beg. of patt.

Turn and continue to work thus: * 3 d.c. around 3 ch., 1 d.c. over each tr., 1 d.c. in 2-ch.sp., 4 ch., 1 d.c. in same 2-ch.sp., 1 d.c. over each tr., 3 d.c. around 3 ch., rep. from * round the hem.
Fasten off.

TO COMPLETE

Starting from the centre back, work in picot (4 d.c., 3 ch., 1 d.c. into last d.c.) along the back, up the side of bra and along the strap. Work along the centre front edges of bra similarly. Cut a piece of elastic a little smaller than your measurement immediately under the bust and place along the 3-row band of tr. on the wrong side, working herringbone over the elastic, and stitching the ends of elastic to the side edge of band.

Work 2 rows of d.c. along the centre back edges and then sew in zip fastener, stitching inside rows of d.c. Sew ends of shoulder straps 3 in. either side of centre back edge.

PANTS
BACK

Using No. 3.00 hook make 82 (84, 88) ch.

1st row: into the 4th ch. from hook work 3 tr., miss 2 ch., work 1 tr. into each ch. to the last 4 ch., miss 2 ch., 3 tr. in next ch., 1 tr. in the last ch., 2 ch.; turn.

2nd row: 3 tr. in first sp., 3 tr. in next sp., miss 2 tr., work in tr. to within 2 tr. of the end, 3 tr. in sp., 3 tr. in last sp., 2 ch.; turn.

Cont. in this way for 9 rows more increasing one group of 3-tr. at each side by missing 2 tr. at the beg. and end of the tr. block on each row and working 3 tr. into the sp. made on the foll. row.

Shape Leg. 12th row: s.s. over 3 grs. of tr., 3 ch., 3-tr. gr. in each of next 3 sps., miss 2 tr., cont. in tr. to within 2 tr. of the end of tr. block, work over sps., 1 tr. into next sp., 3 ch.; turn.

13th row: work 3 grs. of 3 tr., miss 2 tr., work to within 2 tr. of end, work 3 grs. of 3 tr., 1 tr. into next sp., 3 ch.; turn.
Rep. last row until all tr. of centre block are worked off then work over all sts. in tr., dec. 1 tr. at each of every row until 14 rem. Break yarn.

FRONT

Work as for Back until Leg shaping.

Shape Leg. 12th row: s.s. over 6 sps., work 3 ch., miss 2 tr., work in tr. to within 2 tr. of end of tr. block, 1 tr. into first sp., 3 ch.; turn.

13th row: miss first 2 tr., work to within 2 tr. of end, 1 tr. into top of turning ch., 3 ch.; turn.
Rep. this last row until 8 tr. rem.

Work 3 rows straight, and then inc. 1 tr. at each end of every 2nd row until there are 14 tr.
Work 3 more rows. Break yarn.

TO COMPLETE

Join the front to the back as side seams and crutch. Work ¾ in. of d.c. round the waist line and 3 rows of d.c. round the legs.
Cut a length of elastic to the size of your waist, and sew to the inside of the waist line. Herringbone-stitch over it.

Flared tunic—to wear with trousers or as a beach dress (instructions start on page 124).

Flared tunic

(photographed in black and white on page 123)

MATERIALS
9 (10) oz. of Lee Target Motoravia Double Knitting (see note on wools and yarns, page 21); crochet hooks International Standard Sizes 4.00 and 3.50 (see page 9).

MEASUREMENTS
To fit bust size 34 (36) in.; length from top of shoulder 31 in.

TENSION
3-ch.sp. to 2 in. with No. 4.00 hook (see note on tension, page 14).

ABBREVIATIONS
See page 20.

BACK AND FRONT (both alike)
With No. 4.00 hook, make 108 (116) ch.

1st row: 1 d.c. into 8th ch. from hook, * miss 3 ch., 1 d.c. into next ch.; rep. from * to end, 3 ch.; turn: 26 (28) sps.

2nd row: 1 d.c. into 2nd ch. of 3 ch. of previous row (referred to as 2nd ch. throughout), * 3 ch., 1 d.c. into 2nd ch.; rep. from * to last 8 ch., 3 ch., 1 d.c. into 2nd ch., 1 ch., 1 d.c. into 4th ch., 5 ch.; turn.

3rd row: miss 2 d.c., 1 d.c. into 2nd ch., * 3 ch., 1 d.c. into next 2nd ch.; rep. from * to end, 3 ch.; turn.

4th row: 1 d.c. into 2nd ch., * 3 ch., 1 d.c. into next 2nd ch.; rep. from * to last 5 ch., 1 d.c. into 2nd ch., 1 ch., 1 d.c. into 4th ch., 5 ch.; turn.

The 3rd and 4th rows form the patt.

Cont. in patt. until work measures 10 (10½) in., ending with a 4th row, no ch. to turn.

Shape Armholes. 1st row: s.s. over 4 (8) sts., 1 d.c. into next ch., * 3 ch., 1 d.c. into 2nd ch.; rep. from * to last 1 (2) complete ch. sps., 1 ch., 1 d.c. into 2nd ch., 3 ch.; turn.

2nd row: miss 2 d.c., 1 d.c. into 2nd ch., * 3 ch., 1 d.c. into next 2nd ch.; rep. from * to last 2 d.c., 3 ch., 1 d.c. into end d.c., 3 ch.; turn.

Rep. 2nd row once, 1 ch.; turn.

4th row: miss 1 d.c., 1 d.c. into 2nd ch., * 3 ch., 1 d.c. into next 2nd ch.; rep. from * to last 2 d.c., 1 ch., 1 d.c. into end 2nd ch., 5 ch.; turn.

5th row: miss 2 d.c., 1 d.c. into 2nd ch., * 3 ch., 1 d.c. into next 2nd ch.; rep. from * to end, 3 ch.; turn: 20 sps. Work 4th, 3rd then 4th rows of patt.

Shape Neck. Miss 2 d.c., 1 d.c. into next 2nd ch., * 3 ch., 1 d.c. into next 2nd ch.; rep. from * twice, 3 ch.; turn: 4 ch. sps.

Working on these sps. only, cont. in patt. until work measures 8 (8½) in. from armhole shaping. Fasten off. With right side of work facing, miss 11 complete ch. sps., rejoin yarn to next 2nd ch.

Next row: 5 ch., 1 d.c. in next 2nd ch., * 3 ch., 1 d.c. in next 2nd ch.; rep. from * twice: 4 ch. sps.

Complete to correspond with first side.

SKIRT
With right side of work facing, rejoin yarn to lower edge of top.

1st row: with No. 4.00 hook, * 3 ch., 1 d.c. into 2nd ch.; rep. from * to end d.c., 1 ch., 1 d.c. into this d.c., 5 ch.; turn.

2nd row: miss 2 d.c., 1 d.c. into 2nd ch., (3 ch., 1 d.c. into next 2nd ch.) 3 (4) times, * 2 ch., 4 d.c. into next ch. sp., 2 ch., 1 d.c. into next 2nd ch., (3 ch., 1 d.c. into next 2nd ch.) 6 times, rep. from * once, 2 ch., 4 d.c. into next ch. sp., 2 ch., 1 d.c. into next 2nd ch., (3 ch., 1 d.c. into next 2nd ch.) 4 (5) times, 3 ch.; turn.

3rd row: 1 d.c. into 2nd ch., (3 ch., 1 d.c. into next 2nd ch.) 3 (4) times, * 2 ch., miss next d.c., (2 tr. into next d.c.) 4 times, 2 ch., 1 d.c. into next 2nd ch., (3 ch., 1 d.c. into next 2nd ch.) 5 times; rep. from * once, 2 ch., miss next d.c., (2 tr. into next d.c.) 4 times, 2 ch., 1 d.c. into next 2nd ch., (3 ch., 1 d.c. into next 2nd ch.) 3 (4) times, 1 ch., 1 d.c. into 4th ch., 5 ch.; turn.

4th row: miss 2 d.c., 1 d.c. into next 2nd ch., (3 ch., 1 d.c. into next 2nd ch.) 2 (3) times, * 2 ch., (2 tr. into next tr., 1 tr. into next tr.) twice, (1 tr. into next tr., 2 tr. into next tr.) twice, 2 ch., 1 d.c. into next 2nd ch., (3 ch., 1 d.c. into next 2nd ch.) 4 times; rep. from * once, 2 ch., (2 tr. into next tr., 1 tr. into next tr.) twice, (1 tr. into next tr., 2 tr. into next tr.) twice, 2 ch., 1 d.c. into next 2nd ch., (3 ch., 1 d.c. into next 2nd ch.) 3 (4) times, 3 ch.; turn.

5th row: 1 d.c. into 2nd ch., (3 ch., 1 d.c. into next 2nd ch.) 2 (3) times, * 2 ch., * * (1 tr. into next tr.) 3 times, 1 ch.; rep. from * * 3 times, 1 ch., 1 d.c. into next 2nd ch., * * * (3 ch., 1 d.c. into next 2nd ch.) 3 times; rep. from * once, then from * to * * * once, (3 ch., 1 d.c. into next 2nd ch.) 2 (3) times, 1 ch., 1 d.c. into 4th ch., 5 ch.; turn.

6th row: miss 2 d.c., 1 d.c. into next 2nd ch., (3 ch., 1 d.c. into next 2nd ch.) 1 (2) times, * 2 ch., (1 tr. into next tr.) 3 times; rep. from * 3 times, 2 ch., 1 d.c. into next 2nd ch., * * (3 ch., 1 d.c. into next 2nd ch.) twice; rep. from * once, then from * to * * once, (3 ch., 1 d.c. into next 2nd ch.) 2 (3) times, 3 ch.; turn.

7th row: 1 d.c. into 2nd ch., (3 ch., 1 d.c. into next 2nd ch.) 1 (2) times, * 2 ch., * * (1 tr. into next tr.) 3 times, 3 ch.; rep. from * * twice, (1 tr. into next tr.) 3 times, 2 ch., 1 d.c. into next 2nd ch., * *,* 3 ch., 1 d.c. into next 2nd ch.; rep. from * once then from * to * * * once, (3 ch., 1 d.c. into next 2nd ch.) 1 (2) times, 1 ch., 1 d.c. into 4th ch., 5 ch.; turn.

8th row: miss 2 d.c., 1 d.c. into next 2nd ch., (3 ch., 1 d.c. into next 2nd ch.) 1 (2) times, * (3 ch., 1 d.c. into next 2nd tr., 3 ch., 1 d.c. into next 2nd ch.) * * 4 times, (3 ch., 1 d.c. into next 2nd ch.) twice; rep. from * once, then from * to * * once, (3 ch., 1 d.c. into next 2nd ch.) 2 (3) times, 3 ch.; turn.

9th row: 1 d.c. into 2nd ch., * 3 ch., 1 d.c. into next 2nd ch., rep. from * to last 5 ch., 3 ch., 1 d.c. into 2nd ch., 1 ch., 1 d.c. into 4th ch., 5 ch.; turn.

10th row: miss 2 d.c., 1 d.c. into next 2nd ch., (3 ch., 1 d.c. into next 2nd ch.) 9 (10) times, * 2 ch., 4 d.c. into next ch. sp., 2 ch., 1 d.c. into next 2nd ch., (3 ch., 1 d.c. into next 2nd ch.) 8 times; rep. from * once, (3 ch., 1 d.c. into next 2nd ch.) 2 (3) times, 3 ch.; turn.

Keeping ch. patt. correct, complete 2 bells as before: 11th, 12th, 13th, 14th and 15th rows.

16th row: miss 2 d.c., 1 d.c. into next 2nd ch., (3 ch., 1 d.c. into next 2nd ch.) 7 (8) times, * (3 ch., 1 d.c. into next 2nd tr., 3 ch., 1 d.c. into next 2nd ch.) 4 times, (3 ch., 1 d.c. into next 2nd ch.) 4 times; rep. from * once, (3 ch., 1 d.c. into next 2nd ch.) 4 (5) times, 3 ch.; turn.

17th row: work in ch. patt., 5 ch.; turn.

18th row: miss 2 d.c., 1 d.c. into next 2nd ch., (3 ch., 1 d.c. into next 2nd ch.) 4 (5) times, * 2 ch., 4 d.c. into next ch. sp., 2 ch., 1 d.c. into next 2nd ch., (3 ch., 1 d.c. into next 2nd ch.) 10 times; rep. from * once, 2 ch., 4 d.c. into next ch. sp., 2 ch., 1 d.c. into next 2nd ch., (3 ch., 1 d.c. into next 2nd ch.) 5 (6) times, 3 ch.; turn.

Keeping ch. patt. correct, complete 3 bells as before.

24th row: work in ch. patt. (work across tr. as before): 42 (44) ch. sps.

25th row: work in ch. patt., 5 ch.; turn.

26th row: miss 2 d.c., 1 d.c. into next 2nd ch., (3 ch., 1 d.c. into next 2nd ch.) 12 (13) times, * 2 ch., 4 d.c. into next ch. sp., 2 ch., 1 d.c. into next 2nd ch., (3 ch., 1 d.c. into next 2nd ch.) 11 times; rep. from * once, (3 ch., 1 d.c. into next 2nd ch.) 2 (3) times, 3 ch.; turn.

Keeping ch. patt. correct, complete 2 bells as before. Work 2 more rows in ch. patt. Fasten off.

TO COMPLETE

Press each piece carefully, using a damp cloth and warm iron. Sew up shoulder and side seams.

Armbands and Neckband. With No. 3.50 hook and right side of work facing, work 2 rows of d.c. evenly round neck edge and armhole edges. Press all seams.

Mother and daughter beach cover-ups

(photographed in colour on page 132)

MATERIALS

For mother's coat: 16 oz. of Sirdar Pullman in white and 4 oz. in maroon (see note on wools and yarns, page 22); one crochet hook International Standard Size 5.00 (see page 9).

For daughter's coat: 12 oz. of Sirdar Pullman in white and 3 oz. in maroon (see note on wools and yarns, page 22); one crochet hook International Standard Size 4.00 (see page 9).

MEASUREMENTS

Mother's Coat: to fit bust size 34—36 in.; centre back length, including borders, 32 in. **Daughter's coat:** to fit chest size 28—29 in.; centre back length, including borders, 24 in.

N.B. Should larger sizes be required, work motifs with a larger hook. Adding ¼ in. to the width of each motif will add 2½ in. all round to the size. For smaller sizes use a smaller hook.

TENSION

Mother's coat: 1 motif—3¾ in. square; **Daughter's coat:** 1 motif—2¾ in. square (see note, page 14).

ABBREVIATIONS

See page 20; W., white; M., maroon.

MOTIF (make 74 alike)

Using No. 5.00 hook for mother's coat or No. 4.00 for daughter's coat (or size required) and M., beg. with 8 ch., s.s. into 8th ch. from hook to form ring. Work 11 d.c. into circle, cut wool, thread needle and fasten off by making a last loop into the first d.c. (*not* the s.s.): 12 sts. round ring. With W., make a loop on hook, then work 1 tr. into first d.c., 2 tr. into next d.c., * 2 ch., 2 tr. into next d.c., 1 tr. into following d.c., 5 ch., 1 tr. into d.c. last worked into, 2 tr. into next d.c.; rep. from * twice, 2 ch., 2 tr. into next d.c., 1 tr. into foll. d.c. (first d.c. worked into), 5 ch., s.s. into next tr. (first tr. in round); fasten off.

TO COMPLETE

Press work on wrong side.

To Join Motifs. The motifs can either be sewn together at the end or crocheted as you work, which will give a better effect. Motifs are joined as follows: join 10 motifs together for bottom edge of coat, then add 4 more rows of 10 motifs above. Starting at one edge, the 7th row consists of 2 motifs (front), 1-motif space, 4 motifs (back), a 1-motif space, 2 motifs (front). The 8th row is 1-motif space, 1 motif, 1-motif space, 4 motifs, 1-motif space, 1 motif, 1-motif space. The first 2 motifs on each edge of the 8th row are joined together along the top to form the shoulder seams. To crochet motifs tog., work to first 5-ch. loop on second motif and instead of working this work 2 ch., 1 d.c. into corresponding loop of first motif worked, 2 ch., then cont. motif, working 1 ch. and 1 d.c. into corresponding 2-ch. loop on first motif, 1 ch., then join to the 5-ch. loop as before, and cont. to end of motif; fasten off. When adding a 2nd row of motifs, the bottom edge must be joined to the previous row.

Armhole Borders. With right side of work facing and using W., begin with 1 d.c. into 2-ch. sp. at underarm, * 1 d.c. into each of next 3 trs., 1 d.c. into next sp., 1 tr. in joint of motifs, 1 d.c. into next sp., 1 d.c., in each of next 3 tr., 1 d.c. in next 2-ch. sp.; rep. from * all round, omitting last d.c. Work 1 round d.c. over this round. Fasten off. Work other armhole border to match.

Main Border. With right side of work facing and using W., beg. with 1 d.c. into 2-ch. sp. of 3rd motif from edge of right front at bottom and work as given for armhole border to 5-ch. loop at corner, work 5 d.c. into this loop, then continue working as armhole up front, with 5 d.c. in corner at neck edge, work round neck with 5 d.c. in corner of left front at neck edge, then to lower edge, with 5 d.c. at corner, then along lower edge to commencement of work.

Next round: 1 d.c. in each d.c. all round, working 3 d.c. into corner d.c. at lower and neck edges, and missing tr. at each corner of inner turn of neck to shape the neck edge.

Next round: work 1 d.c. over each d.c. of previous round, working only 2 d.c. in the corner sts. at lower and neck edges. Fasten off. Press borders on wrong side, using a warm iron over a damp cloth.

Tie Cords. Take 5 yd. of wool for mother's coat or 3 yd. for daughter's. Fold in half and twist to form a cord. Finish the ends with a small tassel. The cords will tie through the last motif loops at neck edge, and through similar holes at the waist.

More cords may be made if required—use above quantities for each one.

Three-way poncho

(photographed in colour on page 151)

MATERIALS

For mother's poncho: 14 oz. Wendy Double Knit Nylonised in 1st colour, 8 oz. in 2nd colour, 4 oz. in 3rd colour (see note on wools and yarns, page 22); crochet hooks International Standard Sizes 5.00, 4.00 and 3.00 (see page 9).

For daughter's poncho: 8 oz. Wendy 4-ply Nylonised in 1st colour, 4 oz. in 2nd colour, 2 oz. in 3rd colour (see note on wools and yarns, page 22); crochet hooks International Standard Sizes 4.00, 3.00 and 2.50 (see page 9).

For toddler's poncho: 2 oz. Peter Pan 3-ply Bri-Nylon in 1st colour, 2 oz. in 2nd colour, 1 oz. in 3rd colour (see note on wools and yarns, page 22); crochet hooks International Standard Sizes 2.50 and 3.00 (see page 9).

MEASUREMENTS

Mother's poncho: to fit bust size 34—36 in.; length excluding fringe 26 in. Size 38—40 in. bust could be obtained by using hooks one size larger. **Daughter's poncho:** to fit chest size 30—32 in.; length excluding fringe 20 in. Size 28—30 in. chest could be obtained by using hooks one size smaller. **Toddler's poncho:** to fit approx. 10—15 months old; length excluding fringe 11 in.

TENSION

Mother's poncho: 5 tr. grs. to 4 in. and 4 rows to 2 in. with No. 5.00 hook (see note on tension, page 14). **Daughter's poncho:** 3 tr. grs. to 2 in. and 3 rows to 2 in. with No. 4.00 hook (see note on tension, page 14).

Toddler's poncho: 5 tr. grs. to 3 in. and 6 rows to 3 in. (see note on tension, page 14).

ABBREVIATIONS

See page 20.

N.B. Work *centre stitch* as follows: * y.o.h. loosely, insert hook into next sp., y.o.h. and draw yarn thr. to same height as trs., * work from * to * twice more, working into same sp. * *; work from first * to * * all in next sp. (13 loops on hook), y.o.h. and draw thr. all loops on hook, 1 ch. tightly.

MOTHER'S PONCHO

With No. 5.00 hook and 2nd colour, make 255 ch.

1st foundation row: work 2 tr. into 3rd ch. from hook, * miss 3 ch., 3 trs. into next ch., rep. from * to end.

2nd foundation row: 5 ch., * miss 3 sts., 3 tr. into sp., rep. from * to last 3 sts., 5 ch., miss 3 sts., join to top of 3 ch. of first row with s.s.

Mark centre group of trs. on last row with a coloured thread.

1st row: with 1st colour s.s. across first 3 sts. on previous row, 3 ch., work 2 trs. into sp. below, * miss 3 sts., 3 trs. into sp., rep. from * until 3 sts. and sp. before marked group of trs. is reached, miss 3 sts., centre st. (see abbreviations),* * miss 3 sts., 3 trs. into sp., rep. from * * to end.

N.B. On all the foll. rows, centre st. will be worked into space at either side of centre st. worked on previous row.

2nd row: with 1st colour, 5 ch., * miss 3 sts., 3 trs. into sp., rep. from * until group of 3 trs. and centre st. are reached, miss 3 sts., centre st., * * miss 3 sts., 3 trs. into sp., rep. from * * to last 3 sts., 5 ch., miss 3 sts., join to top of 3 ch. of previous row with a s.s.

These 2 rows form the patt.

Cont. in patt. (for colour patt. see below) until there are 20 grs. of trs. either side of centre st., change to hook No. 4.00 and work as patt. for 10 rows, change to hook No. 3.00 and complete.

Colour patt. is as foll.:

6 more rows in 1st colour, 2 rows in 2nd colour, 2 rows in 3rd colour, 2 rows in 1st colour, 4 rows in 2nd colour, 2 rows in 3rd colour, 2 rows in 1st colour, 2 rows in 3rd colour, 4 rows in 2nd colour, 2 rows in 1st colour, 2 rows in 3rd colour, 2 rows in 2nd colour, 8 rows in 1st colour.

NECKBAND

1st row: s.s. across first 3 ch. of previous row, 1 ch., 2 d.c. into sp. below, * miss 3 sts., 3 d.c. into sp., rep. from * until group of 3 trs. and centre st. are reached, miss 3 sts., insert hook into sp. to the right of centre st., draw yarn through, insert hook into sp. at left of centre st., draw yarn through, y.o.h. and draw through all 3 loops on hook, * * miss 3 sts., 3 d.c. into sp., rep. from * * to end.

2nd row: 1 ch., 1 d.c. into every d.c. until d.c. before dec. on previous row, dec. 1 st. as follows: insert hook into next st., draw yarn through twice, y.o.h. and draw through the 3 loops on hook, rep. dec. in next st. then 1 d.c. into every d.c. to end.

Rep. 2nd row 3 times more. Fasten off.

TO COMPLETE

Press on wrong side with warm iron over a damp cloth, join side edges.

Fringe. With 1st colour cut into 10-in. lengths and using 6 lengths for each knot (or more if desired) make knots all round lower edge as follows: fold strands in half, then use a crochet hook to draw the looped ends through the edge of poncho.

Draw ends through loops and pull tight.

DAUGHTER'S PONCHO

Follow directions for Mother's Poncho, but use hook sizes as given and making fringe with 8-in. lengths of yarn.

TODDLER'S PONCHO

Make 199 ch. and follow directions as given for Mother's Poncho, but use hook size 2.50 throughout ending with 4 rows of 2nd colour (30 rows) and completing with 4 rows worked very loosely in 1st colour for the neckband, the last 2 of these worked on hook size 3.00. Make fringe with 6-in. lengths of yarn.

Chapter Six

Clothes for men

Father and son football set

MATERIALS
5 (7) oz. of Sirdar Double Knitting in 1st colour, 5 (7) oz. of Sirdar Double Knitting in 2nd colour (see note on wools and yarns, page 22); crochet hooks International Standard Sizes 4.50 and 3.50 (see page 9).

MEASUREMENTS
Scarf width 7 (10) in., length, excluding fringe, 48 (66) in.; mittens and beret to fit an average size.

TENSION
4 tr. to 1 in. with No. 4.50 hook (see note on tension, page 14).

ABBREVIATIONS
See page 20.

SCARF
MAIN SECTION
With 1st colour and No. 4.50 hook make 30 (42) ch. to measure 7½ (10½) in.

Foundation row: 1 tr. into 4th ch. from hook, 1 tr. into each ch. to end; turn.

Patt. row: 3 ch., miss first tr., 1 tr. into each tr., 1 tr. into 3rd of 3 ch.; turn.

Changing colour on next and every alt. row rep. patt. row until scarf measures 48 (66) in. from beg. ending with a band of 1st colour. Fasten off.

TO COMPLETE
Side Edgings (both alike). With right side of work towards you attach 1st colour to a corner, make 2 d.c. into each row-end along side edge. Fasten off.

Fringe. Cut 1st colour yarn into 12-in. lengths and using 4 strands make a tassel into every alt. st. along both short edges.

BERET
TO MAKE
Wind 1st colour yarn round finger once to form a ring.

Foundation round: with No. 4.50 hook, 3 ch., 17 tr. into ring, draw ring tight.

1st round: 3 ch., 1 tr. into first tr., 2 tr. into each tr., s.s. into 3rd of 3 ch.: 36 sts.

Changing colour on next and every alt. round cont.:

2nd round: 3 ch., miss first tr., * 1 tr. into next tr., 2 tr. into next tr., 1 tr. into next tr.; rep. from * omitting 1 tr. at end of last rep., s.s. into 3rd of 3 ch.: 48 sts.

3rd round: 3 ch., miss first tr., * tr. into each tr. until 2nd tr. of next 2 tr. gr. is reached, 2 tr. into next tr., rep. from * ending with s.s. into 3rd of 3 ch.: 60 sts. inc.

Rep. last round 4 (6) times.

Next round: 3 ch., miss first tr., * 1 tr. into each tr. until next 2 tr.gr. is reached, leaving last loop of each tr. on hook

Make the stripes in the colours of their favourite sporting team!

make 1 tr. into each of next 2 tr., y.o.h. and draw through all loops on hook, (1 dec. made); rep. from * to end, s.s. into 3rd of 3 ch.: 48 sts.

Next round: 3 ch., miss first tr., * 1 tr. into each tr. to within 1 tr. before next dec., a dec. over next 2 sts., rep. from * to end, s.s. into 3rd of 3 ch.: 36 sts.

Rep. last round 3 (4) times.

Next round: 1 d.c. into first tr., 1 d.c. into each st., 1 d.c. into first d.c.

Next round: make 1 d.c. into each d.c.

For large size only: rep. last round twice more.

Both sizes: fasten off.

MITTENS (both alike)
MAIN SECTION

With 1st colour and No. 4.50 hook, make 38 (46) ch. to measure 9½ (11½) in. Work as for scarf for 3 (4) rows. Change to hook No. 3.50 and work 2 (3) rows in patt. Change to hook No. 4.50 and work in patt. until 10 (14) rows are completed from beg.

Divide for Thumb. 3 ch., miss first tr., 1 tr. into each of next 11 (14) tr., 2 tr. into next tr., miss next 10 (12) tr., mark first tr. missed, 2 tr. into next tr., 1 tr. into each of next 11 (14) tr., 1 tr. into 3rd of 3 ch.; turn.

Work 6 (9) rows in patt.

Shape Top. 3 ch., miss first tr., a dec. over next 4 tr., 1 tr. into each of next 5 (8) tr., (dec. over next 4 tr.) twice, 1 tr. into each of next 5 (8) tr., dec. over next 4 tr., 1 tr. into 3rd of 3 ch.

For father's size only: turn; 3 ch., miss first tr., a dec. over next 4 sts., 1 tr. into each of next 2 tr., (a dec. over next 4 tr.) twice, 1 tr. into each of next 2 tr., a dec. over next 4 tr., 1 tr. into 3rd of 3 ch.

Both sizes: fasten off.

To Make Thumb. Attach yarn to first tr. left free, 3 ch., 1 tr. into same place as join, 1 tr. into each tr., 2 tr. into last tr.; turn.

Work 2 (4) rows in patt.

Last row: 3 ch., leaving last loop of each tr. on hook make 1 tr. into each st., y.o.h. and draw thr. all loops on hook, draw tight and secure.

Join side seam, join seam between thumb and main part.

Father and son zipped jerkins

(photographed in colour on page 18)

MATERIALS

For father's jerkin: 15 (16, 17, 18) oz. Robin Vogue Double Knitting (see note on wools and yarns, page 22); crochet hooks International Standard Sizes No. 4.00 and No. 3.50 (see page 9); 16-in. open ended zip fastener.

For son's jerkin: 9 (10, 11, 12) oz. Robin Vogue Double Knitting (see note on wools and yarns, page 22); crochet hooks International Standard Sizes No. 4.00 and No. 3.50 (see page 9); 12 (12, 14, 14)-in. open-ended zip fastener.

MEASUREMENTS

Father's jerkin: to fit chest size 38 (40, 42, 44) in.; length 24½ (25, 25½, 26) in. **Son's jerkin:** to fit chest size 26 (28, 30, 32) in.; length 17 (18½, 20, 21½) in.

TENSION

14 sts. and 10 rows to 3 in. over patt. with No. 4.00 hook (see note on tension, page 14).

ABBREVIATIONS

See page 20.
NB. *These garments are worked from side to side.*

FATHER'S JERKIN
BACK

With No. 4.00 hook make 76 ch.

1st row: tr. into 3rd ch. from hook and into every foll. ch., 2 ch.; turn: 74 sts.

2nd row: d.c. into back loop only of every tr. to end, 3 ch.; turn.

3rd row: tr. into back loop only of every d.c. to end, 3 ch.; turn.

The last 2 rows form the patt. Cont. in patt. as follows:

4th row: patt. to last st., 2 d.c. into last st., 5 ch.; turn.

5th row: tr. into first 2 of the 5 ch., patt. to end, 2 ch.; turn: 78 sts. Rep. the 4th and 5th rows once more.

8th row: patt. to last st., 2 d.c. into last st., 33 (35, 37, 39) ch.; turn.

9th row: tr. into 3rd ch. from hook and into every foll. ch., then patt. to end, 2 ch.; turn: 114 (116, 118, 120) sts.

Work 1 (3, 3, 5) rows without shaping.

Inc. 1 st. at beg. of next row and at this edge on every foll. 3rd row until there are 118 (120, 122, 124) sts., then work 3 (3, 5, 5) rows straight * *: 23 (25, 27, 29) rows from beg. Work 25 (25, 27, 27) rows straight.

Dec. 1 st. at beg. of next row and at this edge on every foll. 3rd row until there are 114 (116, 118, 120) sts., then work 1 (3, 3, 5) rows straight, thus ending with a right side row.

Next row: patt. to last 31 (33, 35, 37) sts.; turn: 83 sts.

Next row: dec. 1 st., patt. to end, 2 ch.; turn.

Next row: patt. to last 3 sts.; turn.

Rep. the last 2 rows once more, then the first of them again:

continued on page 135

Casual choice for the beach—trouser suits in orange (see page 118) and white (page 119).

Above: mother and daughter beach cover-ups
(see page 125).

Opposite: orange sundress with matching
pants (see page 121).

Teenage style—matching sweater, scarf and knee-high socks (see page 74).

74 sts. Work 2 rows without shaping. Fasten off.

LEFT FRONT

Work as given for Back to * * thus ending with a right side row.

Next row: patt. to last 6 (6, 7, 7) sts.; turn.

Next row: dec. 1 st., patt. to end, 2 ch.; turn.

Rep: the last 2 rows twice more.

Next row: patt. to last 6 (7, 7, 8) sts.; turn.

Next row: dec. 1 st., patt. to end, 2 ch.; turn.

Rep. the last 2 rows once more, omitting turning ch. at end of last row. Fasten off.

RIGHT FRONT

With No. 4.00 hook make 76 ch. and work first 3 rows as given for Back.

4th row: inc. in first st., patt. to end, 3 ch.; turn. Join a separate length of wool to beg. of this last row, work 3 ch. Break off.

5th row: patt. to end, then patt. across the 3 ch., 2 ch.; turn.

Rep. the 4th and 5th rows once more, then the 4th row again. Join a separate length of wool to beg. of last row, work 31 (33, 35, 37) ch.; break off.

9th row: patt. to end, then patt. across the 31 (33, 35, 37) ch., 2 ch.; turn: 114 (116, 118, 120) sts.

Work 1 (3, 3, 5) rows.

Inc. 1 st. at end of next row and at this edge on every foll. 3rd row until there are 118 (120, 122, 124) sts., then work 3 (3, 5, 5) rows straight, thus ending with a right side row; break off wool.

Next row: miss first 6 (6, 7, 7) sts., rejoin wool and patt. to end., 3 ch.; turn.

Next row: patt. to last st., miss last st. Break off wool. Rep. these 2 rows twice more.

Next row: miss first 6 (7, 7, 8) sts., rejoin wool and patt. to end, 3 ch.; turn.

Next row: patt. to last st., miss last st. Break off wool. Rep. these 2 rows once more. Fasten off.

TO COMPLETE

Main Edging. Join shoulder and side seams. With No. 4.00 hook and wrong side facing start at left side seam, work in d.c. along lower edge (working 1 d.c. into each row end), work 3 d.c. into corner st.; with No. 3.50 hook patt. up front edge, i.e. d.c. worked into back loops, then up shaped part of front, across back neck and down right front, working 3 d.c. into corner st., then with No. 4.00 hook cont. in d.c. round lower edge to left side seam, s.s. to first d.c.; turn.

Next row: work in d.c. into back loops, and working 3 d.c. into each bottom front corner, using No. 4.00 hook for lower edge and No. 3.50 hook for front edges and back neck, s.s. to first d.c.; turn.

Rep. the last row once more. Fasten off.

Armhole Edging. Work round armholes as given for Main Edging, using No. 3.50 hook.

Sew in zip to centre front edges.

SON'S JERKIN
BACK

With No. 4.00 hook make 56 (60, 65, 69) ch.

1st row: 1 tr. into 3rd ch. from hook and into every foll. ch., 2 ch.; turn: 54 (58, 63, 67) sts.

2nd row: d.c. into back loop only of every st. to last st., 2 d.c. into last st., 4 ch.; turn.

3rd row: tr. into first 2 of the 4 ch., then tr. into back loop only of every d.c. to end, 2 ch.; turn.

Rep. the 2nd and 3rd rows once more.

6th row: d.c. in back loop of every st. to last st., 2 d.c. in last st.: 20 (23, 25, 28) ch.; turn.

7th row: tr. into 3rd ch. from hook and into every foll. ch., then tr. into back loop of every d.c. to end, 2 ch.; turn; 79 (86, 93, 100) sts.

Work 2 (2, 4, 4) rows without shaping.

Inc. 1 st. at end of next row and at this edge on foll. 3rd (3rd, 4th, 4th) row: 81 (88, 95, 102) sts.

Work 2 (4, 3, 5) rows, thus ending with a right side row * *: 15 (17, 19, 21) rows from beg.

Work 20 (22, 21, 23) rows straight.

Dec. 1 st. at shoulder edge on next and foll. 3rd (3rd, 4th, 4th) row, then work 2 (2, 4, 4) rows, thus ending with a right side row.

Next row: patt. to last 18 (21, 23, 26) sts.; turn.

Next row: dec. 1 st., patt. to end, 2 ch.; turn.

Next row: patt. to last 2 sts.; turn.

Rep. the last 2 rows once more then the first of them again, omitting turning ch. at end of last row. Fasten off.

LEFT FRONT

Work as given for Back to * *.

Next row: patt. to last 6 (7, 7, 8) sts.; turn.

Next row: dec. 1 st., patt. to end, 2 ch.; turn.

Rep. these 2 rows twice more.

Next row: patt. to last 6 (6, 8, 8) sts.; turn.

Next row: dec. 1 st., patt. to end. Fasten off.

RIGHT FRONT

With No. 4.00 hook make 56 (60, 65, 69) ch. and work first row as on Back.

2nd row: 2 d.c. into back loop of first st., then d.c. into back loop of every tr. to end, 3 ch.; turn.

Join a separate length of wool to beg. of this last row and work 2 ch. Break off.

3rd row: tr. into back loop of every d.c. to end, then tr. into each of the 2 ch., 2 ch.; turn.

Rep. the 2nd and 3rd rows once more, then the 2nd row again.

Join a separate length of wool to beg. of last row and work 18 (21, 23, 26) ch. Break off.

7th row: tr. into back loop of every d.c. to end, then tr. into each of the 18 (21, 23, 26) ch., 2 ch.; turn: 79 (86, 93, 100) sts.

Work 2 (2, 4, 4) rows.

Inc. 1 st. at beg. of next row and at this edge on foll. 3rd (3rd, 4th, 4th) row. Work 2 (4, 3, 5) rows, thus ending with a right side row. Break off wool.

Next row: miss first 6 (7, 7, 8) sts., rejoin wool and patt. to end, 3 ch.; turn.

Next row: patt. to last st., miss last st. Break off wool. Rep. these 2 rows twice more.

Next row: miss first 6 (6, 8, 8) sts., rejoin wool and patt. to end., 3 ch.; turn.

Next row: patt. to last st., miss last st. Fasten off.

TO COMPLETE

Main Edging. Join shoulder and side seams. With No. 4.00 hook and wrong side facing, start at left side seam, work in d.c. along lower edge (working 1 d.c. into each row end) and 3 d.c. into corner st.; with No. 3.50 hook work in d.c. up front edge into back loops of trs., then d.c. up shaped part of front edge, across back neck and down other front, 3 d.c. into corner st., then with No. 4.00 hook work in d.c. round lower edge to left side seam, s.s. to first d.c.; turn.

Next row: d.c. into back loop of every st., using No. 4.00 hook for lower edge and No. 3.50 hook for front and neck edges, and working 3 d.c. into each bottom front corner, s.s. to first d.c.; turn.

Rep. the last row once more. Fasten off.

Armhole Edging. Work round armholes as given for Main Edging, using No. 3.50 hook.

Sew in zip to centre front edges.

V-necked sweater

(photographed in colour on the front cover)

MATERIALS

31 (33, 35) oz. Sirdar Double Crêpe (see note on wools and yarns, page 22); one crochet hook International Standard Size 3.00 (see page 9).

MEASUREMENTS

To fit chest size 38 (40, 42) in.; length from shoulder to lower edge 29 (29½, 30) in.; sleeve seam, 20 in. (adjustable).

TENSION

5 tr. or d.c. and 4 rows to 1 in. (see note on tension, page 14).

A flecked yarn is particularly attractive for this classic style sweater.

ABBREVIATIONS

See page 20.

N.B. C2., cross 2 tr. (miss 1 d.c., 1 tr. in next d.c., then 1 tr. in missed d.c.).

BACK

Make 103 (109, 113) ch.

1st row: 1 d.c. into 2nd ch. from hook, 1 d.c. in each ch. to end: 102 (108, 112) d.c.; 1 ch.; turn.

2nd row: 1 d.c. in each d.c. to end, 1 ch.; turn.

Rep. last row twice more, turning last row with 3 ch.

1st patt. row: miss first d.c., work 1 tr. in each d.c. to end, 1 ch.; turn.

2nd patt. row: 1 d.c. in each tr. to end, 3 ch.; turn.

These 2 rows form the main patt. Cont. in patt. until work measures 19 in. ending with a tr. row. Omit turning ch.

Shape Armholes. 1st row: s.s. over 6 tr., work in d.c. until 6 tr. rem.; turn.

2nd row: miss first d.c., 1 d.c. in next d.c., then 1 tr. in each d.c. until 2 d.c. rem., 1 d.c. in next d.c.; turn.

3rd row: miss first d.c., 1 d.c. in each tr. to end. Do not work into d.c.; turn.

Rep. last 2 rows until 80 (86, 90) sts. rem. in row.

Cont. straight on these sts. until work measures 9½ (10, 10½) in. from beg. of Armhole Shaping ending with a d.c. row. Omit turning ch.

Shape Shoulders. 1st row: s.s. over 8 (9, 9) d.c., 1 ch., work in tr. until 9 (10, 10) d.c. rem., 1 d.c. in next d.c.; turn.

2nd row: s.s. over 8 (9, 9) sts., work in d.c. until 8 (9, 9) sts. rem.; turn.

3rd row: s.s. over 8 (8, 10) d.c., 1 ch., work in tr. until 9 (9, 11) d.c. rem., 1 d.c. in next d.c. Fasten off.

FRONT

Work as given for Back until first 4 rows d.c. have been worked.

1st patt. row: work 16 tr., * C2, 1 tr. in next d.c., miss 2 d.c., (2 tr., 1 ch., 2 tr.) in next d.c., (one gr. made), miss 2 d.c., 1 tr. in next d.c., * rep. from * to * once, C2, work 30 (36, 40) tr., rep. from * to * twice, C2, then work 16 tr., 1 ch.; turn.

2nd patt. row: 1 d.c. in each st. to end, working 1 d.c. over each 1-ch. sp.

These 2 rows form the patt. for the Front.

Cont. in patt. until work measures 17 in. from beg. ending with a tr. row.

Divide for Neck. 1st row: work 51 (54, 56) d.c., 3 ch.; turn, and work on these sts. only.

2nd row: work in tr. and patt. to end.

3rd row: work in d.c. to end, but do not work into turning ch., 3 ch.; turn.

Rep. last 2 rows twice more, then work 2nd row again. Work should now measure the same as Back to Armhole Shaping, ending with a tr. row, and omitting turning ch.

Shape Armhole. 1st row: s.s. over 6 tr., work in d.c. to end, but do not work into turning ch., 3 ch.; turn.

2nd row: work in tr. and patt. to end, 1 ch.; turn.

3rd row: miss first d.c., work in d.c. to end, omitting turning

ch., 3 ch.; turn.

Rep. last 2 rows until 11 sts. in all have been decreased at armhole edge, and there are 5 tr. remaining at armhole edge. Cont. to dec. at front edge as before until 26 (27, 28) sts. remain in row. Cont. straight on these sts. until armhole is the same depth as Back, ending with a tr. row, omit turning ch.

Shape Shoulder. 1st row: s.s. over 8 (9, 9) tr., work in d.c. to end, 3 ch.; turn. **For sizes 40 and 42 in. only:** dec. 1 st. at beg. of next row. **For all sizes:** work in patt. across this row to the last 8 (9, 9) sts.; turn.

Next row: work in d.c. to end. Fasten off.

With front of work facing, join wool at neck edge of rem. sts. and work in d.c. to end. Now cont. in tr. and patt., dec. 1 st. at beg. of every d.c. row at neck edge until 8 rows in all have been worked.

Shape armhole and cont. working to match first side.

SLEEVES (make 2 alike)

Make 57 (59, 61) ch. and work as given for Back until work measures 3 in. from beg. Now inc. 1 st. at both ends of next d.c. row, and every alt. d.c. row (every 4th row) until 80 (84, 88) d.c. are on row.

Cont. straight on these sts. until sleeve measures 20 in. or length required, ending with a tr. row.

Shape Top. Work the first 3 rows of Back armhole shaping, then rep. the last 2 rows until 34 (36, 38) rem.

Next row: s.s. over 5 sts., work until 5 sts. rem.; turn. Rep. last row twice more. Fasten off.

TO COMPLETE

Press pieces lightly on wrong side, using a damp cloth under a warm iron. Join shoulder, side and sleeve seams. Press seams on wrong side.

Neck Band. With right side of work facing, commence at centre front and work 1 row d.c. up front, round neck and down to V point of left side of neck, turn. Work 5 more rows d.c. over this row, dec. 1 st. at both ends of every row. Fasten off, join the shaped ends of neck band tog. neatly. Sew in sleeves.

For holidays and casual wear—instructions for this vest sweater start on page 140.

Vest-sweater

(photographed in black and white on page 139)

MATERIALS

15 (16) balls Wendy Carolette Double Knitting (see note on wools and yarns, page 22); crochet hooks International Standard Sizes 4.00 and 3.50 (see page 9); four ⅜-in. buttons.

MEASUREMENTS

To fit chest size 38—39 (41—42) in.; sleeve seam 5 (5) in.; length from top of shoulder 27½ (28) in.

TENSION

23 sts. to 4 in., 12 rows to 4 in. in depth, over main patt., using No. 4.00 hook (see note on tension, page 14).

ABBREVIATIONS

See page 20.

FRONT

** With No. 3.50 hook, make 95 (102) ch.
Foundation row: 1 d.c. into 2nd ch. from hook, 1 d.c. into each ch. to end; turn with 1 ch.: 94 (101) sts.
Next row: 1 d.c. into each st. to end; turn with 1 ch.
Rep. the last row 5 times.
Next row: 2 d.c. into each of first 4 (3) sts., 1 d.c. into each of next 2 sts., * 2 d.c. into next st., 1 d.c. into each of next 3 sts., rep. from * to last 4 sts., 2 d.c. into each of last 4 sts.; turn with 3 ch.: 123 (131) sts. Change to No. 4.00 hook.
Next row: 1 tr. into each of first 3 sts. * 1 ch., miss 1 st., 1 tr. into each of next 3 sts., rep. from * to end; turn with 4 ch.
Commence Pattern. 1st row (wrong side): * 1 d.c. into 1-ch. sp., 3 ch., rep. from * to end; 1 d.c. into turning ch. of previous row; turn with 3 ch.
2nd row: (3 tr., 1 ch.) into each 3-ch. loop to end; turn with 4 ch.
These 2 rows form the patt. **
Cont. in patt. until work measures 18 (18) in. from beg. finishing on a right side row.
Divide for Front Opening. Next row: patt. 59 (63) sts., s.s. over 5 sts., patt. to end.
Cont. over the last set of sts. as follows:
Next row: patt. 59 (63) sts., turn with 4 ch.
Work 2 rows.
Shape Armhole. 1st row: patt. to the last 3 sts., d.c. 3 tog. by working 3 d.c. leaving last loop of each st. on hook, y.o.h. and draw through all loops on hook; turn with 3 ch.
2nd row: tr. 3 tog. by working 3 tr. leaving last loop of each st. on hook, y.o.h. and draw through all loops on hook; work to end; turn with 4 ch.
Rep. the 1st and 2nd rows twice more: 47 (51) sts.
Work 12 rows without dec. omitting turning ch. at end of last row.
Shape Neck. 1st row: s.s. over 12 sts., patt. to end; turn with 3 ch.
2nd row: patt. to the last 3 sts., tr. 3 tog.; turn with 1 ch.
3rd row: d.c. 3 tog., work to end; turn with 3 ch.
Rep. the 2nd and 3rd rows once more: 27 (31) sts.
Work 3 rows without dec. finishing at neck edge; turn with 1 ch.
Next row: 1 d.c. into each st. to end; turn.
Shape Shoulder. 1st row: s.s. over first 9 (10) sts., 1 ch., 1 tr. into each st. to end; turn with 1 ch.
2nd row: 1 d.c. into each of first 9 (10) sts. Fasten off.
Miss centre 4 sts., for front opening, rejoin yarn into 5th st. with a s.s. and 3 ch.; patt. to end.
Work 2 rows.
Shape Armhole. 1st row: d.c. 3 tog., work to end; turn with 3 ch.
2nd row: work to last 3 sts., tr. 3 tog.; turn with 1 ch.
Rep. the 1st and 2nd rows twice more then work 12 rows without dec.
Shape Neck. 1st row: work to last 12 sts.; turn with 3 ch.
2nd row: tr. 3 tog., work to end; turn with 4 ch.
3rd row: work to the last 3 sts., d.c. 3 tog.
Rep. the 2nd and 3rd rows once more then work 3 rows without dec. finishing at armhole edge.
Shape Shoulder. 1st row: 1 d.c. into each of first 9 (10) sts., 1 tr. into each st. to end; turn with 1 ch.
2nd row: 1 d.c. into each of first 9 (10) sts. Fasten off.

BACK

Work exactly as instructions given for Front from ** to ** then cont. in patt. until work measures the same as Front to beg. of armhole shaping, finishing on a right side row.
Shape Armholes. 1st row: d.c. 3 tog., work to the last 3 sts., d.c. 3 tog.; turn with 3 ch.
2nd row: tr. 3 tog., work to the last 3 sts., tr. 3 tog.; turn with 1 ch.
Rep. the 1st and 2nd rows twice more: 99 (107) sts.
Work 19 rows without dec. finishing on a wrong side row.
Shape Shoulders and Back of Neck. 1st row: patt. 27 (31) sts.; turn with 1 ch.
2nd row: 1 d.c. into each st. to end; turn.
3rd row: s.s. over first 9 (10) sts., 1 ch., 1 tr. into each st. to end; turn with 1 ch.
4th row: 1 d.c. into each of first 9 (10) sts. Fasten off.
Miss centre 44 sts. for neck edge rejoin yarn into 45th st. with a s.s. and 2 ch., patt. to end; turn with 1 ch.
Next row: 1 d.c. into each of first 9 (10) sts., 1 tr. into each st. to end; turn with 1 ch.
Next row: 1 d.c. into each of first 9 (10) sts. Fasten off.

SLEEVES (make 2 alike)

With No. 3.50 hook, make 57 (57) ch.
Foundation row: 1 d.c. into 2nd ch. from hook, 1 d.c. into each ch. to end: 56 (56) sts. Turn with 1 ch.
Next row: 1 d.c. into each st. to end; turn with 1 ch.

Rep. the last row 5 times more.

Next row: 1 d.c. into first st., 2 d.c. into next st. * 1 d.c. into each of next 2 sts., 2 d.c. into next st., rep. from * to end: 75 (75) sts. Turn with 3 ch.

Change to No. 4.00 hook.

Next row: 1 tr. into each of first 3 sts., * 1 ch., miss 1 st., 1 tr. into each of next 3 sts., rep. from * to end; turn with 4 ch.

Cont. in patt. as given for Front.

Work 2 rows then inc. 1 st. at each end of every row until 91 (91) sts. are on the row.

Shape Top. 1st row: d.c. 3 tog., work to the last 3 sts., d.c. 3 tog.; turn with 3 ch.

2nd row: tr. 3 tog., work to the last 3 sts., tr. 3 tog.; turn with 1 ch.

Rep. the 1st and 2nd rows twice more. Fasten off.

TO COMPLETE

Right Front Edging. With No. 3.50 hook and right side of work towards you, rejoin yarn, work 33 d.c. evenly up right side of front opening; turn with 1 ch.

Next row: 1 d.c. into each st. to end, turn with 1 ch.

Rep. the last row 4 times more. Fasten off.

Left Front Edging. With No. 3.50 hook and right side of work towards you, work 33 d.c. evenly down left side of front opening; turn with 1 ch.

Next row: 1 d.c. into each st. to end; turn with 1 ch.

Rep. the last row once more.

Next row (buttonhole row): 1 d.c. into each of first 5 sts., 2 ch., miss 2 sts., * 1 d.c. into each of next 6 sts., 2 ch., miss 2 sts., rep. from * twice more, 1 d.c. into each of last 2 sts.

Next row: work d.c. to end, working 2 d.c. into each 2 ch. space; turn with 1 ch.

Work 1 row.

Fasten off.

Join shoulder seams by back stitching then work 1 row d.c. evenly round neck edge; turn with 1 ch.

Work 2 more rows d.c. Fasten off.

Join side and sleeve seams by top sewing. Pin sleeves into position, sew in by back stitching. Slip stitch lower edge of under wrap neatly into position. Sew on buttons to correspond with buttonholes. Buttonhole-stitch buttonholes to neaten.

Do not press or dry clean.

Flecked jacket

(photographed in black and white on page 143)

MATERIALS

20 (22, 23) balls of Wendy Diabolo (see note on wools and yarns, page 22); crochet hooks International Standard Sizes 7.00 and 5.50 (see page 9); 6 buttons each 1 in. in diameter; ¼ yd. lining material 36 in. wide for pockets.

MEASUREMENTS

To fit chest size 38 (40, 42) in.; length from shoulder 28 (28½, 29) in.; sleeve seam 18 in.

TENSION

9 d.c. to 3 in. with No. 7.00 hook (see note on tension, page 14).

ABBREVIATIONS

See page 20.

BACK

With No. 7.00 hook, make 61 (64, 67) ch.

1st row: d.c. into 2nd and every foll. ch., 2 ch.; turn: 60 (63, 66) sts. Cont. in d.c. until work measures 18 in. from beg., omitting turning ch. at end of last row and ending with right side facing.

Shape Armholes. Next row: s.s. over first 3 sts., 2 ch., patt. to last 3 sts.; turn. Dec. 1 st. at each end of next and every alt. row until 44 (45, 46) sts. rem. Cont. straight until armhole measures 10 (10½, 11) in., omitting turning ch. at end of last row.

Shape Shoulders. Next row: s.s. over first 4 sts., patt. to last 4 sts.; turn. Rep. this row once.

Next row: s.s. over first 3 sts., patt. to last 3 sts.; turn. Rep. last row once: 16 (17, 18) sts. Fasten off.

LEFT FRONT

With No. 7.00 hook, make 29 (31, 33) ch. and work as given for Back for 6½ in., ending with right side facing: 28 (30, 32) sts.

Pocket Opening. Next row: patt. 12 (13, 14) sts.; turn and cont. on these sts. for 5 in., ending at inside edge. Break off wool, rejoin to inside edge of the 16 (17, 18) sts. which were left and work to match, then cont. across all sts. until work measures the same as Back to armholes, ending with right side facing.

Shape Armhole. Work as Back, but dec. at right edge only, then cont. straight on 20 (21, 22) sts. remaining until armhole measures 7½ (8, 8½) in., ending at armhole edge.

Shape Neck. Next row: patt. to last 3 (4, 5) sts.; turn. Dec. 1 st. at neck edge on next and foll. 2 alt. rows, then cont. straight on remaining 14 sts. until armhole measures the same as on back, ending at armhole edge.

Shape Shoulder. Work as Back but dec. at armhole edge only.

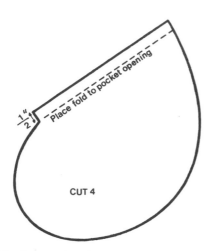

CUT 4

Place fold to pocket opening

1″/2″

Follow this diagram for shape of pocket.

RIGHT FRONT
Work to match Left Front, reversing shaping and pocket position.

SLEEVES (make 2 alike)
With No. 7.00 hook, make 29 (31, 33) ch. and work as for Back: 28 (30, 32) sts.

Inc. 1 st. at each end of 7th and every foll. 8th row until there are 42 (44, 46) sts., then cont. straight until sleeve seam measures 18 in. from beg. Mark this point, then work a further 1 in., omitting turning ch. at end of last row.

Shape Top. Dec. 1 st. at each end of next row then on every alt. row 5 (6, 7) times, 1 st. at each end of next 6 rows, then 2 sts. at each end of next 3 rows: 6 sts. Fasten off.

TO COMPLETE
Right Front Border. With No. 5.50 hook and right side facing, work a row of d.c. along front edge. Turn and work a further 7 rows.

Mark position of buttons with pins: first pin 1 in. from lower edge, 2nd pin ½ in. from top edge, then 4 more pins at equal distances between these two.

Left Front Border. Work to match Right Front Border, making buttonholes at pin positions on 4th row by working 2 ch., miss 2 d.c.

Neck Edging. Join shoulder seams. With No. 5.50 hook and right side facing work 2 rows of d.c. round neck edge.

Pockets. Work 1 row of d.c. along pocket edges nearer to centre opening and stitch to jacket at top and bottom. Cut lining in 4. Shape each piece as in diagram above, with straight edges 1 in. longer than pocket opening, the rest of shape in proportion. Place 2 pieces right sides tog. and stitch round all but straight edge with ½-in. seam allowance. Fold back ½ in. on straight edges and hemstitch neatly. Rep. with other pair of shaped pieces.

To Make Up. Press with a warm iron over a damp cloth. Join side and sleeve seams and sew in sleeves. Press seams. Sew on buttons. Stitch pocket linings in position on wrong side of jacket.

Use a heavy double knitting yarn for extra weight and strength.

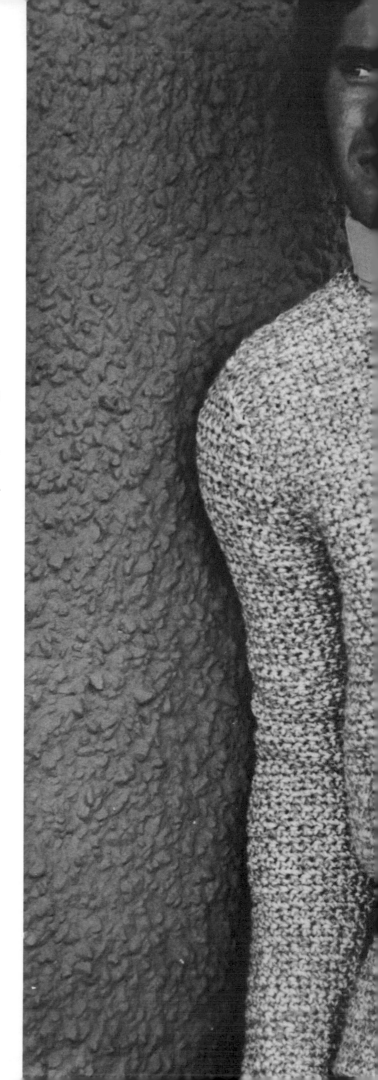

Green jacket

(photographed in colour on page 152)

MATERIALS

23 (24, 25, 26, 27, 28) oz. of Lister Lavenda Double Crêpe or 25 (26, 27, 28, 29, 30) oz. of Lister Lavenda Double Knitting or 25 (26, 27, 28, 29, 30) balls of Lister Bel Air Double Crêpe, Lister Velora Double Knitting or Lister Bri-Nylon Double Knitting (see note on wools and yarns, page 21); crochet hooks International Standard Sizes 3.50 and 3.00 (see page 9); 5 buttons each $\frac{5}{8}$ in. in diameter.

N.B. The jacket shown in the photograph on page 152 was worked in Lister Lavenda Double Crêpe.

MEASUREMENTS

To fit chest size 34 (36, 38, 40, 42, 44) in.; length from shoulder 26 in.; length of sleeve seam 18 in.

TENSION

10 sts. and 8 rows to 2 in. with No. 3.50 hook (see note on tension, page 14).

ABBREVIATIONS

See page 20.

BACK

With No. 3.50 hook commence with 85 (90, 95, 100, 105, 110) ch.

1st row: 1 h.tr. into 2nd ch. from hook, * 1 h.tr. into next ch.; rep. from * to end, 1 ch.; turn.

2nd row: 1 d.c. into 2nd h.tr. from hook, * 1 d.c. into next h.tr.; rep. from * ending with 1 d.c. into turning ch., 3 ch.; turn.

3rd row: 1 tr. into 2nd d.c. from hook, * 1 tr. into next d.c.; rep. from * ending with 1 tr. into turning ch., 2 ch.; turn.

4th row: 1 h.tr. into 2nd tr., * 1 h.tr. into next tr.; rep. from * ending with 1 h.tr. into turning ch., 1 ch.; turn.

The last 3 rows form patt.

Cont. in patt. until work measures $15\frac{1}{2}$ in. from beg., ending with a tr. row and with right side facing.

Next row: s.s. across 2 (4, 6, 7, 8, 9) sts., patt. to last 2 (4, 6, 7, 8, 9) sts., 1 ch.; turn.

Next row: work in patt.

Next row: s.s. across 1 st., patt. to last st.; turn.

Next row: s.s. across 1 st., patt. to last st., 1 ch.; turn.

Next row: work in patt.

Next row: s.s. across 1 st., patt. to last st.; turn.

Next row: s.s. across 1 st., patt. to last st., 1 ch.; turn.

Rep. last 3 rows until 29 (30, 31, 32, 33, 34) sts. rem. Fasten off.

POCKET LININGS (make 2 alike)

With No. 3.50 hook, commence with 25 ch. and work in patt. as for Back until work measures 5 in. Fasten off.

LEFT FRONT

With No. 3.50 hook, commence with 43 (46, 49, 52, 55, 58) ch. and patt. as for Back until work measures 5 in., ending with right side facing.

Next row: patt. 9 (10, 12, 13, 15, 16) sts., patt. across 25 pocket lining sts., miss 25 sts. on Front, patt. to end. Cont. in patt. until work measures $15\frac{1}{2}$ in. from beg., ending with a tr. row and right side facing.

Shape Raglan and Front. Next row: s.s. across 2 (4, 6, 7, 8, 9) sts., patt. to end.

Next row: work in patt.

Next row: s.s. across 1 st., patt. to last st.; turn.

Next row: patt. to last st.; turn.

Next row: patt. to last st.; turn.

Next row: s.s. across 1 st., patt. to last st.; turn.

Rep. last 3 rows, dec. one st. at neck edge on every alt. row and at the same time working raglan dec. until 9 (9, 6, 6, 5, 5) sts. rem.

Now keeping front edge straight, cont. to shape raglan as before until all sts. are worked off.

RIGHT FRONT

With No. 3.50 hook, commence with 43 (46, 49, 52, 55, 58) ch. and work in patt. as Back until work measures 5 in., ending with right side facing.

Pocket Opening. Next row: patt. 9 (11, 12, 14, 15, 17) sts., patt. across 25 pocket lining sts., miss 25 sts. on Front, patt. to end.

Cont. in patt. until work measures $15\frac{1}{2}$ in. from beg., ending with a tr. row and right side facing.

Shape Raglan and Front. Next row: patt. to last 2 (4, 6, 7, 8, 9) sts.; turn.

Next row: work in patt.

Next row: s.s. across 1 st., patt. to last st.; turn.
Next row: s.s. across 1 st., patt. to end, turn.
Next row: s.s. across 1 st., patt. to end, turn.
Next row: s.s. across 1 st., patt. to end, turn.
Next row: s.s. across 1 st., patt. to last st.; turn.
Rep. last 3 rows, dec. 1 st. at neck edge on every alt. row and at the same time working raglan dec. until 9 (9, 6, 6, 5, 5) sts. rem.
Now keeping front edge straight, cont. to shape raglan as before until all sts. are worked off.

SLEEVES (make 2 alike)
With No. 3.50 hook, commence with 50 (52, 54, 56, 58, 60) ch. and patt. as Back for 8 rows.
Now inc. 1 st. at each end of next and every 6th (6th, 6th, 4th, 4th, 4th) row until there are 62 (66, 70, 74, 78, 82) sts. Cont. on these sts. until work measures 18 in. from beg., ending with a tr. row and with right side facing.
Shape Raglan. Work as for Back until 6 sts. rem. Fasten off.

TO COMPLETE
Front Edging. Join raglan seams. With right side of work facing and beg. at lower corner of Right Front, rejoin yarn and with No. 3.00 hook, work d.c. up Right Front, round back of neck, down Left Front and round lower edge, work 1 d.c. into each d.c. of previous row, working 2 d.c. into corners.
Next row: work in d.c. leaving 5 sp. of 2 ch. for button-holes up Left Front, the first one at lower edge and the last one at beg. of neck shaping, the rest evenly spaced between.
Next row: work in d.c., working 2 d.c. into 2-ch. sp. of previous row.
Next row: work in d.c. Fasten off.
Pocket Tops. With No. 3.00 hook, rejoin yarn and work 4 rows in d.c. Fasten off.
Join, side and sleeve seams. Sew pocket linings and pocket tops neatly in position. Sew on buttons to correspond with buttonholes.

Chapter Seven

Accessories and trimmings

Pink handbag

(photographed in colour on back cover and page 153)

MATERIALS
6 balls Coats Mercer-Crochet No. 10 (20 grm.) (see note on wools and yarns, page 20); crochet hook International Standard Size 1.25 (see page 9); a 9-in. handbag frame; $\frac{1}{2}$ yd. backing fabric 36 in. wide (in a colour to tone or contrast with crochet yarn); $\frac{1}{2}$ yd. lining fabric 36 in. wide; $\frac{1}{2}$ yd. bonded fibre interlining 32 in. wide; piece cardboard 9 in. by $4\frac{1}{2}$ in. for stiffening base; Copydex.

MEASUREMENTS
Width 9 in.; depth $4\frac{1}{2}$ in.; height $9\frac{3}{4}$ in

TENSION
1 motif = $2\frac{1}{4}$ in. square (see note on tension, page 14).

ABBREVIATIONS
See page 20.

MAIN SECTION
First Motif. Commence with 6 ch., join with s.s. to form a ring.

1st row: 12 d.c. into ring, 1 s.s. into first d.c.

2nd row: draw loop up approx. $\frac{1}{4}$ in., y.o.h. and draw through, y.o.h. loosely 10 times, insert hook into same place as s.s. and draw yarn through, holding hook against index finger, y.o.h. and draw through all loops on hook, 1 ch. to fasten taking care not to draw yarn up too tightly: a starting bullion st. made; * y.o.h. loosely 10 times, insert hook into next d.c. and draw yarn through, yarn over and draw through all loops on hook, 1 ch., to fasten: another bullion st. made; rep. from * ending with 1 s.s. between first loop made at beginning of row and first bullion st.: 12 bullion sts.

3rd row: working firmly to enable previous row to stand out, work 1 d.c. between each bullion st., 1 s.s. into first d.c.

4th row: draw loop up approx. $\frac{1}{4}$ in. and work starting bullion st. as before, a bullion st. into same d.c., 2 bullion sts. into each d.c., 1 s.s. between first loop and first bullion st.

5th row: 1 d.c. between first 2 bullion sts., * 1 ch., 1 d.c. between last bullion st. and next bullion st.: rep. from * ending with 1 ch., 1 s.s. into first d.c.

6th row: * 1 d.c. into next 1-ch. sp., 5 ch., miss next sp.: rep. from * omitting 5 ch. at end of last rep., 2 ch., 1 tr. into first d.c.

7th row: 1 d.c. into loop just formed, * 5 ch., into centre of next loop work 1 tr., 7 ch. and 1 tr., (5 ch., 1 d.c. into next loop) twice: rep. from * omitting 1 d.c. at end of last rep., 1 s.s. into first d.c. Fasten off.

Second Motif. Work as first motif for 6 rows.

7th row: 1 d.c. into loop just formed, 5 ch., into centre ch. of next loop work 1 tr., 3 ch., 1 s.s. into corresponding loop on first motif, 3 ch. and 1 tr., (2 ch., 1 s.s. into next loop on first motif, 2 ch., 1 d.c. into next loop on second motif) twice, 2 ch., 1 s.s. into next loop on first motif, 2 ch., into centre ch. of next loop on first motif work 1 tr., 3 ch., 1 s.s. into corresponding loop on first motif, 3 ch. and 1 tr., 5 ch. and complete as first motif.

Make 10 rows of 4 motifs joining adjacent sides as second motif was joined to first. Where 4 corners meet, join 3rd and 4th motifs to joining of previous motif.

GUSSET (make 2)

Make 4 rows of 2 motifs joining as before.
Damp and pin out to measurements.
Joining. With wrong sides facing place gussets in position with main section and work a row of d.c. evenly all round, ending with 1 s.s. into first d.c.
Fasten off.

TOP EDGING

1st row: with right side facing, attach yarn to centre stitch at corner of main section, 3 ch., 3 tr. into same sp., * (1 tr. into next st., 5 tr. into next sp.) 3 times, 1 tr. into next st., 3 tr. into next sp., 1 tr. into st. between joining of motifs, 3 tr. into next sp.: rep. from * 3 times omitting 3 tr. at end of last rep. and working last tr. into centre st. at next corner, 4 ch.; turn.
2nd row: miss first 2 tr., * 1 tr. into each of next 5 tr., 1 ch., miss 1 tr.; rep. from * ending with 1 tr. into 3rd of 3 ch., 3 ch.; turn.
3rd row: 1 tr. into first sp., * 1 tr. into each of next 5 tr., 1 tr. into next sp.: rep. from * ending with 1 tr. into 3rd of 4 ch., 1 ch.; turn.
4th row: 1 d.c. into each tr., 1 d.c. into 3rd of 3 ch. Fasten off.
Work other side to correspond.

TO COMPLETE

N.B. ½-in. seam allowance has been given.
Cut 1 piece each of backing, lining and interlining 23½ in. by 10 in. for main section and 2 pieces each 10 in. by 5½ in. for gussets.
Cut 1 piece of lining 7 in. by 9 in. and 1 piece of interlining 6 in. by 3½ in. for pocket.
Pocket. Fold lining widthwise right sides tog.: this will now measure 7 in. by 4½ in. Stitch side seams, press and turn to right side. Insert interlining, turn in raw edges of lining and tack.
Main Section. Place interlining to wrong side of lining and tack. With fold at top, place pocket centrally to right side of lining, approx. 4 in. from top edge. Stitch close to edge, through all layers, along side and bottom edges. Place interlining to wrong side of lining for gussets and tack. Place 2 short ends of main section, right sides tog., pin gussets centrally in position to each side of main section, right sides tog., and machine stitch leaving ½ in. open at top of each side of gussets.
Omitting interlining make another piece in same manner using backing. Press all seams.
Insert lining to backing, placing cardboard in position between 2 sections to form base of bag and gluing lightly in place to interlining with Copydex. Turn in top edges to wrong side and slipstitch.
Insert completed lining to crochet section and stitch in position round top edge.
Insert rods to handbag frame through holes in top edging.

Blue and green handbag

(photographed in colour on page 153)

MATERIALS

2 balls Coats Mercer-Crochet No. 20 (20 grm.) in green (521), 3 balls in dark green (524) and 2 balls in blue (510) (see note on wools and yarns, page 20); steel crochet hook International Standard Size 1.25 (see page 9); 1 yd. fabric 36 in. wide for lining; ½ yd. bonded fibre interlining 32 in. wide; piece of cardboard 4 in. by 9 in. for stiffening base; a 9-in. handbag frame; Copydex.

MEASUREMENTS

Width 9 in.; depth 4 in.; height 10½ in.

TENSION

5 rows to 1 in. over V st. (see note on tension, page 14).

ABBREVIATIONS

See page 20; G., green; D.G., dark green; B., blue.

MAIN SECTION

First Side. With G. make 118 ch.
1st row: 1 tr. into 4th ch. from hook, 1 tr. into each ch. Fasten off; turn.
2nd row: attach B. to last tr. worked; 3 ch., miss next tr., * 1 tr. into each of next 8 tr., into next tr. work 1 tr., 2 ch. and 1 tr. (a V st. made), 1 tr. into each of next 8 tr., miss 2 tr.; rep. from * ending with miss 1 tr., 1 tr. into next ch., 3 ch.; turn.
3rd row: miss first 2 tr., * 1 tr. into each of next 8 tr., V st. into next V st., 1 tr. into each of next 8 tr., miss 2 tr.; rep. from * ending with miss 1 tr., 1 tr. into next ch., 3 ch.; turn.
4th row: miss first 2 tr., * 1 tr. into each of next 8 tr., a V st. into next V st., 1 tr. into each of next 8 tr., miss 2 tr.; rep. from * ending with miss 1 tr., 1 tr. into next ch. Fasten off; turn.
5th row: attach D.G. to last tr. worked, 3 ch., miss 1 tr., * 1

tr. into each of next 8 tr., a V st. into next V st., 1 tr. into each of next 8 tr., miss 2 tr.; rep. from * ending with miss 1 tr., 1 tr. into next ch. Fasten off; turn.

6th row: attach G. to last tr. worked, 3 ch., miss 1 tr., * 1 tr. into each of next 8 tr., a V st. into next V st., 1 tr. into each of next 8 tr., miss 2 tr.; rep. from * ending with miss 1 tr., 1 tr. into next ch., 3 ch.; turn.

7th row: as 4th row.

8th row: attach D.G. to last tr. worked, 3 ch., miss 1 tr., * 1 tr. into each of next 8 tr., a V st. into next V st., 1 tr. into each of next 8 tr., miss 2 tr.; rep. from * ending with miss 1 tr., 1 tr. into next ch., 3 ch.; turn.

9th and 10th rows: as 3rd and 4th rows.

11th row: attach G. to last tr. worked, 3 ch., miss 1 tr., * 1 tr. into each of next 8 tr., a V st. into next V st., 1 tr. into each of next 8 tr., miss 2 tr.; rep. from * ending with miss 1 tr., 1 tr. into next ch. Fasten off; turn.

2nd to 11th rows form colour patt.

Cont. in patt. until work measures $11\frac{1}{2}$ in. or length required ending with an 8th patt. row.

Top Edge. 1st row: miss first 2 tr., * 1 tr. into each of next 8 tr., into next sp. work 1 tr., 4 ch. and 1 tr., 1 tr. into each of next 8 tr., miss 2 tr.; rep. from * ending with miss 1 tr., 1 tr. into next ch., 3 ch.; turn.

2nd to 4th rows: work in patt. omitting turning ch. at end of last row. Fasten off.

Facing for Inside Top Edge. With D.G. make 118 ch.

1st row: 1 tr. into 5th ch. from hook, 1 tr. into each of next 7 tr., * a V st. into next ch., 1 tr. into each of next 8 ch., miss 2 ch., 1 tr. into each of next 8 ch.; rep. from * ending with miss 1 ch., 1 tr. into next ch., 3 ch.; turn.

Rep. 1st to 4th rows of Top Edge once more. Fasten off.

Joining. With D.G. and right side of last rows facing, place Top Edge and facing tog., working with right side of bag facing, attach yarn to first st., 1 d.c. into same place as join, 1 d.c. into each of next 9 sts., * 2 d.c. into next sp., 1 d.c. into each of next 18 sts.; rep. from * omitting 8 d.c. at end of last rep. Fasten off.

Second Side. 1st row: with B. and wrong side facing,

attach yarn to opposite side of foundation ch., 3 ch., miss next ch., * 1 tr. into each of next 8 ch., a V st. into next ch., 1 tr. into each of next 8 ch., miss 2 ch.; rep. from * ending with miss 1 ch., 1 tr. into next ch., 3 ch.; turn and complete to correspond with First Side.

GUSSET (make 2)

With B. make 61 ch.

1st row: 1 tr. into 4th ch. from hook, 1 tr. into each ch., 3 ch.; turn.

Keeping continuity of colours, work in patt. till gusset measures $9\frac{1}{2}$ in. ending with an 8th patt. row. Do not fasten off.

With D.G. cont. in patt. for 4 rows more turning with 1 ch. at end of last row.

Next row: 1 d.c. into each of next 10 sts., * 2 d.c. into next sp., 1 d.c. into each of next 18 sts.; rep. from * omitting 8 d.c. at end of last rep.

Fasten off.

TO COMPLETE

Damp work and pin out to correct measurements.

N.B. $\frac{1}{2}$-in. seam allowance has been given.

Cut 2 pieces of lining fabric and 1 piece of interlining, each 10 in. by 24 in., for main section, 4 pieces of fabric and 2 pieces of interlining, each 10 in. by 5 in., for gussets. Place interlining for main section to wrong side of one lining piece for main section and baste. Similarly baste tog. one interlining piece and one lining piece for each gusset. Place gussets in position to main section, right sides tog., and machine stitch. In a similar way, stitch gussets and main piece of rem. lining fabric. Place both lining sections, wrong sides tog., with cardboard base sandwiched between and glued lightly with Copydex to interlining. Turn in raw edges along top of linings and slipstitch tog. Insert completed lining into bag, and slipstitch top edges of lining to crochet edging.

Insert rods of handbag frame through V sts. on first row of edging.

Beaded evening bag and belt

(photographed in colour on page 153)

MATERIALS

2 oz. Sirdar 4-ply Fontein Crêpe (see note on wools and yarns, page 22); 6 bags of small knitting beads; one crochet hook International Standard Size 3.50 (see page 9); 2 hooks; $5\frac{1}{2}$-in. bag frame; $\frac{1}{2}$ yd. lining material, 36 in. wide.

MEASUREMENTS

Belt width $1\frac{3}{4}$ in.; length 30 in. (to fit average 24—26 in.

waist); bag depth $6\frac{1}{2}$ in.

TENSION

2 patt. to $1\frac{1}{4}$ in. (see note on tension, page 14).

ABBREVIATIONS

See page 20; b.st., bead stitch.

BELT

TO MAKE

Thread all beads on to yarn (see page 15).

Foundation row: make 14 ch., 1 tr. into 6th ch. from hook, * miss 3 ch., (1 tr., 3 ch., 1 tr.) into next ch., rep. from * once more; turn.

1st patt. row: * y.o.h., insert hook into centre ch. of next 3-ch. sp., y.o.h. and draw through, drop 2 beads down behind work, y.o.h. and draw thr. all loops on hook (a b.st. made), 4 b.st. into same place, 1 d.c. into sp. between next 2 tr.; rep. from * working 1 d.c. at end of last repeat into 3rd of 6 ch.; turn.

2nd patt. row: miss first d.c., 1 s.s. into each of next 3 sts., 6 ch., 1 tr. into same place as s.s., * miss next 4 b.sts., (1 tr., 3 ch., 1 tr.) into next b.st., rep. from * to end; turn.

Rep. last 2 rows until work measures 30 in. from beg. ending with first patt. row. Fasten off.

TO COMPLETE

Cut a piece of lining 30½ in. by 2¼ in. Turn in ½ in. round raw edges, and place lining to belt, wrong sides tog. Hem lining to belt, using some of the yarn. Sew 2 hooks to one end of lining and work buttonhole loops with sewing thread on right side of belt at other end.

HANDBAG

TO MAKE

Make 30 ch. to measure 6½ in.

Foundation row: 1 tr. into 6th ch. from hook, * miss 3 ch., (1 tr., 3 ch., 1 tr.) into next ch.; rep. from * to end; turn.

Rep. first and 2nd patt. rows as given for Belt until work measures 13 in. from beg. ending with 2nd patt. row. Fasten off.

TO COMPLETE

Fold work in half and sew to frame. Stitch sides tog. below frame.

Cut a piece of lining 14 in. by 7 in. Fold in half, with right sides tog., and stitch both side seams for 4½ in. up from fold, taking ½ in. turnings. Trim turnings.

Place inside bag, wrong sides tog., turn in ½ in. on remaining raw edges and stitch neatly to inside of bag frame.

Floral bonnet

(photographed in black and white on page 156)

MATERIALS

3 oz. Emu Double Crêpe (see note on wools and yarns, page 21); crochet hooks International Standard Sizes 4.00 and 3.00 (see page 9); 1 yd. ribbon, ¾ in. wide.

MEASUREMENTS

To fit an average-sized head.

TENSION

1 motif 2¾ in. with No. 4.00 hook (see note on tension, page 14).

ABBREVIATIONS

See page 20.

FIRST MOTIF

With No. 4.00 hook, make 5 ch., s.s. into first ch. to form a ring.

1st round: 8 d.c. into ring, s.s. into first d.c.

2nd round: 4 ch., leaving last loop of each d.tr. on hook make 3 d.tr. into same place as s.s., y.o.h. and draw thr. all loops on hook (a cluster formed), * 6 ch., s.s. into 3rd ch. from hook (a picot formed), 3 ch., a 4-d.tr. cl. into next d.c., 5 ch., a 4-d.tr. cl. into next d.c., rep. from * 3 times omitting 2nd cl. of last repeat, s.s. into top of first cl. Fasten off.

SECOND MOTIF

With No. 4.00 hook work as for first motif until 2nd round is reached.

2nd round: 4 ch., a 3 d.tr. into same place as s.s., 3 ch., 1 d.c. into a p. on first motif, 3 ch., a 4-d.tr. cl. into next d.c. on 2nd motif, 2 ch., 1 d.c. into appropriate 5 ch. loop on first motif, 2 ch., a 4-d.tr. cl. into next d.c. on 2nd motif, 3 ch., 1 d.c. into next p. on first motif, 3 ch., complete as first motif.

TRIANGLE MOTIF

With No. 4.00 hook make 4 ch., s.s. into first ch. to form a ring.

1st round: 6 d.c. into ring, s.s. into first d.c.

2nd round: 3 ch., a 3-tr. cl. into same place as s.s., * 6 ch., s.s. into 3rd ch. from hook (a p. formed), 3 ch., a 4-tr. cl. into next d.c., 5 ch., a 4-tr. cl. into next d.c., rep. from * twice omitting last cl. of 2nd repeat, s.s. into top of first cl., fasten off. Join triangles to previous motifs in the same way as for 2nd motifs.

TO COMPLETE

Join tog. a line of 6 motifs. To this join a row of 1 triangle motif, 4 motifs, 1 triangle motif. To this join a row of 1 motif, a triangle motif, 2 motifs, a triangle motif, 1 motif. Join last row tog. with 1 motif.

The face edge of bonnet is the edge with 6 motifs.
Edging. 1st round: with No. 3.00 hook and right side facing attach yarn to p. at right hand corner, * (3 d.c. into next sp., 1 d.c. into next cl.) twice, 3 d.c. into next sp., 1 d.c. into next p.; rep. from * all round omitting last d.c. of last repeat, s.s. into first d.c.; turn.
2nd round: 5 ch., miss first 2. d.c., * 1 d.tr. into next d.c., 1 ch., miss next d.c.; rep. from * along neck edge, 1 d.tr. into next d.c. at 2nd corner; 1 d.c. into top of d.tr. just formed, 3 ch., s.s. into top of last d.c., 2 d.c. into sp., ** 3 ch., s.s. into top of last d.c., 1 d.c. into each of next 2 d.c.; rep. from ** along face edge to corner, 3 ch., s.s. into top of last d.c., 2 d.c. into sp. Then along neck edge work *** 3 ch., s.s. into top of last d.c., 2 d.c. into next sp.; rep. from *** omitting last d.c. of last repeat, s.s. into first d.c. Fasten off. Thread length of ribbon round neck edge to tie under chin.

Chequered beret
(photographed in black and white on page 156)

MATERIALS
2 balls Sirdar Courtelle Crêpe Double Knitting in white and 2 balls Sirdar Courtelle Crêpe Double Knitting in orange (see note on wools and yarns, page 22); crochet hooks International Standard Sizes 5.50, 4.50 and 3.50 (see page 9); ½-in. button mould. (Any 2 colours may be used.)

MEASUREMENTS
To fit an average-sized head.

TENSION
4 tr. to 1 in. with No. 4.50 hook and yarn used double (see note on tension, page 14).

ABBREVIATIONS
See page 20; W., white; O., orange.

MAIN PIECE
Use double yarn throughout. With No. 4.50 hook and O., make 8 ch. and join with s.s. to form a ring.
1st round: 16 tr. into ring, s.s. to first tr.
2nd round: with W., 2 tr. into each tr., s.s. to first tr.: 32 sts.
3rd round: with O., * miss 1 tr., 2 tr. into next tr.; rep. from * to end, s.s. to first tr. Change to No. 5.50 hook.
4th round: with W., 2 tr. into sp. between grs. of 2 tr., * 1 ch., 2 tr. into next sp.; rep. from * to end, 1 ch., s.s. to first tr.
5th round: with O., 2 tr. into sp., * 2 ch., 2 tr. into next sp.; rep. from * to end, 2 ch., s.s. to first tr.
6th round: with W., 3 tr. into sp., * 1 ch., 3 tr. into next sp.; rep. from * to end, 1 ch., s.s. to first tr.
7th round: with O., 3 tr. into sp., * 2 ch., 3 tr. into next sp.; rep. from * to end, 2 ch., s.s. to first tr.
8th round: with W., 4 tr. into sp., * 1 ch., 4 tr. into next sp.; rep. from * to end, 1 ch., s.s. to first tr.
9th round: with O., 4 tr. into sp., * 2 ch., 4 tr. into next sp.; rep. from * to end, 2 ch., s.s. to first tr.
10th round: as 8th round.
11th round: as 7th round.
12th round: as 6th round.
13th round: as 5th round.
Change to No. 4.50 hook.
14th round: as 4th round.
15th round: with O., * 1 d.c. into next 2 tr., 1 d.c. into sp.; rep. from * to end: 48 d.c.
16th round: with O., 1 d.c. into each d.c.; fasten off.

BUTTON COVER
Use single yarn. With No. 3.50 hook and W., make 4 ch. and join with s.s. to form a ring.
1st round: 8 d.c. into ring.
2nd round: 2 tr. into each d.c.: 16 sts.
3rd round: 1 tr. into each tr.
4th round: * 1 tr. into first tr., miss 1 tr.; rep. from * to end: 8 sts.

TO COMPLETE
Place button mould inside cover, draw up yarn and fasten off securely. Sew button to top of beret.

Panelled hat
(photographed in black and white on page 156)

MATERIALS
2 oz. each of 3 contrasting colours of Emu Supercrimp Bri-Nylon 4-ply (see note on wools and yarns, page 21); crochet hooks International Standard Sizes 5.00 and 6.00 (see page 9); facing ribbon (optional), ¾ in. wide, to fit round inside of hat, approx. 22 in. plus turnings.

MEASUREMENTS
To fit an average-sized head.

TENSION
2 grs. and 1 d.c. to 2 in., 3 rows to 1¾ in. with No. 5.00 hook (see note on tension, page 14). *continued on page 155*

Colourful ponchos for all the family —mother, daughter and toddler. Instructions on page 126.

Above: green jacket worked in alternate rows of
double crochet and trebles (see page 144).

Opposite: sparkling beaded evening bag and
belt (see page 148).

Above: pink handbag (see page 146).

Above: blue and green handbag (see page 147).

Scarves to beat the winter winds—instructions for both are on page 166.

ABBREVIATIONS

See page 20.

N.B. Group (gr.), work into same st. (1 tr., y.o.h. insert hook into st., y.o.h. and draw through, y.o.h. insert hook into st., y.o.h. and draw through, y.o.h. and draw through 4 sts. on hook, y.o.h. and draw through last 2 sts., 1 tr.).

PANEL (make 6 alike, 2 in each colour)

1st row: 3 ch., 1 gr. into centre ch., 2 ch.; turn.

2nd row: omitting first tr. make 1 gr. into first st., 1 d.c. into next st., 1 gr. into last st., 2 ch.; turn.

3rd row: omitting first tr. make 1 gr. into first st., 1 d.c. into centre st. of gr. from previous row, 1 gr. into next d.c., 1 d.c. into next centre st. of gr., 1 gr. into last st., 2 ch.; turn.

4th row: omitting first tr. make 1 gr. into first st., 1 d.c. into centre st. of next gr., 1 gr. into next d.c., 1 d.c. into centre st. of next gr., 1 gr. into next d.c., 1 d.c. into centre st. of next gr., 1 gr. into last st., 2 ch.; turn.

5th row: 1 d.c. into centre st. of gr., (1 gr. into next d.c., 1 d.c. into centre st. of next gr.) twice, 1 gr. into next d.c., 1 d.c. into centre st. of last gr., 2 ch.; turn.

6th row: omitting first tr. make 1 gr. into first d.c., (1 d.c. into centre st. of next gr., 1 gr. into next d.c.) twice, 1 d.c. into centre st. of next gr., 1 gr. into last d.c., 2 ch.; turn.

Repeat 5th and 6th rows until 20 patt. rows from beg.

Shape Brim. Inc. as follows: omitting first tr. make 1 gr.

into first st., 1 d.c. into centre st. of gr., work across row as before and inc. in the same way at the beg. of the next row. You will now have 2 more grs.

Work next row without increasing then work as follows:

1st row: 1 tr. into every st., 1 ch.; turn.

2nd row: miss first tr., work 1 tr. into each st. until 2 sts. remain, miss next tr., 1 tr. in last st.

3rd row: 1 tr. into each of next 4 tr., * 1 tr. into each of next 4 tr., miss 1 tr., rep. from * to the end of the row. Fasten off.

TO COMPLETE

With a warm iron press all sections under a damp cloth. Join seams with colours alternating and the corresponding colours opposite one another. Fold brim to inside along last line of groups and slip-stitch in place. Press seams. With No. 6.00 hook work trimming for seams as follows: work along seam line starting at bottom edge. Make 1 d.c., * 3 ch., 1 d.c. into first ch. (picot), 1 d.c. into seam ½ in. from last d.c., 2 ch., 1 d.c. ½ in. from last d.c.

Repeat from * to crown then cont. down other side on corresponding section. Alternate trimming colours if wished or use only one colour. Now work one row of double crochet in the corresponding colour of each section along the lower edge, holding it in slightly while working. If wished, sew ribbon to inside of hat where the upturned brim ends.

Brimmed hat

(photographed in black and white on page 158)

MATERIALS

3 oz. Hayfield Courtier Bri-Nova Crêpe Double Knitting (see note on wools and yarns, page 21); one crochet hook International Standard Size 3.00 (see page 9); 2 yd. milliners' wire.

MEASUREMENTS

To fit an average-sized head.

TENSION

5 sts. and 5 rows to 1 in. over d.c. (see note on tension, page 14).

ABBREVIATIONS

See page 20.

TO MAKE

Commence with 6 ch. and join with s.s. to form a ring.

1st round: 12 d.c. into ring, s.s. into first d.c.

2nd round: 2 d.c. into each d.c., s.s. into first d.c.: 24 sts.

3rd round: * 1 d.c. into first d.c., 2 d.c. into next d.c.; rep. from * to end of round, s.s. into first d.c.: 36 sts.

4th round: as 3rd round.

5th round: 5 ch., leaving last loop of each on hook work 3 ch., tr. into same place as 5 ch., y.o.h. and pull through all loops on hook, 2 ch., miss 2 d.c., * leaving last loop of each on hook work 4 d.tr. into next d.c., y.o.h. and pull through all loops on hook: cl. made; 2 ch., miss 2 d.c.; rep. from * to end of round, s.s. into 5th of 5 ch.

6th round: 2 ch., 1 d.c. into top of cl., 3 d.c. into next sp., * 2 d.c. into top of cl., 3 d.c. into next sp., rep. from * to end of round, s.s. into 2nd of 2 ch.

7th round: 2 ch., 1 d.c. into each d.c. to end of round, s.s. into 2nd of 2 ch.

8th round: as 7th round.

9th round: 5 ch., 3 d.tr. cl., 2 ch., miss 2 d.c., * cl. into next d.c., 2 ch. miss 2 d.c.; rep. from * to end of round, s.s. into 5th of 5 ch.

10th round: 2 ch., 1 d.c. into top of cl., 2 d.c. into next sp., * 2 d.c. into top of cl., 2 d.c. into next sp., rep. from * to

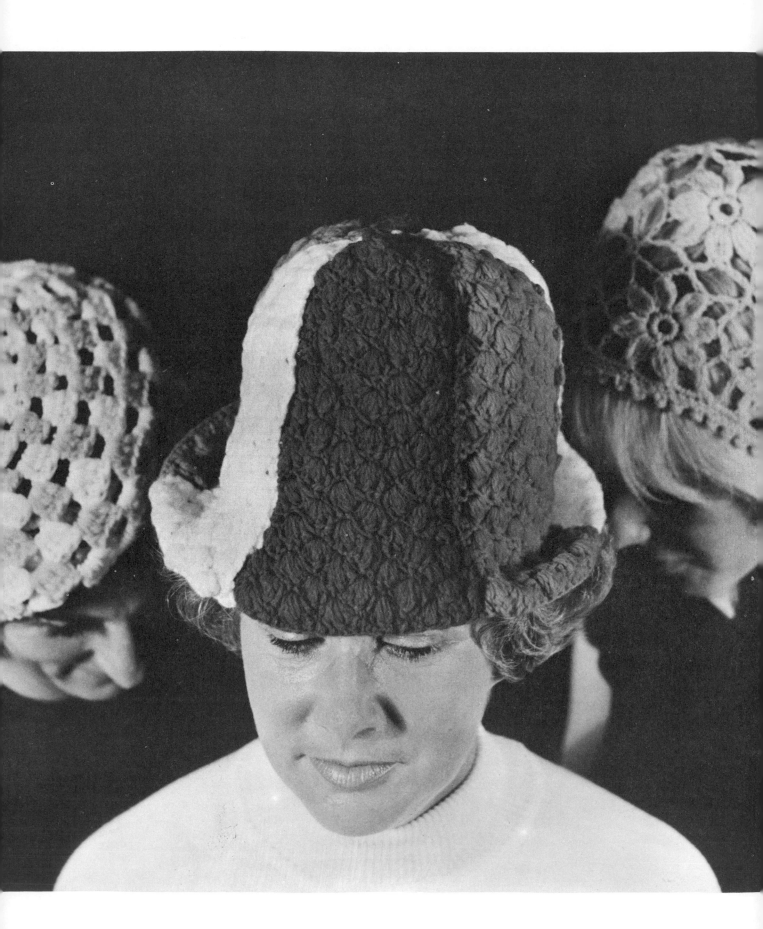

end of round, s.s. into 2nd of 2 ch.
11th round: as 7th round.
12th round: as 7th round.
13th round: as 9th round.
14th round: 2 ch., 2 d.c. into next sp.; * 1 d.c. into top of cl., 2 d.c. into next sp.; rep. from * to end of round, s.s. into 2nd of 2 ch.
15th round: 2 ch., 1 d.c. into each d.c. to end of round, s.s. into 2nd of 2 ch.
16th round: as 15th round.
17th round: as 9th round.
18th round: as 14th round.
19th round: as 15th round.
20th round: as 15th round.
21st round: as 15th round.
22nd round: 2 ch., 1 d.c. into next d.c., 2 d.c. into next

d.c., * 1 d.c. into each of next 2 d.c., 2 d.c. into next d.c., rep. from * ending round with 1 d.c. into last d.c., s.s. into 2nd of 2 ch. .
23rd round: 2 ch., 1 d.c. into each d.c. to end of round, s.s. into 2nd of 2 ch.
24th round: 2 ch., 1 d.c. into each of next 2 d.c., 2 d.c. into next d.c., * 1 d.c. into each of next 3 d.c., 2 d.c. into next d.c.; rep. from * ending round with 1 d.c. into next d.c., s.s. into 2nd of 2 ch.
25th round: as 9th round.
26th round: as 14th round.
27th round: place milliners' wire on top of sts., work as 23rd round, working d.c. round wire.
28th round: place milliners' wire on top of sts., work as 27th round.
Fasten off.

Buckled beret

(photographed in black and white on page 158)

MATERIALS
1 ball Sirdar Candytwist (see note on wools and yarns, page 22); one crochet hook International Standard Size 7.00 (see page 9); a small buckle.

MEASUREMENTS
To fit average-sized head.

TENSION
3 tr. to 1 in. (see note on tension, page 14).

ABBREVIATIONS
See page 20.

TO MAKE
Make 4 ch., and join with s.s. into a ring.
1st round: 2 ch., 7 d.c. into ring, s.s. to 2nd of 2 ch.; 8 sts.
2nd round: 3 ch., 1 tr. into first d.c., 2 tr. into every d.c., s.s. to 3rd of 3 ch.: 16 sts.
3rd round: 3 ch., 2 tr. between first and 2nd tr., 3 tr. between each pair of 2 tr., s.s. to 3rd of 3 ch.: 24 sts.
4th round: 3 ch., 4 tr. on next tr., 1 d.c. between grs. of tr., * 5 tr. on middle tr. of next gr. of 3, 1 d.c. between the grs. of 3 tr., rep. from * to end: 48 sts.

5th round: 3 ch., 2 tr. into same place, * 1 ch., 1 d.c. on 3rd of 5 tr., 1 ch., 3 tr. on d.c., rep. from * to end, finish with 1 ch., 1 d.c. on 3rd of 5 tr., 1 ch., s.s. to 3rd of 3 ch.: 48 sts.
6th round: s.s. along to first ch. sp., 3 ch., 2 tr. into this sp., 3 tr. into each ch. sp. to end, s.s. to 3rd of 3 ch.: 48 sts.
7th round: 3 ch., * 3 tr. on 2nd of 3 tr., 1 tr. between gr. of 3 tr.; rep. from * to last gr., 3 tr. on 2nd tr. of gr., s.s. to 3rd of 3 ch.: 64 sts.
8th round: 3 ch., * 2 tr. on 2nd of 3 tr., 1 tr. on single tr., rep. from * to last gr., 2 tr. on 2nd of 3 tr., s.s. to 3rd of 3 ch.: 48 sts.
9th round: 3 ch., * 2 tr. between 2 tr., 1 tr. on single tr., rep. from * to last gr., 2 tr. between 2 tr., s.s. to 3rd of 3 ch.
10th round: as 9th round.
11th round: 2 ch., 1 d.c. on each tr., s.s. to 2nd of 2 ch.
12th round: 3 ch., 1 tr. on each d.c., s.s. to 3rd of 3 ch.
13th round: 2 ch., * 1 d.c. on next 5 d.c., miss next d.c.; rep. from * to end, s.s. to 2nd of 2 ch.
Work 2 rows in d.c.
Fasten off.

TO COMPLETE
Sew buckle to band of cap. Make small tassel and sew under one side of buckle.

White cloche hat

(photographed in black and white on page 158)

MATERIALS
3 oz. Sirdar Double Crêpe (see note on wools and yarns, page 22); one crochet hook International Standard Size 3.00 (see page 9).
Left to right: chequered beret (page 150), panelled hat (page 150), floral bonnet (149).

MEASUREMENTS
To fit an average head; depth from centre of crown to lower edge 10 in.

TENSION
About 5 d.c. to 1 in. (see note on tension, page 14).

TO MAKE

Commence at centre of crown and work 2 ch., then 6 d.c. into 2nd ch. from hook.

The beg. of round should be marked with a coloured thread, and carried up after each round.

1st round: 2 d.c. into each d.c.: 12 d.c.

2nd round: * 2 d.c. into first d.c., 1 d.c. into next d.c., rep. from * to end of round: 18 d.c.

3rd round: * 2 d.c. into first d.c., 1 d.c. into each of next 2 d.c.; rep. from * to end of round: 24 d.c.

Cont. in this manner inc. 6 each round until there are 12 d.c. between inc.: 84 d.c.

Work 1 round in d.c.

Next round: * 2 d.c. into first d.c., 1 d.c. into each of next 13 d.c.; rep. from * to end of round: 90 d.c.

Work 2 rounds in d.c.

Next round: * 2 d.c. into first d.c., 14 d.c.; rep. from * to end of round: 96 d.c.

Work 5 rounds in d.c.

1st patt. round: * miss 2 d.c., (2 tr., 2 ch., 1 d.tr., 2 ch., 2 tr.) into next d.c., miss 2 d.c., 1 d.c. into next d.c.; rep. from * to end of round.

2nd patt. round: 6 ch., * 1 d.c. into d.tr., 2 ch., 1 d.tr. into next d.c., 2 ch.; rep. from * to end of round, s.s. into 4th of 6 ch. at beginning of round.

3rd patt. round: * 2 d.c. into 2-ch. sp., 1 d.c. into d.c., 2 d.c. into 2-ch. sp., 1 d.c. into d.tr.; rep. from * to end of round: 96 d.c.

Work 3 rounds in d.c.

Rep. last 6 rounds twice, but omit last round on second rep. Fasten off.

Cotton socks

(photographed in black and white on page 160)

MATERIALS

4 oz. of Twilley's Lyscordet (see note on wools and yarns, page 22); crochet hooks International Standard Sizes 2.50 and 3.00 (see page 9).

MEASUREMENTS

To fit stocking size 8½ (9, 9½) in. (Continental 36, 37, 38); length from lower edge of heel to top 14 in.

TENSION

1 patt. to 1 in. with No. 2.50 hook (see note on tension, page 14).

ABBREVIATIONS

See page 20.

N.B. When working into trebles pick up 3 loops.

MAIN SECTION

Working from the top down and with No. 2.50 hook make 60 ch. to measure 10 in., s.s. into first ch.

Foundation round: 3 ch., 1 tr. into next ch., * 2 ch., miss next ch., 1 d.c. into next ch., 2 ch., miss next ch., 1 tr. into each of next 3 tr.; rep. from * omitting last 2 tr. at end of last rep., s.s. into 3rd of 3 ch.: 10 patt.

1st patt. round: 3 ch., 1 tr. into next tr., * 1 ch., 1 d.c. into next 2-ch. sp., 3 ch., 1 d.c. into next 2-ch. sp., 1 ch., 1 tr. into each of next 3 tr.; rep. from * omitting last 2 tr. at end of last rep., s.s. into 3rd of 3 ch.

Left to right: buckled beret (page 157), brimmed hat (page 155), white cloche hat (157).

2nd patt. round: 3 ch., 1 tr. into next tr., * 2 ch., 1 d.c. into next 3-ch. loop, 2 ch., 1 tr. into each of next 3 tr.; rep. from * omitting last 2 tr. at end of last rep., s.s. into 3rd of 3 ch. Rep. last 2 rounds until work measures 7 in. from beg. ending with a 2nd round.

Next round: 3 ch., * 1 ch., 1 d.c. into next 2-ch. loop, 3 ch., 1 d.c. into next 2-ch. loop, 1 ch., 1 tr. into next tr., leaving last loop of each tr. on hook make 1 tr. into each of next 2 tr., yarn over hook and draw through all loops on hook; rep. from * ending last rep. with 1 tr. into next tr., s.s. into 3rd of 3 ch.

3rd patt. round: 3 ch., * 2 ch., 1 d.c. into next 3-ch. loop, 2 ch., 1 tr. into each of next 2 tr., rep. from * omitting last tr. at end of last rep., s.s. into 3rd of 3 ch.

4th patt. round: 3 ch., * 1 ch., 1 d.c. into next 2-ch. loop, 3 ch., 1 d.c. into next 2-ch. loop, 1 ch., 1 tr. into each of next 2 tr., rep. from * omitting last tr. at end of last rep., s.s. into 3rd of 3 ch.

Rep. last 2 rounds until work measures 11½ in. from beg.

Shape foot. Change to No. 3.00 hook and make 24 ch., miss next five 3-ch. loops, miss next tr., 1 s.s. into next tr.

Next round: work as for 3rd patt. round across first 5 patts., then work as rep. of foundation round across chain length (working only 2 tr. instead of 3 tr.), s.s. into 3rd of 3 ch.; 10 patts.

Work 4th and 3rd patt. rounds twice more, then change to No. 2.50 hook and cont. to rep. same rounds until work measures 4 (4½, 5) in. from beg. of foot shaping.

Shape Toe. 1st row: work d.c. evenly across first 5 patts.; turn.

2nd row: miss first d.c., 1 d.c. into each d.c. to within last d.c.; turn.

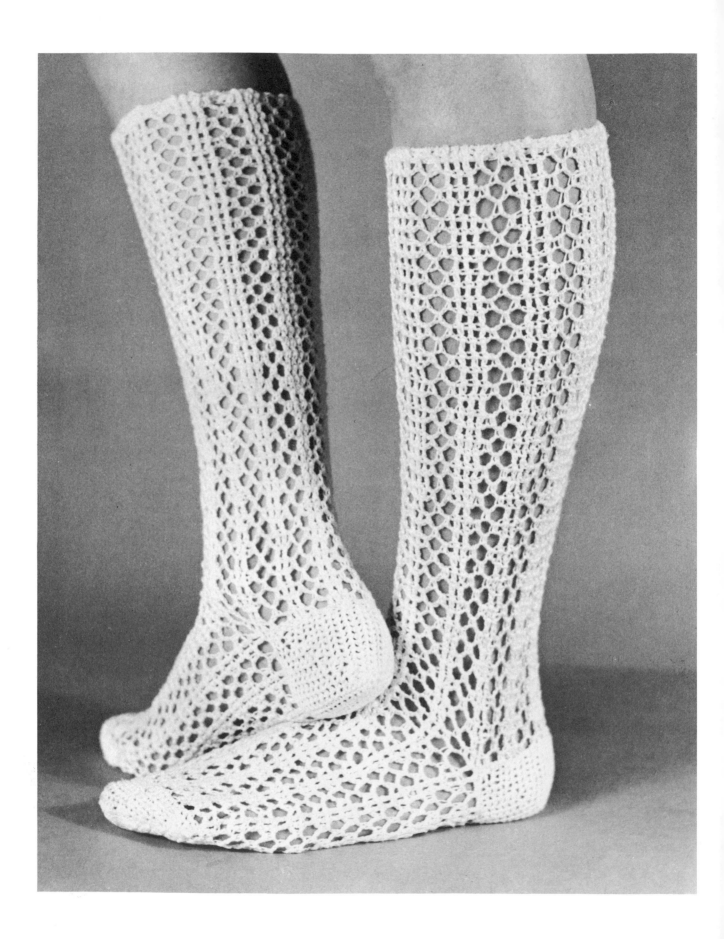

Rep. last row until toe shaping measures 1 in. Fasten off.
Bottom of Toe Shaping. 1st row: attach yarn to first free tr. and work to correspond with top of Toe Shaping. Fasten off.

HEEL

With No. 3.00 hook make 2 ch.
Foundation row: 1 d.c. into 2nd ch. from hook; turn.
1st row: 3 d.c. into d.c.; turn.
2nd row: 1 d.c. into first d.c., 3 d.c. into next d.c., 1 d.c. into next d.c.; turn.
3rd row: 1 d.c. into first d.c., 1 d.c. into each d.c. until 2nd of 3 d.c. group is reached, 3 d.c. into next d.c., 1 d.c. into each d.c. to end; turn.
Rep. last row until work measures $1\frac{3}{4}$ in. from beg.
Next row: 1 d.c. into first d.c., 1 d.c. into each d.c. to end; turn.
Rep. last row until work measures $2\frac{1}{4}$ in. measuring along

edge then cont. as follows:
Next row: 1 d.c. into first d.c., 1 d.c. into each d.c. to within 1 st. before centre st., (insert hook into next st. and draw a loop through) 3 times, y.o.h. and draw through all loops on hook (a dec. formed), 1 d.c. into each d.c. to end; turn.
Next row: 1 d.c. into first d.c., 1 d.c. into each d.c. to within 3 centre sts., 1 dec., 1 d.c. into each d.c. to end; turn.
Rep. last row until only 1 st. remains. Fasten off.

TO COMPLETE

Sew in heel and sew up toe.
Top Edging. 1st round: with No. 2.50 hook and right side facing attach yarn to a ch., then work 1 d.c. into each ch., 1 d.c. into first d.c.
2nd and 3rd rounds: working in continuous rounds make 1 d.c. into each d.c., s.s. into first d.c. Fasten off.
Make another sock the same.

Lacy-look tights

(photographed in black and white on page 163)

MATERIALS

7 balls Coats Mercer-Crochet No. 40 (20 grm.) (see note on wools and yarns, page 20); steel crochet hooks International Standard Sizes 1.00 and 1.25 (see page 9); length of $\frac{1}{4}$-in. elastic to fit waist.

MEASUREMENTS

To fit stocking size 9–10 in. (Continental 37–39); hip size 36–38 in.

TENSION

12 tr. and 6 rows to 1 in., 8 rows of 4 ch. loops to 1 in. with 1.00 hook (see note on tension, page 14).

ABBREVIATIONS

See page 20; pc.st., popcorn stitch.
N.B. If extra width is required, more ch. may be added to ch. loops.

TO MAKE

Heel. With No. 1.00 hook make 25 ch.
1st row: 1 tr. into 7th ch. from hook, 1 tr. into each of next 18 ch., 3 ch., working along opposite side of foundation ch., 1 tr. into each of next 18 ch., 1 s.s. into 3rd of turning ch.
2nd row: 3 ch., into next sp. work 2 tr., 3 ch. and 2 tr. (side of heel), 1 tr. into each of next 23 tr., into next sp. work 2

Lacy patterned cotton socks—instructions start on the previous page

tr., 3 ch. and 2 tr., 1 tr. into each of next 20 tr., 1 s.s. into 3rd of 3 ch.
Cont. in this manner working 2 tr., 3 ch. and 2 tr. into each side of heel, 1 tr. into each tr. and having 4 tr. more between sides of heel on each row until 11 rows have been worked. Fasten off.
Toe. Work as heel until 9 rows have been completed. Fasten off.
Foot. 1st row: attach yarn to any corner loop on toe, 1 d.c. into same place as join, * (4 ch., miss 3 tr., 1 d.c. into next tr.) 12 times, 4 ch., 1 d.c. into next loop; rep. from * once more omitting 4 ch. and 1 d.c. at end of repeat, 1 ch., 1 tr. into first d.c.
2nd row: 1 d.c. into loop just formed, * 4 ch., 1 d.c. into next loop, rep. from * ending with 1 ch., 1 tr. into first d.c.
3rd row: 1 d.c. into loop just formed, 4 ch., into next loop work 1 d.c., 4 ch. and 1 d.c., (4 ch., 1 d.c. into next loop) 12 times, 4 ch., into next loop work 1 d.c., 4 ch. and 1 d.c., (4 ch., 1 d.c. into next loop) 11 times, 1 ch., 1 tr. into first d.c.
4th row: 1 d.c. into loop just formed, 4 ch., 1 d.c. into next loop, 4 ch., into next loop work 1 d.c., 4 ch. and 1 d.c., (4 ch., 1 d.c. into next loop) 13 times, 4 ch., into next loop work 1 d.c., 4 ch. and 1 d.c., (4 ch., 1 d.c. into next loop) 11 times, 1 ch., 1 tr. into first d.c.
5th row: 1 d.c. into loop just formed, (4 ch., 1 d.c. into next loop) twice, * 4 ch., into next loop work 6 tr., remove loop from hook, insert hook into first tr. of treble group then into dropped loop and draw it through (a pc.st. made), (4 ch., 1 d.c. into next loop) 4 times, rep. from * twice more,

4 ch., 1 pc.st. into next loop, (4 ch., 1 d.c. into next loop) 11 times, 1 ch., 1 tr. into first d.c.

6th to 9th rows: 1 d.c. into loop just formed, * 4 ch., 1 d.c. into next loop, rep. from * ending with 1 ch., 1 tr. into first d.c.

10th row: 1 d.c. into loop just formed, (4 ch., 1 d.c. into next loop) 7 times, * 4 ch., a pc.st. into next loop (4 ch., 1 d.c. into next loop) 4 times, rep. from * once more, 4 ch., a pc.st. into next loop, (4 ch., 1 d.c. into next loop) 11 times, 1 ch., 1 tr. into first d.c.

11th to 14th rows: as 6th to 9th rows.

15th row: 1 d.c. into loop just formed, (4 ch., 1 d.c. into next loop) 7 times, * 4 ch., a pc.st. into next loop, (4 ch., 1 d.c. into next loop) 4 times, rep. from * twice more, 4 ch., a pc.st. into next loop, (4 ch., 1 d.c. into next loop) 6 times, 1 ch., 1 tr. into first d.c.

16th to 19th rows: as 6th to 9th rows.

20th row: 1 d.c. into loop just formed, (4 ch., 1 d.c. into next loop) 12 times, * 4 ch., a pc.st. into next loop, (4 ch., 1 d.c. into next loop) 4 times, rep. from * once more, 4 ch., a pc.st. into next loop, (4 ch., 1 d.c. into next loop) 6 times, 1 ch., 1 tr. into first d.c.

21st to 24th rows: as 6th to 9th rows.

25th row: 1 d.c. into loop just formed, (4 ch., 1 d.c. into next loop) 12 times, * 4 ch., 1 pc.st. into next loop, (4 ch., 1 d.c. into next loop) 4 times, rep. from * twice more, 4 ch., a pc.st. into next loop, 4 ch., 1 d.c. into next loop, 1 ch., 1 tr. into first d.c.

26th to 29th rows: as 6th to 9th rows.

30th row: 1 d.c. into loop just formed, (4 ch., 1 d.c. into next loop) 17 times, * 4 ch., a pc.st. into next loop, (4 ch., 1 d.c. into next loop) 4 times; rep. from * once more, 4 ch., a pc.st. into next loop, 4 ch., 1 d.c. into next loop, 1 ch., 1 tr. into first d.c.

Close-up of tights stitch pattern.

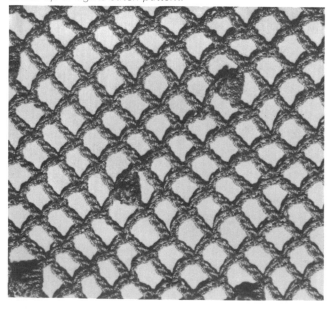

31st to 34th rows: as 6th to 9th rows.

35th row: 1 d.c. into loop just formed, (4 ch., 1 d.c. into next loop) twice, 4 ch., a pc.st. into next loop, (4 ch., 1 d.c. into next loop) 14 times, * 4 ch., a pc.st. into next loop, (4 ch., 1 d.c. into next loop) 4 times; rep. from * once more, 4 ch., a pc.st. into next loop, 4 ch., 1 d.c. into next loop, 1 ch., 1 tr. into first d.c.

36th to 39th rows: as 6th to 9th rows.

40th row: 1 d.c. into loop just formed, (4 ch., 1 d.c. into next loop) twice, 4 ch., a pc.st. into next loop, (4 ch., 1 d.c. into next loop) 19 times, 4 ch., a pc.st. into next loop, (4 ch., 1 d.c. into next loop) 4 times, 4 ch., a pc.st. into next loop, 4 ch., 1 d.c. into next loop, 1 ch., 1 tr. into first d.c.

41st to 44th rows: as 6th to 9th rows.

45th row: 1 d.c. into loop just formed, (4 ch., 1 d.c. into next loop) twice, 4 ch., a pc.st. into next loop, (4 ch., 1 d.c. into next loop) 4 times, 4 ch., a pc.st. into next loop, (4 ch., 1 d.c. into next loop) 14 times, 4 ch., a pc.st. into next loop 4 times, 4 ch., a pc.st. into next loop, 4 ch., 1 d.c. into next loop, 1 ch., 1 tr. into first d.c.

46th to 49th rows: as 6th to 9th rows.

50th row: 1 d.c. into loop just formed, (4 ch., 1 d.c. into next loop) twice, 4 ch., a pc.st. into next loop, (4 ch., 1 d.c. into next loop) 4 times, 4 ch., a pc.st. into next loop, (4 ch., 1 d.c. into next loop) 19 times, 4 ch., a pc.st. into next loop, 4 ch., 1 d.c. into next loop, 1 ch., 1 tr. into first d.c.

51st row: as 6th row.

Heel Joining. 1st row: 1 d.c. into loop just formed, (5 ch., 1 d.c. into next loop) 11 times, 2 ch., 1 d.c. into any corner loop on heel, (2 ch., 1 d.c. into next loop on foot, 2 ch., miss 3 tr. on heel, 1 s.s. into next tr.) 14 times, 2 ch., 1 d.c. into next loop on foot, 2 ch., 1 d.c. into next corner loop on heel, 2 ch., 1 d.c. into next loop on foot, (5 ch., 1 d.c. into next loop) twice, 2 ch., 1 tr. into first d.c.

2nd row: 1 d.c. into loop just formed, (5 ch., 1 d.c. into next loop) 11 times, 5 ch., 1 d.c. into d.c. at join of heel, (5 ch., miss 3 tr., 1 d.c. into next tr.) 14 times, 5 ch., 1 d.c. into d.c. at join of heel, (5 ch., 1 d.c. into next loop, twice, 2 ch., 1 tr. into first d.c.

Leg. 1st row: 1 d.c. into loop just formed, * 5 ch., 1 d.c. into next loop, rep. from * ending with 2 ch., 1 tr. into first d.c.

2nd row: 1 d.c. into loop just formed, (5 ch., 1 d.c. into next loop) twice, * 5 ch., a pc.st. into next loop, (5 ch., 1 d.c. into next loop) 4 times, rep. from * 4 times more, 5 ch., a pc.st. into next loop, 5 ch., 1 d.c. into next loop, 2 ch., 1 tr. into first d.c.

3rd to 6th rows: as 1st row of Leg.

7th row: 1 d.c. into loop just formed, (5 ch., 1 d.c. into next loop) twice, * 5 ch., a pc.st. into next loop, (5 ch., 1 d.c. into next loop) 4 times, rep. from * 4 times more, 5 ch., a pc.st. into next loop, 5 ch., 1 d.c. into next loop, 2 ch., 1 tr. into first d.c.

Rep. last 5 rows 11 times.

Change to No. 1.25 hook, rep. last 5 rows 11 times more.

Rep. last 5 rows having 6-ch. loops 7 times more.

Rep. last 5 rows having 7-ch. loops twice more.

Rep. last 5 rows having 8-ch. loops 5 times more.

Rep. last 5 rows having 9-ch. loops twice more or for length required to within approx. 1 in. of inside leg measurement.

Next row: 1 d.c. into loop just formed, (9 ch., 1 d.c. into next loop) twice, * 9 ch., into next loop work 1 d.c., 9 ch., and 1 d.c., (9 ch., 1 d.c. into next loop) 4 times, rep. from * 4 times more, 9 ch., into next loop work 1 d.c., 9 ch., 1 d.c. into next loop, 5 ch., 1 d.c. into first d.c.

Next row: 1 d.c. into loop just formed, * 9 ch., 1 d.c. into next loop, rep. from * all round ending with 5 ch., 1 d.tr. into first d.c.

Rep. last row 3 times more. Fasten off.

Work another section in same manner. Mark centre back of both legs with a coloured thread.

Leg Joining and Pants. 1st row: miss 4 loops to left of coloured thread on first leg, attach yarn to next loop, 1 d.c. into same loop, 9 ch., 1 d.c. into next loop, 26 ch., miss 5 loops to right of coloured thread on other leg, 1 d.c. into next loop, (9 ch., 1 d.c. into next loop) 29 times, 26 ch., 1 d.c. into corresponding loop on first leg, (9 ch., 1 d.c. into next loop) 27 times, 5 ch., 1 d.tr. into first d.c.

2nd row: 1 d.c. into loop just formed, 9 ch., 1 d.c. into next loop, * 9 ch., 1 d.c. into 4th of 26 ch., (9 ch., miss 8 ch., 1 d.c. into next ch.) twice, (9 ch., 1 d.c. into next loop) 29 times, rep. from * omitting (9 ch. and 1 d.c.) twice at end of repeat, 5 ch., 1 d.tr. into first d.c.

3rd row: 1 d.c. into loop just formed, * 9 ch., 1 d.c. into next loop, rep. from * all round ending with 5 ch., 1 d.tr. into first d.c.

Rep. last row 36 times more or for length required to waist omitting 5 ch. and 1 d.tr. at end of last row, 9 ch., 1 d.c. into first d.c.

Next row: 1 s.s. into first loop, 5 ch., * into same loop work (1 d.tr., 1 ch.) 4 times, into next loop work (1 d.tr., 1 ch.) 5 times, rep. from * all round, 1 s.s. into 4th of 5 ch. Fasten off.

Gusset. 1st row: attach yarn to corner d.c. on right of any long side, (9 ch., 1 d.c. into next loop) 6 times, 9 ch., 1 d.c. into next corner loop, 9 ch.; turn.

2nd row: 1 d.c. into first loop, (9 ch., 1 d.c. into next loop) 6 times, 5 ch., 1 d.tr. into same d.c. as join, 1 ch.; turn.

3rd row: 1 d.c. into loop just formed, (9 ch., 1 d.c. into next loop) 6 times, 9 ch., 1 d.c. into 5th of next loop, 9 ch.; turn.

4th row: 1 d.c. into first loop, (9 ch., 1 d.c. into next loop) 6 times, 5 ch., 1 d.tr. into first d.c. on previous row, 1 ch.; turn.

Rep. last 2 rows twice more then 3rd row again omitting 9 ch. at end of last row, 4 ch.; turn.

Next row: join to opposite leg as follows: 1 d.c. into corner d.c. on opposite leg, (4 ch., 1 d.c. into next loop on leg, 4 ch., 1 d.c. into next loop on gusset) 6 times, 4 ch., 1 d.c. into next corner d.c., 4 ch., 1 d.c. into next d.c. on gusset. Fasten off.

TO COMPLETE

Neatly sew row-ends of gusset to 26 ch. on leg joinings. Thread elastic between d.tr. sps. at waist, draw up to fit neatly and secure.

Slippers

(photographed in colour on back cover and page 171)

MATERIALS

2 balls Coats Mercer-Crochet No. 20 (20 grm.) in blue (508), 1 ball in red (469) and 1 ball in beige (625) (see note on wools and yarns, page 20); one crochet hook International Standard Size 1.25 (see page 9); ½ yd. tubular elastic; 1 pair soles size 4 (American 5½, Continental 36½) or required size; about 12 in. by 18 in. blue felt to line slippers (optional).

MEASUREMENTS

To fit shoe size 4 (American 5½, Continental 36½) approx.

TENSION

Front: 20 d.tr. to 2 in. and 6 rows to 1 in. *Side:* 10 ch. to 1 in. (see note on tension, page 14).

ABBREVIATIONS

See page 20; Bl., blue; R., red; B., beige.

SIDE (make 2)

With Bl. make 223 ch., or length required to fit round soles, having a multiple of 3 ch., plus 1, and 10 ch. to 1 in.; being careful not to twist, join with s.s. to form a ring.

1st row: 1 d.c. into each ch., 1 s.s. into first d.c., 1 ch.; turn.
2nd row: 1 d.c. into same place as s.s., * 3 ch., miss 2 d.c., 1 d.c. into next d.c.; rep. from * omitting 1 d.c. at end of last repeat, 1 s.s. into first d.c.; turn.
3rd row (right side): 1 s.s. into first loop, 4 ch., 4 d.tr. into same loop, * 1 ch., miss next loop, 5 d.tr. into next loop; rep. from * omitting 5 d.tr. at end of last repeat, 1 s.s. into 4th of 4 ch.; fasten off; turn.
4th row: with B. and working over previous row, attach yarn to first loop on 2nd row, 6 ch., 1 tr. into same loop, * 3 ch., miss 5 d.tr., into next free loop on 2nd row work 1 tr., 3 ch. and 1 tr.: a V st. made; rep. from * omitting a V st. at end of last repeat, 1 s.s. into 3rd of 6 ch.; fasten off; turn.
5th row: with R., attach yarn to first V st. on previous row, 4 ch., 4 d.tr. into same V st., * 1 ch., miss next loop, 5 d.tr. into next V st.; rep. from * omitting 5 d.tr. at end of last repeat, 1 s.s. into 4th of 4 ch.; fasten off; turn.
6th row: with B. attach yarn to first free loop on 4th row, 6 ch., 1 tr. into same loop, * 3 ch., miss 5 d.tr., a V st. into next free loop on 4th row; rep. from * omitting a V st. at end of last repeat, 1 s.s. into 3rd of 6 ch.; fasten off; turn.
7th row: using Bl., attach yarn to first V st. on previous row, 4 ch., 4 d.tr. into same V st., * 1 ch., miss next loop, 5 d.tr. into next V st.; rep. from * omitting 5 d.tr. at end of last repeat, 1 s.s. into 4th of 4 ch.; fasten off.

FRONT (make 2)

With Bl., commence with 17 ch.

1st row: 1 d.c. into 2nd ch. from hook, * 3 ch., miss 2 ch., 1 d.c. into next ch.; rep. from * to end; turn.
2nd row: 1 s.s. into first loop, 4 ch., 4 d.tr. into same loop, * 1 ch., miss next loop, 5 d.tr. into next loop; rep. from * to end; fasten off; turn.
3rd row: with B., attach yarn to first d.c. on second last row, 6 ch., 1 tr. into same d.c., 1 s.s. into next d.tr., * 3 ch., a V st. into next free loop on second last row; rep. from * ending with 3 ch., 1 s.s. into 4th of 4 ch. on last row, a V st. into next d.c. on previous row; fasten off; turn.
4th row: with R., attach yarn to first tr. on previous row, 1 d.c. into same place as join, 1 s.s. into next loop, 4 ch., 4 d.tr. into same loop, * 1 ch., 5 d.tr. into next V st.; rep. from * to within last V st., 4 d.tr. into next V st., 4 ch., 1 s.s. into same V st., 1 d.c. into 3rd of 6 ch.; fasten off; turn.
5th row: with B., attach yarn to first d.c. on last row, 6 ch., 1 tr. into same d.c. 1 s.s. into 4th of 4 ch., * 3 ch., a V st. into next free loop on second last row; rep. from * ending with 3 ch., 1 s.s. into 4th of 4 ch., a V st. into next d.c. on previous row; fasten off; turn.
6th row: with Bl., attach yarn to first tr. on previous row, 1 d.c. into same place as join and work as 4th row. Rep. 3rd to 6th rows twice, then 3rd and 4th rows again.
17th row: with B., attach yarn to 4th of 4 ch., 1 d.c. into same place as join, * 3 ch., a V st. into next free loop on second last row; rep. from * ending with 3 ch., miss 4 d.tr., 1 d.c. into 4th of 4 ch.; fasten off; turn.
18th row: with Bl., attach yarn to first V st. on previous row, 4 ch., 4 d.tr. into same loop, * 1 ch., 5 d.tr. into next V st.; rep. from * to end: fasten off; turn.
19th row: with B., attach yarn to first free loop on second last row, 6 ch., 1 tr. into same loop, 1 s.s. into next d.tr., * 3 ch., a V st. into next free loop on second last row; rep. from * to within last loop, 3 ch., 1 s.s. into 4th of 4 ch., a V st. into last loop on second last row; fasten off; turn.
20th row: with R., attach yarn to first V st. on previous row, 4 ch., 4 d.tr. into same loop, * 1 ch., 5 d.tr. into next V st.; rep. from * to end; fasten off; turn.
Repeat 17th to 20th rows once.
Damp and pin out to measurements.

Joining. Place Front centrally to side, wrong sides tog. With Bl., attach yarn to last d.tr. on last row of Front and work a row of d.c. round Front only. Fasten off.

EDGING

1st row: with Bl., and with right side facing, attach yarn to last d.c. of joining and work a row of d.c. round opening ending with 1 s.s. into first d.c.
2nd row: 3 ch., 1 tr. into each d.c., 1 s.s. into 3rd of 3 ch.
3rd row: 1 d.c. into same place as s.s., 1 d.c. into each tr., 1 s.s. into first d.c.
Rep. last 2 rows once.
6th row: 2 ch., 1 tr. into next d.c., leaving the last loop of each on hook work 1 tr. into each of next 2 d.c., y.o.h. and draw through all loops on hook; a joint tr. made, 1 tr. into each d.c. to within 4 d.c. at next corner; (a joint tr. over next 2 d.c.) twice, 1 tr. into each d.c., 1 s.s. into first tr.

165

7th row: insert hook into same place as s.s. and draw loop through, insert hook into next st. and draw loop through, y.o.h. and draw through all loops on hook (a joint d.c. made), (a joint d.c. over next 2 sts.) twice, 1 d.c. into each tr. to within 4 tr. before next dec., (a joint d.c. over next 2 sts.) 3 times, 1 d.c. into each tr., drop Bl., pick up R., 1 s.s. into first st.

8th row: 2 ch., 1 tr. into next st., a joint tr. over next 2 sts., 1 tr. into each d.c. to within 1 d.c. before next dec., (a joint tr. over next 2 sts.) 4 times, 1 tr. into each d.c. to within last 4 d.c., (a joint tr. over next 2 d.c.) twice, 1 s.s.

into first tr.

9th row: working over elastic, a joint d.c. over first 2 sts., a joint d.c. over next 2 sts., 1 d.c. into each tr. to within 2 tr. before next dec., (a joint d.c. over next 2 sts.) 4 times, 1 d.c. into each tr. to within last 4 sts., (a joint d.c. over next 2 sts.) twice, 1 s.s. into first st. Fasten off. Adjust elastic and secure.

Work other slipper to match.

TO COMPLETE

Stitch crocheted slippers to soles. Line with felt if wished.

Navy scarf

(photographed in colour on page 154)

MATERIALS

7 oz. Sirdar Double Knitting wool (see note on wools and yarns, page 22); one crochet hook International Standard Size 4.00 (see page 9).

MEASUREMENTS

Length 77 in. (adjustable); width 7½ in.

TENSION

One pattern to 1¼ in. (see note on page 14).

ABBREVIATIONS

See page 20.

TO MAKE

Using No. 4.00 hook make 40 ch.

Foundation row: 1 d.c. into 2nd ch. from hook, miss 2 ch., 3 tr. into next ch., * 3 ch., miss 3 ch., 1 d.c. into next ch., miss 2 ch., 3 tr. into next ch.; rep. from * 5 times; turn.

Pattern row: 1 ch., 1 d.c. into first tr., 3 tr. into next d.c., * 3 ch., 1 d.c. into 3-ch.sp., 3 tr. into next d.c.; rep. from * to end.

Rep. this row until scarf measures 70 in. (allow for 2-in. drop when complete) or length required. Fasten off.

TO COMPLETE

Work 1 row of d.c. up each long edge.

Fringe. Cut wool into 6-in. lengths, place two lengths tog. and fold in half, insert hook into first st. at the end of scarf and draw through the double loop, pass ends through this loop and pull knot tightly. Cont. along the edge. When complete trim evenly. Work the other end the same.

Red scarf

(photographed in colour on page 154)

MATERIALS

9 oz. Lister Lavenda Double Knitting (see note on wools and yarns, page 21); one crochet hook International Standard Size 4.00 (see page 9).

MEASUREMENTS

Width 12 in.; length 56 in. (including fringe).

TENSION

3 p. patts. to 2½ in., 4 patt. rows to 1¾ in. approx. (see note on tension, page 14).

ABBREVIATIONS

See page 20.

MAIN PIECE

Begin with 63 ch.

1st row: 1 tr. into 8th ch. from hook, 3 ch., 1 s.s. into 3rd ch. from hook (p. made), 1 tr. into same place as last tr., * 2 ch., miss 3 ch., into next ch. work 1 tr., 1 p., 1 tr.; rep. from * 12 times, 2 ch., miss 2 ch., 1 tr. into next ch., 6 ch.; turn.

2nd row: 1 s.s. into 3rd ch. from hook, 1 tr. into first 2 ch. sp., * 2 ch., into next 2 ch. sp. work 1 tr., 1 p., 1 tr.; rep. from * ending with 2 ch., 1 tr. into last sp., 1 p., 1 tr. into 3rd of turning ch., 5 ch.; turn.

3rd row: * into next 2 ch. sp., work 1 tr., 1 p., 1 tr., 2 ch.; rep. from * ending with 1 tr. into 3rd of turning ch., 6 ch.; turn.

The last 2 rows form patt.
Cont. in patt. until work measures 48 in. from beg. ending with a 2nd patt. row and omitting 6 turning ch. at end of last row.

EDGE
Next row: * 3 ch., s.s. to top of next p.; rep. from * to last

p. 3 ch., 1 tr. into 3rd of turning ch.; fasten off.

FRINGE
Wind wool round piece of cardboard $4\frac{1}{2}$ in. wide and length of short edge of scarf. Cut through wool at one edge. Using 3 strands tog. knot through short edges of scarf at intervals of $\frac{1}{2}$ in. Trim fringe.

Red, white and blue hairband and watchstrap
(photographed in colour on page 171)

MATERIALS
1 oz. of Sirdar 4-ply Fontein Crêpe in blue, 1 oz. in white and 1 oz. in red (see note on wools and yarns, page 22); one crochet hook International Standard Size 4.00 (see page 9); 4-in. length of elastic; 2 press studs.

MEASUREMENTS
Length 7 (16) in.

TENSION
5 sts. to 1 in. (see note on tension, page 14).

ABBREVIATIONS
See page 20; B., blue; W., white; R., red.
N.B. Figures in brackets refer to hairband. Where only one figure is given this refers to both hairband and watchstrap.

TO MAKE
With B., commence with 36 (81) ch. to measure 7 (16) in.
Foundation row: 1 d.c. into 2nd ch. from hook, 1 d.c. into each ch. to end; fasten off and turn.
1st row: attach W. to first d.c., 1 d.c. into same place as join, 1 d.c. into each d.c. to end; turn.
2nd row: 1 d.c. into first d.c., 1 d.c. into each d.c. to end; fasten off and turn.
3rd row: attach R. to first d.c., 1 d.c. into same place as join, 1 d.c. into each d.c. to end; fasten off.
4th row: attach B. to first d.c., 1 d.c. into same place as join, 1 d.c. into each d.c. to end; fasten off, and turn.
Rep. 3rd, first, 2nd and 4th rows once. Fasten off.
Sew elastic to each end of hairband.
Thread watchstrap on to watch. Fasten ends with press studs to fit wrist size.

Red and white hairband and watchstrap
(photographed in colour on page 171)

MATERIALS
1 oz. of Sirdar 4-ply Fontein Crêpe in red and 1 oz. of white (see note on wools and yarns, page 22); one crochet hook International Standard Size 4.00 (see page 9); 4-in. length of elastic; 2 press studs.

MEASUREMENTS
Length 7 (16) in.

TENSION
5 sts. to 1 in. (see note on tension, page 14).

ABBREVIATIONS
See page 20; R., red; W., white.

N.B. Figures in brackets refer to hairband. Where only one figure is given this refers to both hairband and watchstrap.

TO MAKE
With R., commence with 36 (81) ch. to measure 7 (16) in.
Foundation row: 1 d.c. into 2nd ch. from hook, * 1 tr. into next ch., 1 d.c. into next ch.; rep. from * ending with 1 tr. into last ch.; fasten off and turn.
1st row: attach W. to first tr., 1 d.c. into same place as join, * 1 tr. into next d.c., 1 d.c. into next tr.; rep. from * ending with 1 tr. into last d.c.; fasten off and turn.
Changing colour on every row, rep. first row 3 times. Fasten off. Sew elastic to each end of hairband. Thread watchstrap on to watch. Fasten ends with press studs.

White hairband and watchstrap

(photographed in colour on page 171)

MATERIALS

1 oz. of Sirdar 4-ply Fontein Crêpe (see note on wools and yarns, page 22); one crochet hook International Standard Size 4.00 (see page 9); 4-in. length of elastic; 2 press studs.

MEASUREMENTS

Length 6½ (17½) in.

TENSION

2 patt. to 3¼ in. (see note on tension, page 14).

ABBREVIATIONS

See page 20.

N.B. Figures in brackets refer to hairband.

TO MAKE

Commence with 35 (91) ch. to measure 7 (18) in.

Foundation row: into 7th ch. from hook work (y.o.h., insert hook into ch. and draw up a loop) 4 times, y.o.h. and draw through all loops on hook, secure with 1 ch.: a puff st. made; 3 puff sts. into same place, * miss 3 ch., 1 tr. into next ch., miss 3 ch., 4 puff sts. into next ch.; rep. from * ending with 3 ch., 1 s.s. into last ch.; working along other other side of commencing ch., 3 ch., * * miss 3 ch., 4 puff sts. into next ch., miss 3 ch., 1 tr. into next ch.; rep. from * * ending with miss 3 ch., 4 puff sts. into next ch., 3 ch.

2nd round: * 2 d.c. into end of commencing ch., 2 d.c. into each sp.; rep. from * once, s.s. into first d.c.; fasten off. Sew elastic to each end of hairband. Thread watchstrap on to watch. Fasten ends with press studs.

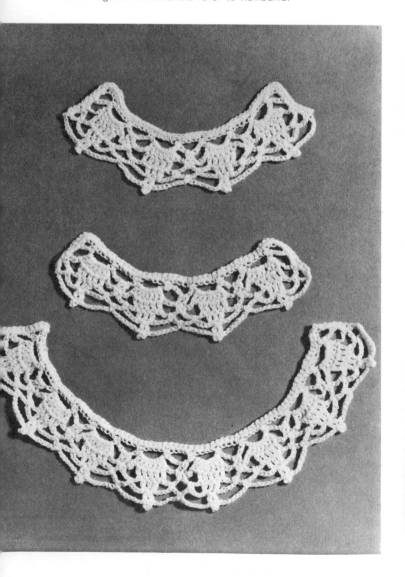

Scalloped collar and cuffs

MATERIALS
1 oz. Sirdar 4-ply Fontein Crêpe (see note on wools and yarns, page 22); one crochet hook International Standard Size 4.00 (see page 9).

MEASUREMENTS
Collar: length of neck edge 16 in.; depth 3 in.
Cuffs: length of wrist edge 8 in.; depth 3 in.

TENSION
1 patt. to 2 in. (see note on tension, page 14).

ABBREVIATIONS
See page 20.
N.B. Figures in brackets refer to collar. Where only one figure is given this refers to both collar and cuffs.

TO MAKE (make 2 cuffs, 1 collar)
Commence with 46 (86) ch. to measure 8½ (16½) in. For every additional 2 in. required add 10 extra ch.
Foundation row: 1 d.c. into 8th ch. from hook, * 6 ch., miss 4 ch., 1 d.c. into next ch.; rep. from * to within last 3 ch., end with 3 ch., 1 tr. into last ch.; turn 7 (15) 6-ch. loops.
2nd row: 1 d.c. into first tr., * 4 ch., miss next tr., 1 tr. into each of next 5 tr., 4 ch., miss next tr., 1 d.c. into each of next 2 tr.; rep. from * ending with 4 ch., miss next tr., 1 tr. into each of next 5 tr., miss next tr., 4 ch., 1 d.c. into 3rd of 6 ch.; turn.
3rd row: 6 ch., * 1 d.c. into next 4-ch. loop, 4 ch., miss next tr., 1 tr. into each of next 3 tr., 4 ch., 1 d.c. into next 4-ch. loop, 5 ch., miss next tr., 1 tr. into each of next 3 tr., 3 ch., 1 tr. into last d.c.; turn.
4th row: * 7 ch., (1 tr., 3 ch., 1 s.s. into last tr. made, 1 tr.) all into centre tr. of 3 tr., 7 ch., 1 d.c. into next 5-ch. loop; rep. from * to end working 1 d.c. at end of last rep. into 3rd of 6 ch.

TO COMPLETE
Edging. Make d.c. evenly down side edge, 3 d.c. into corner, make 1 d.c. into each ch. along lower edge, 3 d.c. into 2nd corner, complete to correspond with first side. Fasten off. Stitch cuffs and collar to dress, blouse or jumper, as required.

Motif collar and cuffs

MATERIALS
1 oz. of Sirdar 4-ply Fontein Crêpe (see note on wools and yarns, page 22); one crochet hook International Standard Size 4.00 (see page 9).

MEASUREMENTS
Collar: length of neck edge 16 in.; depth 2 in.
Cuffs: length of wrist edge 8 in.; depth 2 in.

TENSION
1 motif to 2 in. (see note on tension, page 14).

ABBREVIATIONS
See page 20.

FIRST MOTIF
Commence wirh 6 ch., s.s. into first ch. to form a ring.
1st round: 12 d.c. into ring, 1 d.c. into first d.c.
2nd round: * 6 ch., y.o.h., insert hook into next d.c. and draw up a loop, (y.o.h., insert hook into same place and *Far left: scalloped collar and cuffs. Left: motif collar and cuffs.* draw up a loop) 4 times, y.o.h. and draw through all loops on hook: puff st. made, 6 ch., 1 d.c. into next d.c.; rep. from * all round omitting 1 d.c. at end of last rep., s.s. into first d.c.; fasten off.
Mark 5th petal made.

SECOND MOTIF
Work as First Motif to 2nd round.
2nd round: 6 ch., a puff st. into next d.c., 6 ch., 1 d.c. into next d.c., 4 ch., 1 d.c. into appropriate loop on marked petal of First Motif, 1 ch., a puff st. into next d.c., 6 ch., 1 d.c. into next d.c., then work rep. and ending of 2nd round of First Motif.
Work and join 3 more motifs for each Cuff and 8 more motifs for Collar.

EDGING. 1st row:
with wrong side facing attach yarn to first loop of First Motif, 1 d.c. into same place as join, * 3 ch., 1 d.c. into last loop made on 6th petal, 5 ch., 1 d.c. into first loop made on next motif; rep. from * ending with 3 ch., 1 d.c. into last loop on 6th petal; turn.
2nd row: 1 d.c. into each st. to end; fasten off.

Long jabot and cuffs

MATERIALS
2 oz. of Sirdar 4-ply Fontein Crêpe (see note on wools and yarns, page 22); one crochet hook International Standard Size No. 4.00 (see page 9).

MEASUREMENTS
Jabot: width 5 in.; length 12 in.
Cuffs: length of wrist edge 8 in.; depth 3 in.

TENSION
1 patt. to 1½ in. (see note on tension, page 14).

ABBREVIATIONS
See page 20.

JABOT
TO MAKE
Commence with 50 ch. to measure 10 in.
Foundation row: 1 d.c. into 2nd ch. from hook, * miss 3 ch., 8 d.tr. into next ch., miss 3 ch., 1 d.c. into next ch.; rep. from * 5 times, then, working along other side of commencing ch., * * miss 3 ch., 8 d.tr. into next ch., miss 3 ch., 1 d.c. into next ch.; rep. from * * 5 times; turn: 6 sh. made on each side.
1st row: * 5 ch., miss next d.tr., 1 d.c. into next d.tr.; rep. from * over first 5 shs., * * 5 ch., 1 d.c. into next d.tr.; rep. from * * round both sides of last sh., * * * 5 ch., miss next

d.tr., 1 d.c. into next d.tr.; rep. from * * * over last 5 shs., ending with 3 ch., 1 tr. into last d.c.; turn.
2nd row: * 6 ch., 1 d.c. into next loop; rep. from * to within last loop, ending with 3 ch., 1 d.tr. into last loop; turn.
3rd row: * 7 ch., 1 d.c. into next loop; rep. from * to within last loop, ending with 4 ch., 1 d.tr. into last loop; turn.
4th row: * 7 ch., 1 s.s. into 3rd ch. from hook, 4 ch., 1 d.c. into next loop; rep. from * to end; fasten off.

CUFFS (make 2 alike)
TO MAKE
Commence with 42 ch. to measure 8½ in.
Foundation row: 1 d.c. into 2nd ch. from hook, * miss 3 ch., 8 d.tr. into next ch., miss 3 ch., 1 d.c. into next ch.; rep. from * 4 times; turn.
1st row: * 5 ch., miss first d.tr., 1 d.c. into next d.tr.; rep. from * to within last 2 d.tr., ending with 3 ch., 1 tr. into last d.tr.; turn.
Work 2nd and 3rd rows of Jabot once.
4th row: * 7 ch., 1 s.s. into 3rd ch. from hook, 4 ch., 1 d.c. into next loop; rep. from * ending with 7 ch., 1 s.s. into 3rd ch. from hook, 1 ch., 1 d.c. into last d.c.
Edging. Make d.c. evenly down side, 3 d.c. into corner, 1 d.c. into each ch., 3 d.c. into 2nd corner, complete to correspond with first side; fasten off.

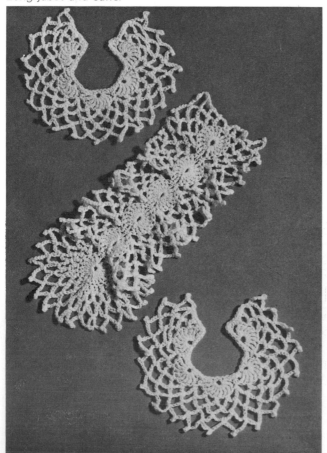

Long jabot and cuffs.

Short jabot and cuffs (see page 175).

Above: red, white and blue slippers (page 165).   *Below: hairbands and watchstraps (167–8).*

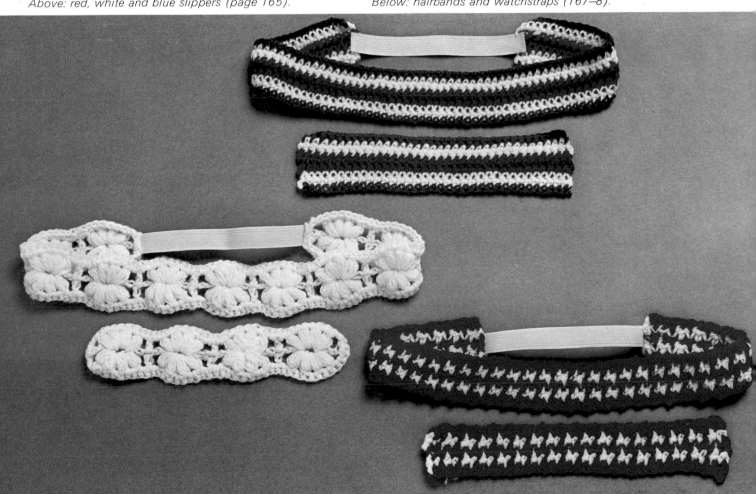

Above: crochet edging for bed linen (page 182).

Opposite: a pretty trimming for a circular tablecloth (see page 184).

So romantic —an unusual edging worked in crochet for a parasol (see page 184).

Short jabot and cuffs

(photographed in black and white on page 170)

MATERIALS
1 oz. of Sirdar 4-ply Fontein Crêpe (see note on wools and yarns, page 22); one crochet hook International Standard Size 4.00 (see page 9).

MEASUREMENTS
Jabot: width 7 in.; depth 5 in.
Cuffs: length of wrist edge 8 in.; depth 3 in.

TENSION
1 patt. to 1 in. (see note on tension, page 14).

ABBREVIATIONS
See page 20.

JABOT
MAIN PIECE
Commence with 9 ch.
Foundation row: 1 d.c. into 2nd ch. from hook, 1 d.c. into each ch. to end; turn.
1st row: working into back loops only make 1 d.c. into first d.c., 1 d.c. into each d.c. to end; turn.
2nd row: 1 d.c. into first d.c., * 5 ch., 1 d.c. into next d.c.; rep. from * to within last d.c., end with 2 ch., 1 d.tr. into last d.c.; turn.
3rd row: 3 ch., 4 tr. into first d.tr., 5 tr. into centre ch. of each 5-ch. loop to end; turn.
4th row: * 3 ch., 1 tr. into centre tr. of next gr., 3 ch., 1 d.c. into sp. before next gr.; rep. from * ending with 3 ch., 1 tr. into centre tr. of next gr., 1 d.tr. into 3rd of 3 ch.; turn.
5th row: 3 ch., 4 tr. into first d.tr., 5 tr. into each tr. to end; turn.

Rep. 4th and 5th rows twice, then 4th row once.
Last row: 3 ch., into first d.tr. work 2 tr., 3 ch., 1 s.s. into last tr. made and 3 tr., into each tr. to end work 3 tr., 3 ch., 1 s.s. into last tr. made and 3 tr.
Fasten off.

TOP FRILL
1st row: working into loops left free on first row attach yarn to first loop, 1 d.c. into same place as join, * 5 ch., 1 d.c. into next loop; rep. from * ending with 2 ch., 1 d.tr. into last d.tr.; turn: 7 loops. Work 2nd to 5th rows, then work 4th, 5th and 4th rows, then last row. Fasten off.
Gather up commencing ch. and secure.

CUFFS (make 2 alike)
TO MAKE
Commence with 38 ch. to measure 8½ in.
Foundation row: 1 d.c. into 2nd ch. from hook, * 3 ch., miss 1 ch., 1 tr. into next ch., 3 ch., miss 1 ch., 1 d.c. into next ch.; rep. from * to within last 4 ch., ending with 3 ch., miss 1 ch., 1 tr. into next ch., miss 1 ch., 1 d.tr. into last ch.; turn: 9 tr.
Work 5th and 4th rows of Jabot once.
3rd row: 3 ch., 4 tr. into first d.tr., 6 tr. into each loop to end; turn.
4th row: * 3 ch., 1 tr. into centre sp. of next gr., 3 ch., 1 d.c. into sp. before next gr.; rep. from * ending with 3 ch., 1 tr. into centre tr. of last gr., 1 d.tr. into 3rd of 3 ch.; turn.
Work last row of Jabot once. Fasten off.
Edging. With right side facing, attach yarn to first commencing ch., 1 d.c. into same place as join, * 1 d.c. into next sp., 1 d.c. into next ch.; rep. from * to end; fasten off.

Ear-rings

(photographed in black and white on page 176)

MATERIALS
1 ball Coats Mercer-Crochet No. 20 (20 grm.) (see note on wools and yarns, page 20); one steel crochet hook International Standard Size 1.25 (see page 9); 1 pair ear-ring clips; 36 beads or sequins.

MEASUREMENTS
Length excluding clips 3 in (at deepest point).

TENSION
Half moon motif ⅝ in. deep; small motif ¾ in. in diameter (see note on tension, page 14).

ABBREVIATIONS
See page 20.

RIGHT EAR-RING
Half Moon Motif Front. Make 14 ch.
1st row (right side): 2 d.c. into 2nd ch. from hook, * * 2 h.tr. into next ch., 2 tr. into each of next 2 ch., 2 d.tr. into each of next 2 ch., 3 t.tr. into next ch., 2 d.tr. into each of next 2 ch., 2 tr. into each of next 2 ch., 2 h.tr. into next ch., 2 d.c. into next ch., 1 ch.; turn.
2nd row: miss first d.c., 1 d.c. into each of next 10 sts., 2 d.c. into next st., 1 d.c. into each of next 3 sts., 2 d.c. into

next st., 1 d.c. into each of next 9 sts., miss next d.c., 1 d.c. into next d.c., 1 ch.; turn.

3rd row: miss first d.c., 1 d.c. into each of next 24 d.c., miss next d.c., 1 d.c. into next d.c. Fasten off. * *

Back. With right side facing attach yarn to first foundation ch., 2 d.c. into same place as join, rep. from * to * on Front. Join Front and Back tog. by working through both sections at the same time as follows: with Front facing attach yarn to first row-end, into next row-end work 1 d.c., 2 ch. and 1 d.c. (a p. made), * working into loops at centre only of each d.c. work a p. into next d.c., miss next d.c., rep. from * working 7th, 8th and 9th p. on Front only to leave opening for clip and ending with a p. into centre row-end, 1 s.s. into next row-end. Fasten off.

Motif may be slightly padded with cotton wool if desired. Insert clip and secure firmly.

Small Motif (make 9). Make 5 ch., join with a s.s. to form a ring.

1st row: * 1 d.c. into ring, 5 ch., 1 d.c. into 2nd ch. from hook, 1 d.c. into each ch.; rep. from * 4 times, 1 s.s. into first d.c. Fasten off. * * *

With Front of Half Moon Motif facing, miss first 6 ps., attach yarn to next p. and work 14 ch. Fasten off. Miss next 2 ps., attach yarn to next p. and work 25 ch. Fasten off. Miss next 2 ps., attach yarn to next p. and work 32 ch. Fasten off.

TO COMPLETE

Attach small motifs to lengths of ch. as shown in illustration opposite. Sew one bead or sequin to each side at centre of each small motif.

LEFT EAR-RING

Work as Right Ear-ring to * * *.

With Front of Half Moon Motif facing, miss first 2 ps., attach yarn to next p. and work 32 ch. Fasten off. Miss next 2 ps., attach yarn to next p. and work 25 ch. Fasten off. Miss next 2 ps., attach to next p. and work 14 ch. Fasten off. Complete as for Right Ear-ring.

Lacy stole

(photographed in black and white on page 178)

MATERIALS

23 balls Coats Mercer-Crochet No. 20 (20 grm.) (see note on wools and yarns, page 20); one crochet hook International Standard Size 1.25 (see page 9).

MEASUREMENTS

24½ in. by 73½ in.

TENSION

1 motif, 1¾ in. in diameter (see note on tension, page 14).

ABBREVIATIONS

See page 20.

FIRST MOTIF

Commence with 6 ch.

1st row: into 6th ch. from hook work (1 tr., 2 ch.) 7 times, 1 s.s. into 4th of 6 ch.

2nd row: 1 s.s. into first sp., 1 d.c. into same sp., * (5 ch., 1 s.s. into 4th ch. from hook: picot made) twice, 1 ch., 1 d.c. into next sp.; rep. from * omitting 1 d.c. at end of last rep., 1 s.s. into first d.c.

Jewellery, crochet style—sequin-studded ear-rings are easy to make.

3rd row: s.s. along to ch. between next 2 ps. on next loop, 1 d.c. into same loop, * 7 ch., 1 d.c. between ps. of next loop; rep. from * omitting 1 d.c. at end of last rep., 1 s.s. into first d.c.

4th row: into each loop work (1 d.c., 1 h.tr., 9 tr., 1 h.tr. and 1 d.c.), 1 s.s. into first d.c.: 8 scallops; fasten off.

SECOND MOTIF

Work as first motif for 3 rows.

4th row: into first loop work (1 d.c., 1 h.tr., 4 tr.), 1 s.s. into centre tr. of any scallop of first motif, (5 tr., 1 h.tr. and 1 d.c.) into same loop on second motif, into next loop work (1 d.c., 1 h.tr., 4 tr.), 1 s.s. into centre of tr. of next scallop on first motif, (5 tr., 1 h.tr. and 1 d.c.) into same loop on second motif; complete as for first motif.

Make 14 rows of 42 motifs, joining each as second motif was joined to first motif.

FILLING

Commence with 7 ch., join with a s.s. to form a ring.

1st row: 1 d.c. into ring, 4 ch., 1 s.s. into any join between motifs, 4 ch., (1 d.c. into ring, 4 ch., 1 s.s. into next joining between motifs, 4 ch.) 3 times, 1 s.s. into first d.c.; fasten off.

Fill in all spaces between motifs in same manner. Damp and pin out to measurements.

Dress trimming

(photographed in black and white on page 180)

MATERIALS

5 balls Coats Mercer-Crochet No. 20 (20 grm.) (see note on wools and yarns, page 20); one crochet hook International Standard Size 1.25 (see page 9); a caftan-style dress, with a plain front and long bell sleeves, or similar suitable style.

MEASUREMENTS

Depth of edging 2½ in. approx. The above quantities are enough to make 2 sleeve trimmings, each 17 in. long approx.; centre trimming 31 in. long approx.; lower trimming, 50 in. long approx.

TENSION

Depth of edging 2½ in. (see note on page 14).

ABBREVIATIONS

See page 20.

RINGS

First Strip. 1st row: beg. with 10 ch., join with a s.s. to form a ring, 3 ch., turn, 10 tr. into ring (righthand side), * 10 ch., turn, 1 s.s. into 10th ch. from hook, 3 ch., turn, remove loop from hook, insert hook into 3rd last tr. worked and draw dropped loop through, 10 tr. into new ring; rep. from * for length required having a multiple of 2 rings plus 1; fasten off.

2nd row: with wrong side facing, attach yarn to 3rd of 3 ch. in first ring, 11 tr. into same ring, * 1 s.s. into next ring, 3 ch., remove loop from hook, insert hook into 3rd last tr. worked and draw dropped loop through, 10 tr. into ring; rep. from * ending with 1 s.s. into last tr. of first row; fasten off.

Second Strip. 1st row: beg. with 10 ch., join with a s.s. to form a ring, 3 ch., turn, 5 tr. into ring, remove loop from hook, insert hook into centre st. of first ring of first strip and draw dropped loop through, 5 tr. into same ring, * 10 ch., turn, 1 s.s. into 10th ch. from hook, 3 ch., turn, remove loop from hook, insert hook into 3rd last tr. worked and draw dropped loop through, 5 tr. into ring, remove loop from hook, insert hook into centre st. of next ring of first strip and draw dropped loop through, 5 tr. into same ring; rep. from * to end; fasten off.

2nd row: as 2nd row of first strip.

EDGING

1st row: with right side facing, attach yarn to centre st. of first ring, 4 ch., leaving the last loop of each on hook work 2 d.tr. into same place as join, y.o.h. and draw through all loops on hook (a 2-d.tr.cl. made), (3 ch., a 3-d.tr.cl. into same place as join) 3 times, * 4 ch., 1 d.c. into centre st. of

Lacy stole is made up from two different motifs (instructions on page 177).

next ring, 4 ch., into centre st. of next ring work (a 3-d.tr.cl., 3 ch.) 3 times and a 3-d.tr.cl.; rep. from * to end; fasten off.
2nd row: with right side facing, attach yarn to first sp., into each sp. work 2 d.c., 3 ch. and 2 d.c.; fasten off. Work edging on other side to correspond.

TO COMPLETE

Make required number of trimming lengths. Damp and pin out to measurements. Stitch to dress, down centre front, round lower edge and round each sleeve edge, as in photograph below.

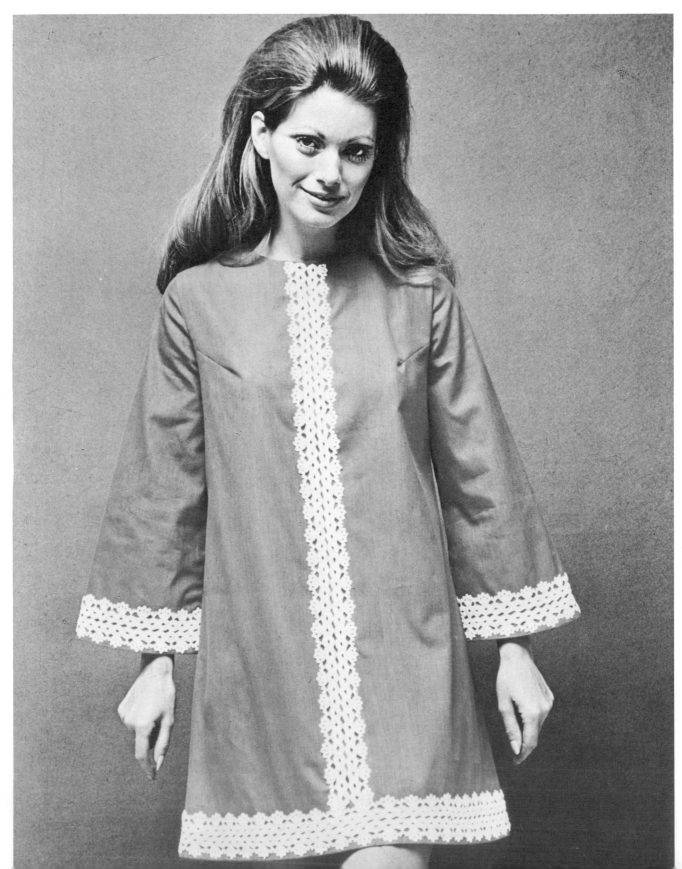

Chapter Eight

Gift ideas and novelties

Place mats and matching napkins

(photographed in colour on page 191)

MATERIALS
3 balls Coats Mercer-Crochet No. 20 (20 grm.) (see note on wools and yarns, page 20); one crochet hook International Standard Size 1.25 (see page 9); ½ yd. heavy linen 48 in. wide.

MEASUREMENTS
Place mat 12 in. by 16 in.; napkin 12 in. square; depth of edging 1¼ in. approx. The above quantities are sufficient to make and trim two place mats and two napkins.

TENSION
6 sps. to 1¾ in. approx. (see note on tension, page 14).

ABBREVIATIONS
See page 20.

PLACE MAT EDGING (make 2)
Beg. with 8 ch.
1st row: 1 tr. into 8th ch. from hook, * 5 ch., turn, miss 2 ch., then into the next ch. work 1 tr., and 5 ch. and 1 tr. (a corner has been turned), * * 5 ch., turn, miss 2 ch., 1 tr. into next ch.; rep. from * * 44 times, 5 ch., turn, miss 2 ch., into next ch. work 1 tr., 5 ch. and 1 tr. (another corner turned), * * * 5 ch., turn, miss 2 ch., 1 tr. into next ch.; rep. from * * * 62 times; rep. from * omitting 2 sps. at end of repeat, 3 ch., turn, 1 s.s. into first of foundation ch., 1 s.s. into each of next 3 ch., 3 ch., miss 2 ch. of previous sp., 1 s.s. into next ch.; fasten off

2nd row: attach yarn to any corner sp., 4 ch., leaving the last loop of each on hook work 4 d.tr. into same sp., y.o.h. and draw through all loops on hook (a 4-d.tr. cl. made), 5 ch., a 5-d.tr.cl. into same sp., * 5 ch., leaving the last loop of each on hook work 2 d.tr. into next sp., 1 d.tr. into same place as tr. of first row and 2 d.tr. into next sp. (a 5-d.tr.cl. made over 2 sps.); rep. from * along side, 5 ch., into next corner sp. work a 5-d.tr.cl., 5 ch. and a 5-d.tr.cl.; rep. from * omitting a corner at end of last repeat, 1 s.s. into first cl.

3rd row: 4 ch., into same place as s.s. work 1 d.tr., 5 ch. and 2 d.tr., * 1 d.c. into next loop, into next cl. work 2 d.tr., 5 ch. and 2 d.tr.; rep. from * ending with 1 d.c. into next loop, 1 s.s. into 4th of 4 ch.

4th row: 1 d.c. into same place as s.s., * into next loop work 2 d.c., 3 ch., 1 d.c., 5 ch., 1 d.c., 3 ch. and 2 d.c., miss next st., 1 d.c. into each of next 3 sts.; rep. from * omitting 1 d.c. at end of last repeat, 1 s.s. into first d.c.; fasten off.

NAPKIN EDGING (make 2)
Work as for Place Mat having 46 sps. along each side and 1 sp. at each corner.

TO COMPLETE
Damp crochet and pin out to measurements.
Cut 2 pieces of linen each 12 in. by 16 in. for place mats and 2 pieces each 12 in. square for napkins. Make ½-in. hems all round each piece, mitre corners and slip stitch in position.
Sew edgings in place to linen.

Bed linen trimming

(photographed in colour on page 172)

MATERIALS

4 balls Coats Mercer-Crochet No. 20 (20 grm.) (see note on wools and yarns, page 20); one crochet hook International Standard Size 1.25 (see page 9).

MEASUREMENTS

Width of trimming 2¾ in. The above quantity is sufficient to trim one single bed sheet and one pillowcase as shown in photograph on page 172.

TENSION

43 ch. to 3½ in.; 9 rows to 2¾ in. (see note on tension, page 14).

ABBREVIATIONS

See page 20.

TO MAKE

Commence with a length of foundation ch. (as long as length of trimming required) having a multiple of 14 ch. plus 9.

1st row: 1 t.tr. into 6th ch. from hook, * into next ch. work 1 t.tr., 4 ch. and 1 t.tr., 1 t.tr. into next ch., ** leaving the last loop of each on hook work 1 t.tr. into next ch., miss 4 ch. and 1 t.tr. into next ch., y.o.h. and draw through all loops on hook (a joint t.tr.), 4 ch., a joint t.tr. first into same place as last t.tr., missing 4 ch. and then into next ch., 1 t.tr. into next ch.; rep. from * ending last repeat at **, 1 t.tr. into next ch., 5 ch.; turn.

2nd row: miss first t.tr., * 1 t.tr. into each of next 2 t.tr., 4 ch., leaving the last loop of each on hook work 3 t.tr. into same place as last t.tr., and 3 t.tr. into next t.tr., y.o.h. and draw through all loops on hook (a joint cl. made), 4 ch., 1 t.tr. into same place as last cl., 1 t.tr. into next t.tr., a joint t.tr. over next 2 joint t.tr.; rep. from * omitting a joint t.tr. at end of last repeat, 1 t.tr. into next ch., 5 ch.; turn.

3rd row: miss first t.tr., * 1 t.tr. into next t.tr., leaving the last loop of each on hook work 1 t.tr. into next t.tr. and 3 t.tr. into next joint cl., y.o.h. and draw through all loops on hook, 4 ch., leaving the last loop of each on hook work 3 t.tr. into same place as last cl. and 1 t.tr. into next t.tr., y.o.h. and draw through all loops on hook, 1 t.tr. into each of next 2 sts., 4 ch., 1 t.tr. into same place as last t.tr.; rep. from * omitting 4 ch. and 1 t.tr. at end of last rep., 5 ch.; turn.

4th row: miss first t.tr., * 1 t.tr. into next t.tr., a joint t.tr. over next 2 cl., 1 t.tr. into each of next 2 t.tr., ** 4 ch., a joint t.tr. into same place as last t.tr. and into next t.tr., 4 ch., 1 t.tr. into same place as last t.tr.; rep. from * ending last rep. at ** and working last t.tr. into 5th of 5 ch.; turn.

5th row: 1 d.c. into each of first 5 sts., * 4 ch., into next joint t.tr. work 1 d.tr., 3 ch. and 1 d.tr., 4 ch., miss 4 ch., 1 d.c. into each of next 5 sts.; rep. from * ending with 6 ch.; turn.

6th row: miss first 4 d.c., * 1 tr. into next d.c., (2 ch., miss 1 ch., 1 tr. into next ch.) 5 times, 2 ch., 1 tr. into next d.c., 3 ch., miss 3 d.c.; rep. from * ending with 1 tr. into next d.c., 1 ch.; turn.

7th row: 1 d.c. into first tr., * 3 d.c. into next sp., 1 d.c. into next tr., (2 d.c. into next sp.) 6 times, 1 d.c. into next tr.; rep. from * ending with 3 d.c. into next sp., 1 d.c. into 3rd of 6 ch.; fasten off.

8th row: with right side facing attach thread to first of foundation ch., 1 d.c. into same place as join, 1 d.c. into each of next 4 ch., * 4 ch., miss 4 ch., into next ch. work 1 d.tr., 3 ch. and 1 d.tr., 4 ch., miss 4 ch., 1 d.c. into each of next 5 ch.; rep. from * ending with 6 ch.; turn.

9th and 10th rows: as 6th and 7th rows.

TO COMPLETE

Damp and pin out to measurements.

Make 1 length of trimming for sheet and 2 lengths for pillowcase and sew in position as shown in photograph on page 172.

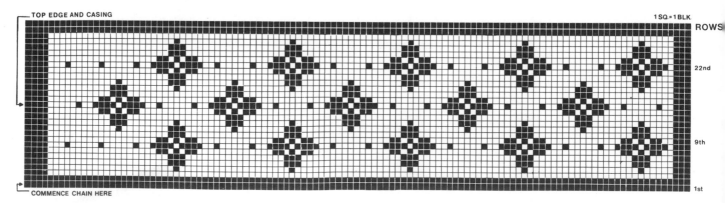

Pattern chart for curtain in filet crochet (see opposite).

Patterned curtain

MATERIALS
8 balls Coats Mercer-Crochet No. 40 (20 grm.) (see note on wools and yarns, page 20); one crochet hook International Standard Size 1.50 (see page 9); 1⅝ yd. seam binding ½ in. wide.

MEASUREMENTS
19 in. by 54 in. approx.

TENSION
6 sps. and 6 rows to 1 in. (see note on tension, page 14).

ABBREVIATIONS
See page 20.

MAIN CURTAIN
Commence with 348 ch.

1st row: 1 tr. into 4th ch. from hook, 1 tr. into each of next 344 ch.: 115 blks.; 3 ch.; turn.

2nd row: miss first tr., 1 tr. into each of next 344 tr., 1 tr. into top of turning ch.: 115 blks. made over 115 blks.; 3 ch.; turn.

3rd row: miss first tr., 1 tr. into each of next 9 trs.: 3 blks. made at beg. of row; * 2 ch., miss 2 tr., 1 tr. into next tr.; rep. from * 107 times: 108 sps. made over 108 blks.; 1 tr. into each of next 11 tr., 1 tr. into 3rd of 3 ch.: 4 blks. made at end of row, 3 ch.; turn.

4th row: 4 blks., * 2 ch., 1 tr. into next tr.; rep. from * 21 times: 22 sps. made over 22 sps.; 2 tr. into next sp., 1 tr. into next tr.: blk. made over sp., * * 19 sps., 1 blk.; rep. from * * 3 times; 5 sps., 3 blks., 3 ch.; turn.

Follow diagram opposite from 5th to 22nd rows, repeat 9th to 22nd row 20 times, then 9th row to end. Fasten off

TO COMPLETE
Damp and pin out to measurements.
Place seam binding to top of curtain (see diagram) and sew in position to form casing.

Parasol trimming

(photographed in colour on page 174)

MATERIALS
3 balls Coats Mercer-Crochet No. 40 (20 grm.) (see note on wools and yarns, page 20); one crochet hook International Standard Size 1.00 (see page 9); umbrella or parasol.

MEASUREMENTS
Depth of frill 1¼ in.

TENSION
5 sps. to 1 in. on backing (see note on tension, page 14).

ABBREVIATIONS
See page 20.

BACKING
Commence with 20 ch.
1st row: 1 tr. into 8th ch. from hook, * 2 ch., miss 2 ch., 1 tr. into next ch.; rep. from * to end, 5 ch.; turn.
2nd row: miss first tr., 1 tr. into next tr., * 2 ch., 1 tr. into next tr.; rep. from * to within last sp., 2 ch., miss 2 ch., 1 tr. into next ch., 5 ch.; turn. Rep. last row until work measures 100 in. or length required, having an even number of rows ending last row with 3 ch. Do not turn.

FRILL
1st row: 4 tr. over bar of last tr. worked, 5 tr. into next 2-ch. sp. on second last row, 5 tr. over bar of next tr. on second last row, 5 tr. into next 2-ch. sp. on third last row, 5 tr. over bar of next tr. on third last row, cont. to end of row working last 5 tr. over foundation ch.; fasten off.
2nd row: attach yarn to bar of second last tr. on last row of Backing, 3 ch., 4 tr. over bar of same tr., 5 tr. into next 2-ch. sp. on second last row and complete to correspond with first row.
Rep. last row 3 times.
Fasten off.

TO COMPLETE
Sew neatly to edge of umbrella or parasol.

Circular tablecloth

(photographed in colour on page 173)

MATERIALS
12 balls Coats Mercer-Crochet No. 20 (20 grm.) (see note on wools and yarns, page 20); steel crochet hooks International Standard Sizes 1.25 and 1.50 (see page 9); 2 yd. medium weight linen 72 in. wide; 6⅓ yd. bias binding to match linen.

MEASUREMENTS
Finished cloth 70 in. in diameter.

TENSION
Motif 2½ in. in diameter (see note on tension, page 14).

ABBREVIATIONS
See page 20.

TRIMMING
First Motif. 1st row: begin by winding yarn round a pencil 6 times, slip off pencil and with No. 1.25 hook work 24 d.c. into ring.
2nd row: working into back loop only work * 1 d.c. into each of next 4 d.c., 7 ch., 1 s.s. into last d.c., into ring just made work 1 d.c., 1 h.tr., 7 tr., 1 h.tr. and 1 d.c., 1 s.s. into same d.c. as last s.s.; rep. from * to end.
3rd row: 1 s.s. into each of next 2 d.c., 6 ch., * inserting hook from back of ring, 1 tr. into back loop of d.c. at base of ring, 3 ch., 1 tr. into 2nd of next 3 d.c., 3 ch.; rep. from * omitting 1 tr. and 3 ch. at end of last rep., 1 s.s. into 3rd of 6 ch.
4th row: 3 ch., * 5 tr. into next sp., 1 tr. into next tr.; rep. from * omitting 1 tr. at end of last rep., 1 s.s. into 3rd of 3 ch.
5th row: 1 d.c. into same place as s.s., working into back loop only, 1 d.c. into each tr.
6th row: * 1 d.c. into each of next 2 d.c., 6 ch., miss 4 d.c.; rep. from * ending with 1 s.s. into first d.c.
7th row: 1 s.s. into next d.c., 8 d.c. into each loop.
8th row: * (working into back loop only throughout, work 1 d.c. into each of next 2 d.c., 3 ch., 1 d.c. into same place as last d.c.) 3 times, 1 d.c. into each of next 2 d.c.; rep. from * ending with 1 s.s. into first d.c. Fasten off.
Second Motif. Work as first motif for 7 rows.
8th row: working into back loop only throughout, work 1 d.c. into each of next 2 d.c., 3 ch., 1 d.c. into same place as last d.c., 1 d.c. into each of next 2 d.c., 1 ch., 1 d.c. into corresponding 3 ch. loop on first motif, 1 ch., 1 d.c. into

same place as last d.c. on second motif, 1 d.c. into each of next 2 d.c. and complete as first motif.

Make 70 more motifs joining each as second motif was joined to first having 5 loops free on each side between joinings and joining last motif to first motif to form a circle.

SINGLE MOTIFS

First Motif. Work as first motif of trimming for 7 rows.

8th row: picking up back loop only throughout, work 1 d.c. into each of next 2 d.c., 3 ch., 1 d.c. into same place as last d.c., 1 d.c. into each of next 2 d.c., 1 ch., 1 s.s. into 6th free 3 ch. loop to right of any join on trimming, 1 ch., 1 d.c. into same place as last d.c., 1 d.c. into each of next 2 d.c., 3 ch., 1 d.c. into same place as last d.c., 1 d.c. into each of next 4 d.c., (3 ch., 1 d.c. into same place as last d.c., 1 d.c. into each of next 2 d.c.) three times, 1 d.c. into each of next 2 d.c., 3 ch., 1 d.c. into same place as last d.c., 1 d.c. into each of next 2 d.c., 1 ch., 1 s.s. into 6th free 3 ch. loop to left of same joining on trimming, 1 ch., 1 d.c. into same place as last d.c. and complete motif as before.

Miss next 2 motifs on trimming. Make 1 more motif

joining to next 2 motifs on trimming as before. Make 16 more motifs having 2 motifs free between joinings.

BRAID

With double yarn and No. 1.50 hook commence with 2 ch., holding this between finger and thumb of left hand, work 1 d.c. into 2nd ch. from hook; turn. Inserting hook into back of loop work 1 d.c. into foundation loop of 2nd ch. made, * turn, insert hook into 4 loops at side, yarn over and draw through 4 loops on hook, yarn over and draw through remaining 4 loops; rep. from * until work measures 6 yd. 6 in. approx. or length required. Fasten off.

TO COMPLETE

Cut a circle of linen 72 in. in diameter. Face edges with bias binding to form a circle 70 in. in diameter. Place motifs around edge of cloth as in illustration on page 173, and sew in position. Mark scalloped outline on cloth, having lower curve of scallop approx. 15½ in. from edge of cloth; upper curve approx. 28 in. from edge. Sew crochet braid in place following scallop outline.

Round cushion

(photographed in colour on the back cover and in black and white on page 186)

MATERIALS

4 balls Coats Mercer-Crochet No. 20 (20 grm.) (see note on wools and yarns, page 20); one steel crochet hook International Standard Size No. 1.25 (see page 9); 1 round cushion pad 13 in. in diameter.

MEASUREMENTS

Finished size approx. 14 in. in diameter.

TENSION

First 3 rows approx. 1½ in. (see note on tension, page 14).

ABBREVIATIONS

See page 20; pc.st., popcorn stitch.

BACK AND FRONT (both alike)

Commence with 8 ch., join with s.s. to form a ring.

1st row: 3 ch., 19 tr. into ring, 1 s.s. into 3rd of 3 ch.

2nd row: 4 ch., * 1 tr. into next tr., 1 ch.; rep. from * ending with 1 s.s. into 3rd of 4 ch.

3rd row: 6 ch., * 1 d.tr. into next tr., 2 ch., rep. from * ending with 1 s.s. into 4th of 6 ch.

4th row: 1 s.s. into first sp., 4 ch., 1 d.tr. into same sp., * 3 ch., 2 d.tr. into next sp., rep. from * ending with 3 ch., 1 s.s. into 4th of 4 ch.

5th row: 1 s.s. into first st., 1 s.s. into next sp., 4 ch., 2 d.tr. into same sp., * 4 ch., 3 d.tr. into next sp., rep. from * ending with 4 ch., 1 s.s. into 4th of 4 ch.

Close-up of stitch pattern.

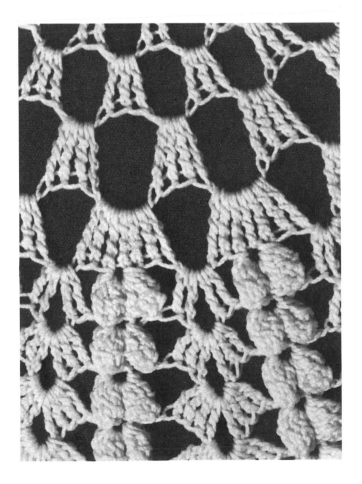

6th row: 1 s.s. into each of first 2 sts., 1 s.s. into next sp., 5 ch., 3 t.tr. into same sp., * 5 ch., 4 t.tr. into next sp., rep. from * ending with 5 ch., 1 s.s. into 5th of 5 ch.

7th row: 1 s.s. into each of first 3 sts., 1 s.s. into next sp., 5 ch., 6 t.tr. into same sp., * 2 ch., 7 t.tr. into next sp., rep. from * ending with 2 ch., 1 s.s. into 5th of 5 ch.

8th row: 1 s.s. into each of first 3 t.tr., 4 ch., 4 d.tr. into same place as last s.s., remove loop from hook, insert hook into 4th of 4 ch. and draw dropped loop thr. (a starting pc.st. made), 1 d.tr. into same place as last s.s., 5 d.tr. into same place as last s.s., remove loop from hook, insert hook into 5th last d.tr. and draw dropped loop thr. (another pc.st. made), * 1 ch., into next sp. work 2 d.tr., 3 ch. and 2 d.tr., 1 ch., miss next 3 t.tr. into next t.tr., work a pc.st., 1 d.tr. and a pc.st., rep. from * omitting a pc.st., 1 d.tr. and a pc.st. at end of last rep., work 1 s.s. into starting pc.st.

9th row: 1 s.s. into first d.tr., into same place work a starting pc.st., 1 d.tr. and a pc.st., * 2 ch., into next 3-ch. sp., work 3 d.tr., 3 ch. and 3 d.tr., 2 ch., miss next pc.st., into next d.tr. work a pc.st., 1 d.tr. and a pc.st., rep. from * omitting a pc.st., 1 d.tr. and a pc.st. at end of last rep., 1 s.s. into starting pc.st.

10th row: 1 s.s. into first d.tr., into same place work a starting pc.st., 1 d.tr. and a pc.st., * 2 ch., into next 3-ch. sp., work 4 d.tr. work a pc.st., 1 d.tr. and a pc.st., rep. from * omitting a pc.st., 1 d.tr. and a pc.st. at end of last rep., 1 s.s. into starting pc.st.

11th row: 1 s.s. into first d.tr., into same place work a starting pc.st., 1 d.tr. and a pc.st., * 2 ch., into next 3-ch. sp. work 5 d.tr., 3 ch. and 5 d.tr., 2 ch., miss next d.tr. work a pc.st., 1 d.tr. and a pc.st., rep. from * omitting a pc.st., 1 d.tr. and a pc.st. at end of last rep., 1 s.s. into starting pc.st.

12th row: 1 s.s. into first d.tr., into same place work a starting pc.st., 1 d.tr. and a pc.st., * 3 ch., into next 3-ch. sp. work 3 d.tr., 3 ch., 4 d.tr., 3 ch. and 3 d.tr., 3 ch., miss next pc.st., into next d.tr. work a pc.st., 1 d.tr. and a pc.st., rep. from * omitting a pc.st., 1 d.tr. and a pc.st. at end of last rep., 1 s.s. into starting pc.st.

13th row: 1 s.s. into first d.tr., into same place work a starting pc.st., 1 d.tr. and a pc.st., * 2 ch., miss next sp., into next sp. work 3 d.tr., 3 ch. and 2 d.tr., 4 ch., into next sp. work 2 d.tr., 3 ch. and 3 d.tr., 2 ch., miss next pc.st., into next d.tr. work a pc.st., 1 d.tr. and a pc.st., rep. from * omitting a pc.st., 1 d.tr. and a pc.st. at end of last rep., 1 s.s. into starting pc.st.

14th row: 1 s.s. into first d.tr., into same place work a starting pc.st., 1 d.tr. and a pc.st., * 1 ch., into next 3-ch. sp. work 2 d.tr., 2 ch. and 2 d.tr., 6 ch., into next 3-ch. sp. work 2 d.tr., 2 ch. and 2 d.tr., 1 ch., miss next pc.st., into next d.tr. work a pc.st., 1 d.tr. and a pc.st., rep. from * omitting a pc.st., 1 d.tr. and a pc.st. at end of last rep., 1 s.s. into starting pc.st.

15th row: 1 s.s. into first d.tr., a starting pc.st. into same place, * 2 ch., 3 d.tr. into next 2-ch. sp., 9 ch., 3 d.tr. into

Choose a cushion pad in a colour to contrast with crochet yarn.

next 2-ch. sp., 2 ch., miss next pc.st., a pc.st. into next d.tr., rep. from * omitting a pc.st. at end of last rep., 1 s.s. into starting pc.st.

16th row: into same place work a starting pc.st. having 3 d.tr. instead of 4, * 2 d.tr. into next d.tr., 17 ch., miss 4 d.tr., 2 d.tr. into next d.tr., into next pc.st. work a pc.st. having 4 d.tr. instead of 5, rep. from * omitting a pc.st. at end of last rep., 1 s.s. into starting pc.st.

17th row: into same place work a starting pc.st. having 2 d.tr. instead of 4, * 2 d.tr. into next d.tr., 9 ch., miss 8 ch., 1 tr. into next ch., 9 ch., miss next d.tr., 2 d.tr., 2 d.tr. into next d.tr., into next pc.st. work a pc.st. having 3 d.tr. instead of 5; rep. from * omitting a pc.st. at end of last rep., 1 s.s. into starting pc.st.

18th row: 3 ch., 1 d.tr. into same place as s.s., * 1 d.tr. into next d.tr., 9 ch., into next tr. work 1 tr., 3 ch. and 1 tr., 9 ch., miss next d.tr., 1 d.tr. into next d.tr., leaving the last loop of each on hook work 2 d.tr. into next pc.st., y.o.h. and draw through all loops on hook (a 2-d.tr. cl. made), rep. from * omitting a cl. at end of last rep., 1 s.s. into first d.tr.

19th row: 4 ch., * 1 d.tr. into next d.tr., 10 ch., 1 tr. into next tr., 3 ch., 1 tr. into next tr., 10 ch., 1 d.tr. into next d.tr., 1 d.tr. into next cl., rep. from * omitting 1 d.tr. at end of last rep., 1 s.s. into 4th of 4 ch.

20th row: 3 ch., 1 d.tr. into next d.tr., * 13 ch., leaving the last loop of each on hook work 1 d.tr. into each of next 2 tr., y.o.h. and draw through all loops on hook (a joint d.tr. made), 13 ch., a 3-d.tr. cl. over next 3 d.tr., rep. from * omitting a cl. at end of last rep., leaving the last loop on hook work 1 d.tr. into next d.tr., insert hook into first d.tr. and draw yarn through all loops on hook.

21st row: 18 ch., * 1 d.tr. into next joint d.tr., 14 ch., 1 d.tr. into next cl., 14 ch., rep. from * omitting 1 d.tr. and 14 ch. at end of last rep., 1 s.s. into 4th of 18 ch.

22nd row: 3 ch., 1 tr. into each st., 1 s.s. into 3rd of 3 ch. Fasten off.

When making the second piece, do not fasten off.

TO COMPLETE

Edging. Join Back and Front by placing wrong sides tog. and working thr. both sections at the same time as follows: into same place as s.s. work 1 d.c., 3 ch. and 1 d.c., * miss next tr., into next tr. work 1 d.c., 3 ch., and 1 d.c., rep. from * for approximately two-thirds of circumference, leave opening for pad by working over front section only and ending with 1 s.s. into first d.c. Fasten off.

Striped cushion is worked in rows of trebles (instructions on opposite page).

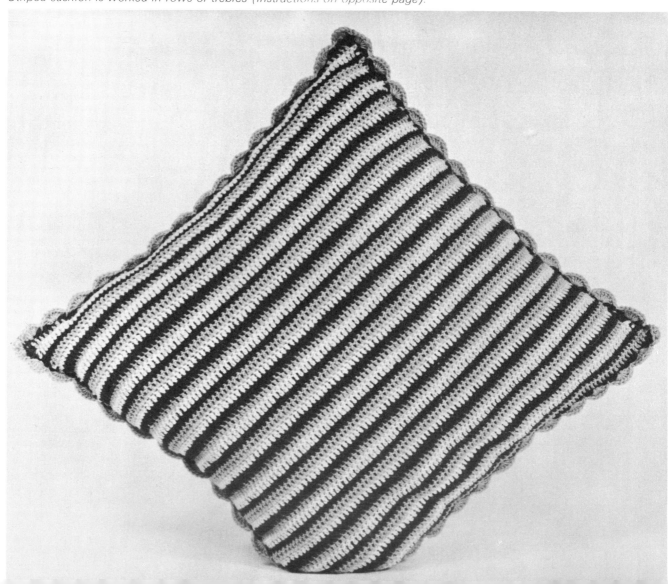

Striped cushion

(photographed in colour on the back cover and in black and white opposite)

MATERIALS

$1\frac{1}{2}$ oz. of Hayfield Beaulon 4-ply in 1st colour, 1 oz. in 2nd colour, 1 oz. in 3rd colour (see note on wools and yarns, page 21); one crochet hook International Standard Size 2.50 (see page 9); a 16-in. cushion pad with plain-coloured fabric cover to fit it (choose a fabric colour to match one of crochet yarns).
N.B. Our cushion is made up in royal blue, lime green and beige, with a royal blue covered cushion pad.

MEASUREMENTS

17 in. square (including edging).

TENSION

3 rows and 6 tr. to 1 in. (see note on tension, page 14).

ABBREVIATIONS

See page 20.

TO MAKE

With first shade make 85 ch.

1st row: 1 tr. in 3rd ch. from hook, 1 tr. in each ch. to end of row.
2nd row: join in 2nd shade, 3 ch., 1 tr. in 2nd tr. from hook, 1 tr. in each tr. to end of row.
3rd row: join in 3rd shade, 3 ch., 1 tr. in 2nd tr. from hook, 1 tr. in each tr. to end of row.
4th row: with first shade, 3 ch., 1 tr. in 2nd tr. from hook, 1 tr. to end of row.
Rep. 2nd, 3rd and 4th rows until work makes a square when folded corner-wise: 16 in. from beg.
With 3rd shade work 1 row d.c. round all 4 sides of square. Fasten off.

TO COMPLETE

Press lightly and stitch square to one side of cushion cover, then work shell pattern round all 4 sides thus: with first shade 3 ch., 6 tr. in same sp., * miss 1 d.c., 1 d.c. in next d.c., miss 1 d.c., 7 tr. in next d.c. Rep. from * to end. Finish with s.s.
Fasten off.
Place cover on cushion pad.

Long jacket

(photographed in black and white on page 8)

MATERIALS

23 (25, 27) oz. Sirdar Summer Breeze (see note on wools and yarns, page 22); crochet hooks International Standard Sizes 3.00 and 2.50 (3.00, 3.50 and 3.00) (see page 9).

MEASUREMENTS

To fit bust size 34 (36, 38) in.; length from shoulder 30 ($30\frac{1}{2}$, 31) in.; sleeve seam $18\frac{1}{2}$ in.

TENSION

1 patt. = $1\frac{3}{4}$ in. with No. 3.00 hook; 3 patts. = $5\frac{3}{4}$ in. with No. 3.50 hook (see note on tension, page 14).

ABBREVIATIONS

See page 20.

BACK

With No. 3.00 (3.00, 3.50) hook commence with 113 ch. to measure 20 (21, 22) in.

Foundation row: 4 tr. into 7th ch. from hook: a gr. formed; * 1 ch., 1 tr. into next ch., 1 ch., 4 tr. into next ch.: another gr. formed; miss 3 ch., 1 tr. into next ch., miss 3 ch., 4 tr. into next ch.: another gr. formed; rep. from *, 1 ch., 1 tr. into next ch., 1 ch., 4 tr. into next ch.: another gr. formed; 1 tr. into last ch.; turn: 11 patts. altogether.
Pattern row: 3 ch., * 1 gr. into next 1 ch.sp., 1 ch., 1 tr. into next tr., 1 ch., 1 gr. into next 1 ch.sp., 1 tr. into next tr.; rep. from * working last tr. of last rep. into 3rd of 3 ch.; turn.
Rep. last row until work measures 18 in. from beginning then change to No. 2.50 (3.00, 3.00) hook and continue to work patt. row until work measures $22\frac{1}{2}$ in. from beginning (adjust length here if required).
Shape Armholes. 1st row: 1 s.s. into each of first 12 sts., patt. to within last patt.; turn.
Work patt. row until armhole measures $7\frac{1}{2}$ (8, $8\frac{1}{2}$) in. from beginning ending with an even row.
Last row: 6 ch., * 1 d.c. into next 1 ch.sp., 1 d.c. into next tr., 1 d.c. into next tr., 1 d.c. into next 1 ch.sp., 3 ch., 1 tr.

into next tr., 3 ch.; rep. from *, 1 d.c. into next 1 ch.sp., 1 d.c. into next tr., 1 d.c. into next 1 ch.sp., 2 ch., 1 tr. into 3rd of 3 ch.
Fasten off.

RIGHT FRONT
With No. 3.00 (3.00, 3.50) hook, commence with 63 ch. to measure 11 (11½, 12) in.
Work as for Back until armhole shaping is reached.
Shape Armhole. 1st row: 1 s.s. into each of first 12 sts., patt. to end; turn.
Work patt. until 5 rows less than Back are completed.
Shape Neck. 1st row: 1 s.s. into each of first 12 sts., patt. to end; turn.
2nd row: patt. to within last patt.; turn.
3rd row: 1 s.s. into each of first 6 sts., patt. to end; turn.
Work 2 rows in patt.
Last row: 1 d.c. into first tr., 1 d.c. into next 1 ch.sp., 3 ch., miss 4 tr., 1 tr. into next tr., 3 ch., then work rep. and ending of last row of Back.
Fasten off.

LEFT FRONT
Work as for Right Front until armhole shaping is reached.
Shape Armhole. 1st row: patt. to within last patt.; turn.
Work in patt. until 5 rows less than Back are completed.
Shape Neck. 1st and 2nd rows: work as for 2nd and first Right Front neck shaping rows.
3rd row: patt. to within last 6 sts.; turn.
Work 2 rows in patt.
Last row: work as for last row of Back but ending with

1 d.c. into next 1 ch.sp., 1 d.c. into 3rd of 4 ch.
Fasten off.

SLEEVES (make 2 alike)
With No. 2.50 (3.00, 3.00) hook commence with 53 ch., to measure 10½ (11, 11½) in.
Work as for Back until work measures 8 in. Change to No. 3.00 (3.00, 3.50) hook and continue in patt. until work measures 10 in. from beginning.
1st increasing row: 4 ch., 5 tr. into first tr., then work rep. of patt. row to within last patt., 1 gr. into next ch.sp., 1 ch., 1 tr. into next tr., 1 ch., 1 gr. into next 1 ch.sp., into 3rd of 3 ch. work 4 tr., 1 ch., 1 tr.; turn.
Work in patt. until work measures 14 in. from beginning.
2nd increasing row: 3 ch., into first tr. work 4 tr., 1 ch., 1 tr., patt. to within turning ch., into 3rd of 4 ch. work 1 tr., 1 ch., 5 tr.; turn.
Work in patt. until sleeve measures 18½ in. from beginning (adjust length here if required).
Work last row of Back once.
Fasten off.

TO COMPLETE
Join side and shoulder seams, set in sleeves, join sleeve seams.
Edgings (all alike). With No. 2.50 (3.00, 3.00) hook and right side facing, attach yarn to edge, * 1 d.c. into edge, 3 ch., 1 s.s. into top of last d.c., 2 d.c. into edge; rep. from * all round edge of jacket, s.s. into first d.c.
Fasten off.
Lightly press.

Waste paper bin

(photographed in colour on the back cover)

MATERIALS
2 oz. of Twilley's Goldfingering or Lyscordet (see note on wools and yarns, page 22); one crochet hook International Standard Size 2.50 (see page 9); one waste paper bin 10 in. high with circumference at top 27½ in. and at bottom 21½ in.; 11 in. by 29 in. lining material if required.

MEASUREMENTS
Height 10 in.; diameter at top 8½ in. approx.; circumference at top 27½ in.; circumference at bottom 21½ in.

TENSION
6 sts. to 1 in. (see note on tension, page 14).

ABBREVIATIONS
See page 20.

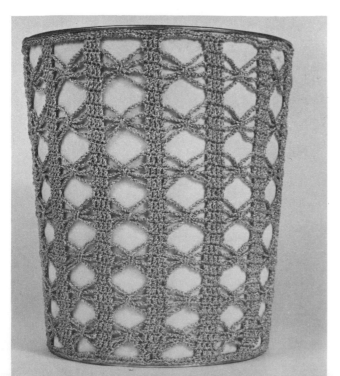

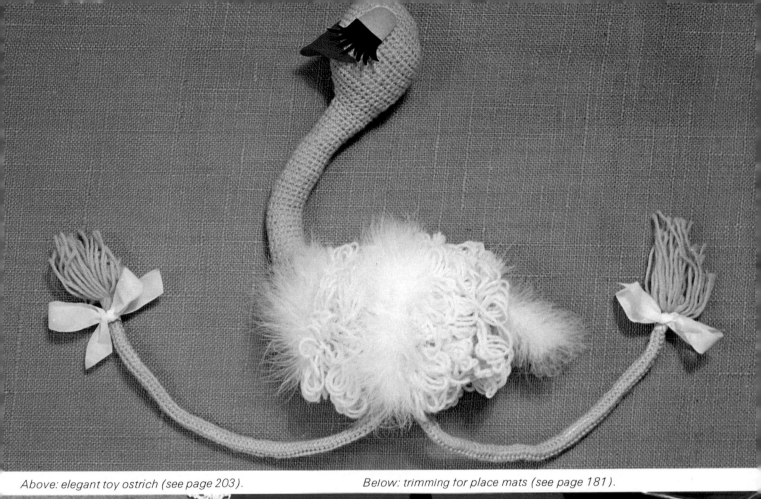

Above: elegant toy ostrich (see page 203).   Below: trimming tor place mats (see page 181).

TO MAKE

Commence with 126 ch., s.s. into first ch. to form a ring.

1st round: 3 ch., miss first ch., 1 tr. into each of next 3 ch., * 11 ch., miss 5 ch., 1 tr. into each of next 4 ch.; rep. from * to within last 5 ch., 11 ch., s.s. into 3rd of 3 ch.: 14 patts.

2nd round: 3 ch., miss first tr., 1 tr. into each of next 3 tr., * 8 ch., 1 tr. into each of next 4 tr.; rep. from * ending with 8 ch., s.s. into 3rd of 3 ch.

3rd round: rep. last round.

4th round: 3 ch., miss first tr., 1 tr. into each of next 3 tr., * 5 ch., 1 d.c. over ch. lengths of last 3 rounds, 5 ch., 1 tr. into each of next 4 tr.; rep. from * ending with 5 ch., 1 d.c. over ch. length of last 3 rounds, 5 ch., 1 s.s. into 3rd of 3 ch.

5th round: 3 ch., miss first tr., 1 tr. into each of next 3 tr., * 11 ch., 1 tr. into each of next 4 tr.; rep. from * ending with 11 ch., s.s. into 3rd of 3 ch.
Rep. 2nd to 4th rounds once.

9th round: 3 ch., miss first tr., 1 tr. into each of next 3 tr., * 13 ch., 1 tr. into each of next 4 tr.; rep. from * ending with 13 ch., s.s. into 3rd of 3 ch.

10th round: 3 ch., miss first tr., 1 tr. into each of next 3 tr., * 10 ch., 1 tr. into each of next 4 tr.; rep. from * ending with 10 ch., s.s. into 3rd of 3 ch.

11th round: rep. last round.

12th round: 3 ch., miss first tr., 1 tr. into each of next 3 tr., * 6 ch., 1 d.c. over ch. lengths of last 3 rounds, 6 ch., 1 tr. into each of next 4 tr.; rep. from * ending with 6 ch., 1 d.c.

over ch. length of last 3 rounds, 6 ch., 1 s.s. into 3rd of 3 ch.
Rep. last 4 rounds twice.

21st round: 3 ch., miss first tr., 1 tr. into each of next 3 tr., * 15 ch., 1 tr. into each of next 4 tr.; rep. from * ending with 15 ch., s.s. into 3rd of 3 ch.

22nd round: 3 ch., miss first tr., 1 tr. into each of next 3 tr., * 12 ch., 1 tr. into each of next 4 tr.; rep. from * ending with 12 ch., s.s. into 3rd of 3 ch.

23rd round: rep. last round.

24th round: 3 ch., miss first tr., 1 tr. into each of next 3 tr., * 7 ch., 1 d.c. over ch. lengths of last 3 rounds, 7 ch., 1 tr. into each of next 4 tr.; rep. from * ending with 7 ch., 1 d.c. over ch. lengths of last 3 rounds, 7 ch., 1 s.s. into 3rd of 3 ch.
Rep. last 4 rounds once.

Next round: 3 ch., miss first tr., 1 tr. into each of next 3 tr., * 8 ch., 1 tr. into each of next 4 tr.; rep. from * ending with 8 ch., 1 s.s. into 3rd of 3 ch.

Last round: 1 d.c. into same place as s.s., * 1 d.c. into each of next 3 tr., 8 d.c. into 8-ch. sp., 1 d.c. into next tr.; rep. from * omitting last d.c. of last rep., s.s. into first d.c.; fasten off.

Bottom Edging. With right side facing attach yarn to a 5-ch. sp., 5 d.c. into same place, * 1 d.c. into each of next 4 tr., 5 d.c. into next ch. sp.; rep. from * omitting last 5 d.c. at end of last rep., s.s. into first d.c.; fasten off.
Slide crochet on to bin, with lining glued on to bin underneath if liked.

Turquoise lampshade

(photographed in colour on the back cover and in black and white on page 194)

MATERIALS
4 oz. of Twilley's Lyscordet or Goldfingering (see note on wools and yarns, page 22); one crochet hook International Standard Size 2.50 (see page 9); one lampshade frame 8 in. high and 38 in. in circumference; 9 in. by 39 in. lining material.

MEASUREMENTS
Height 8 in.; diameter 12 in.; circumference 38 in.

TENSION
1 motif to 3½ in. when stretched (see note on tension, page 14).

ABBREVIATIONS
See page 20.

Outfit for a favourite doll —hat, cape, dress, vest and panties (see page 204)

FIRST MOTIF
Yarn round finger 12 times to form a ring.

1st round: work 16 d.c. into ring, s.s. into first d.c.

2nd round: draw loop up on hook approx. ¾ in., into same place work y.o.h., insert hook into st. and draw loop up, (y.o.h., insert hook into same st., and draw loop up) 3 times, y.o.h. and draw through all loops on hook: puff st. made; * 3 ch., a puff st. into next d.c.; rep. from * ending with 3 ch., 1 s.s. into top of first puff st.

3rd round: s.s. into centre of first loop, 1 d.c. into same place, * 5 ch., 1 d.c. into next loop; rep. from * omitting last d.c. of last rep., s.s. into first d.c.

4th round: 5 d.c. into each loop, s.s. into first d.c.

5th round: 1 s.s. into each of first 2 d.c., 1 d.c. into same place as last s.s., * 9 ch., 1 s.s. into 3rd ch. from hook: a p. made; 6 ch., miss 4 d.c., 1 d.c. into next d.c., 7 ch., miss 4 d.c., 1 d.c. into next d.c., 5 ch., miss 4 d.c., 1 d.c. into next d.c., 7 ch., miss 4 d.c., 1 d.c. into next d.c.; rep. from * omitting last d.c. of last rep., s.s. into first d.c.; fasten off.

SECOND MOTIF
Work as First Motif until 5th round is reached.

5th round: 1 s.s. into each of first 2 d.c., 1 d.c. into same

193

place as last s.s., 6 ch., 1 d.c. into a p. on first motif, 6 ch., miss 4 d.c., 1 d.c. into next d.c. on second motif, 3 ch., 1 d.c. into appropriate 7-ch. loop on first motif, 3 ch., miss 4 d.c., 1 d.c. into next d.c. on second motif, 2 ch., 1 d.c. into appropriate 5-ch. loop on first motif, 2 ch., miss 4 d.c., 1 d.c. into next d.c. on second motif, 3 ch., 1 d.c. into appropriate 7-ch. loop on first motif, 3 ch., miss 4 d.c., 1 d.c. into next d.c. on second motif, 6 ch., 1 d.c. into next p. on first motif, 6 ch., miss 4 d.c., 1 d.c. into next d.c. on second motif, complete as for first motif; fasten off.

Make a rectangle of 2 motifs by 11, joining in similar manner.

EDGING

This is worked on top and bottom.

1st round: with right side facing attach yarn to edge, then work 231 d.c. evenly round, 1 d.c. into first d.c.

2nd to 5th rounds: working in continuous rounds make 1 d.c. into each d.c., s.s. into first d.c.; fasten off.

TO COMPLETE

Press work lightly on the wrong side with a warm iron over a damp cloth. Line frame. Cover with crochet and sew into position by turning in last round of edging and hemming this to lining.

Duchesse set

MATERIALS

2 balls (25 grm.) of Twilley's Lystra (see note on wools and yarns, page 22); one crochet hook International Standard Size 1.25 (see page 9).

MEASUREMENTS

Centre mat 17 in. by 11 in.; side mats 6 in. by 7 in. The above quantity is sufficient to make one large centre mat and two small side mats.

TENSION

1 motif—$4\frac{1}{2}$ in. from point to point (see note on tension, page 14).

ABBREVIATIONS

See page 20.

FIRST MOTIF

6 ch., s.s. into first ch. to form a ring.

1st round: (1 d.c. into ring, 5 ch.) 6 times, s.s. into first d.c. 6 sps.

2nd round: into each loop make 1 d.c., 1 h.tr., 5 tr., 1 h.tr. and 1 d.c. ending with s.s. into first d.c.

3rd round: * 5 ch. behind petals, 1 d.c. between 2 d.c. of previous row; rep. from *, s.s. into first d.c.

4th round: into next loop work 1 ch., 1 h.tr., 7 tr., 1 h.tr. and 1 d.c., ending with s.s. into first d.c.

5th round: 1 s.s. into each of first 3 sts. of next petal, * 1 d.c. into next st., 4 ch., 1 s.s. into 3rd ch. from hook, 5 ch., miss 3 sts., 1 d.c. into next st., 4 ch., 1 s.s. into 3rd ch. from hook, 5 ch., miss 3 sts. on next petal; rep. from * ending with 1 s.s. into first d.c., s.s. into centre of next loop.

6th round: 4 ch., 3 d.tr. into same loop, * into next loop make 2 d.tr., 3 ch. and 2 d.tr., 4 d.tr. into next loop; rep. from * omitting 4 d.tr. at end of last rep., s.s. into 4th of 4 ch.

7th round: 3 ch., 1 tr. into each of next 5 d.tr.,* into next 3-ch. loop work 3 tr., 3 ch. and 3 tr., 1 tr. into each d.tr.; rep. from *, s.s. into 3rd of 3 ch.

8th round: 1 s.s. into each of first 3 sts., 1 d.c. into next tr., * 5 ch., into next 3-ch. loop work 2 tr., 3 ch. and 2 tr., (5 ch., miss 4 tr., 1 d.c. into next tr.) twice; rep. from * omitting 1 d.c. at end of last rep., s.s. into first d.c.; fasten off.

SECOND MOTIF

As first motif until 8th round is reached.

8th round: 1 s.s. into each of first 3 sts., 1 d.c. into next st., 5 ch., 2 tr. into next 3-ch. loop, 1 ch., 1 d.c. into appropriate 3-ch. loop on first motif, 1 ch., 2 tr. into same place as last 2 tr. on second motif, (2 ch., 1 d.c. into appropriate 5-ch. loop on first motif, 2 ch., miss 4 tr. on second motif, 1 d.c. into next tr.) twice, 2 ch., 1 d.c. into appropriate 5-ch. loop on first motif, 2 ch., 2 tr. into next 3-ch. loop, on second motif, 1 ch., 1 d.c. into appropriate

3-ch. loop on first motif, 1 ch., 2 tr. into same place as last 2 tr. on second motif, complete as 8th round of first motif; fasten off.

TO COMPLETE

Join motifs as given in instructions below and also see photograph below.

Centre mat (9 motifs). Join 3 motifs in a line, then 1 line of 2 motifs on each side, then 1 motif each side of last 2 lines.

Side mats (3 motifs each). Join 2 motifs in a line, then 1 motif on one side.

Starch and press.

Motif bedspread

MATERIALS

50 balls Coats Mercer-Crochet No. 60 (20 grm.) (see note on wools and yarns, page 20); one crochet hook International Standard Size 5.50 (see page 9).

MEASUREMENTS

78¾ in. by 72 in., to fit a single bed.

TENSION

1 motif, 2¼ in. in diameter (see note on tension, page 14).

ABBREVIATIONS

See page 20.

MOTIF

Commence with 8 ch., join with a s.s. to form a ring.

1st row: 3 ch., 23 tr. into ring, 1 s.s. into 3rd of 3 ch.

2nd row: 4 ch., * 1 tr. into next tr., 1 ch.; rep. from * ending with 1 s.s. into 3rd of 4 ch.

3rd row: s.s. into 1-ch. sp., 3 ch., 1 tr., 1 ch., and 2 tr. into same place as last s.s.: sh. made, * 1 ch., miss next sp., 2 tr., 1 ch. and 2 tr. into next sp.: another sh. made; rep. from * ending with 1 ch., 1 s.s. into 3rd of 3 ch.

4th row: s.s. to centre of first sh., 3 ch., 1 tr., 1 ch. and 2 tr. into same place as last s.s.: sh. over sh., * 2 ch., sh. over next sh.; rep. from * ending with 2 ch., 1 s.s. into 3rd of 3 ch.

Close-up of bedspread pattern

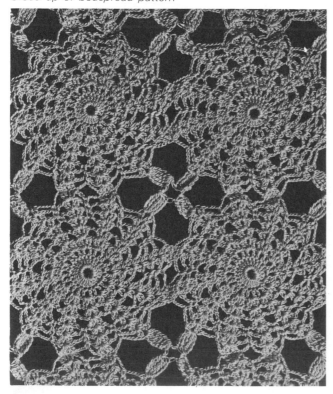

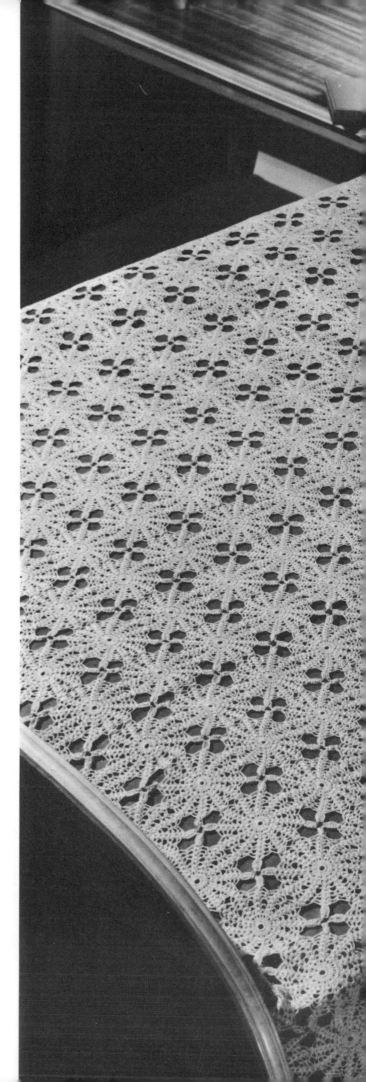

5th row: as 4th row but having 3 ch. between sh.

6th row: s.s. to centre of first sh., 3 ch., 1 tr., 1 ch., and 2 tr. into same place as last s.s., * 2 ch., 1 d.c. into 3-ch. sp., 2 ch., sh. over sh.; rep. from * omitting sh. over sh. at end of last rep., 1 s.s. into 3rd of 3 ch.

7th row: s.s. to centre of first sh., 3 ch., 1 tr., 1 ch. and 2 tr. into same place as last s.s., * 3 ch., 1 d.c. into next d.c., 3 ch., sh. over sh.; rep. from * omitting sh. over sh. at end of last rep., 1 s.s. into 3rd of 3 ch.

8th row: as 7th row, but having 4 ch. instead of 3 ch. between shs.; fasten off.

TO COMPLETE

Make 35 rows of 32 motifs. Sew 2 shs. of each motif to 2 shs. of adjacent motifs, leaving 1 free sh. on each motif between joinings.

Filling. Attach yarn to centre of any free sh., 5 ch., leaving the last loop of each on hook work 4 qd. tr. into same sh., y.o.h. and draw through all loops on hook: cl. made, 1 ch., * into next free sh. work a 5-qd. tr., 1 ch.; rep. from * twice, join with 1 s.s. into 5th of 5 ch.; fasten off. Fill in all sps. between motifs in this manner.

Damp and press.

Matching tea and egg cosies

(photographed in colour on the back cover and in black and white opposite)

MATERIALS

For tea cosy: 3 balls Robin Vogue Double Knitting in navy, ½ ball Robin Vogue 4-ply in red (see note on wools and yarns, page 22); crochet hooks International Standard Sizes 3.00 and 4.00 (see page 9); a 2-in. curtain ring for tea cosy loop; two pieces foam each 10 in. by 8 in. (optional); piece lining material 18 in. by 12 in. (optional).

For four egg cosies: 2 balls Robin Vogue Double Knitting in navy, ½ ball Robin Vogue 4-ply in red; one crochet hook International Standard Size 4.00 (see page 9). *N.B. Any 2 contrasting shades may be used.*

MEASUREMENTS

Tea cosy: width (at widest part) 11 in.; height 8½ in.
Egg cosy: width (at widest part) 2¾ in.; height 3½ in.

TENSION

10 tr. to 2 in. with No. 4.00 hook (see note on tension, page 14).

ABBREVIATIONS

See page 20; N., navy; R., red.

TEA COSY
MAIN PIECE

With No. 4.00 hook and N., make 52 ch.

Work 1 tr. into 3rd ch. from hook, work 1 tr. into each ch. to end, 3 ch. to turn.

Next row: work 1 tr. into each tr. to end, 3 ch.; turn.

Rep. last row 8 times more.

Dec. 1 tr. at each end of the next and foll. 2 alt. rows, then work 5 rows straight.

Dec. 1 tr. at each end of the next 2 rows, then dec. 2 tr. at each end of the next 2 rows. Fasten off.

Make another piece in the same way.

FLOWER

With No. 3.00 hook and R. make 9 ch., s.s. to form a ring. Work 19 tr. into ring, s.s. to top of 3 ch.: 20 tr.

Next round: * make 20 ch., 1 d.c. into 2nd ch. from hook, 1 d.c. into next ch., 1 h.tr. into next 2 ch., 1 tr. into next 15 ch. (1 petal made); miss 1 tr., s.s. over next tr.; rep. from * 9 times more. Fasten off.

Rings for End of Petals (make 10). With No. 3.00 hook and R. make 5 ch. Join with s.s. Work 10 tr. into ring, s.s. to join. Fasten off.

LOOP

With No. 4.00 hook and N., work in d.c. to cover curtain ring. Fasten off.

TO COMPLETE

Press work on wrong side using a warm iron over a damp cloth. If required, cut 2 pieces of lining the same shape as the tea cosy, but ½ in. larger all round; cut 2 pieces of foam the same shape and size as cosy. Stitch shaped edges of lining tog., right sides facing and with ½-in. turnings. Join shaped edges of foam tog., using an edge-to-edge stitch (i.e. no turnings allowed). Sew flower into place on one side of cosy, positioning as in photograph opposite. Stitch each crocheted ring just beyond the tip of each petal. Join shaped edges of cosy tog. Place foam inside cosy, then put lining, so wrong side is against foam. Turn in remaining raw edges of lining and slip stitch neatly to cosy. Attach ring to top of cosy, sewing through cosy and lining.

EGG COSIES
MAIN PIECE (make 4)

With No. 4.00 hook and R. make 27 ch.

Work 1 tr. into 2nd ch. from hook, work 1 tr. into each ch. to end, break R., join in N., turn with 3 ch.

Next row: work 1 tr. into each tr. to end, turn with 3 ch. Rep. the last row 5 times more, then dec. 6 sts. evenly over the next row.

Next row: work in tr., missing every alt. st. Fasten off.

LOOP (make 4)

With No. 4.00 hook and N. make 15 ch.

Work 1 d.c. into each ch., join with a s.s. Fasten off.

TO COMPLETE

Press work on wrong side, using a warm iron over a damp cloth. Fold each piece in half, so curved edges are tog., stitch along this seam. Attach loop to the top of each cosy.

Spare toilet roll cover

MATERIALS

¾ oz. (approx.) of Hayfield Bri-Nylon Double Knitting in 1st colour and ½ oz. (approx.) Hayfield Bri-Nylon Double Knitting in 2nd colour (see note on wools and yarns, page 21); crochet hooks International Standard Sizes 3.00, 2.50 and 2.00 (see page 9); one baby doll 4½ in. tall.

MEASUREMENTS

Dress: length 5½ in., diameter at bottom 6 in.
Bonnet: height 2 in.

TENSION

5 sts. to 1 in. and 3 rows to ⅝ in. over d.c. with No. 2.00 hook (see note on tension, page 14).

ABBREVIATIONS

See page 20.

DRESS

With No. 2.00 hook and 2nd colour, commence with 22 ch.
1st row: 1 d.c. into 2nd ch. from hook, 1 d.c. into each

ch. to end; turn.

2nd row: 2 ch., 1 d.c. into 2nd d.c. from hook, 1 d.c. into each d.c. to end; fasten off; turn.

Join 1st colour.

3rd row: 2 ch., 2 d.c. into 2nd d.c. from hook, 2 d.c. into each d.c. to end of row, 2 d.c. into 2nd of 2 ch.; change to No. 2.50 hook, 2 ch.; turn.

4th row: 1 d.c. into each st. to end of row; 3 ch.; turn.

5th row: 2 tr. into 2nd d.c. from hook, * 1 tr. into next st., 2 tr. into next st.; rep. from * to end of row; change to No. 3.00 hook, 3 ch.; turn.

6th row: 1 tr. into 2nd tr., 1 tr. into each tr. to end of row, join with s.s. to form a ring.

1st round: 4 ch., 1 d.tr. into each tr. to end of round, s.s. into top of 4 ch.

Rep. last round 8 times.

Join 2nd colour.

Next round: 3 ch., 1 tr. into same place as 3 ch., 2 tr. into each sp. to end of round, s.s. into top of 3 ch.

Frills. Join 2nd colour on 2nd and every alt. round of d.tr. and work 2 tr. into each sp. to end of each round, s.s. into first tr. Fasten off.

BONNET

With No. 3.00 hook and 2nd colour, commence with 4 ch., join with s.s. to form a ring.

1st round: 2 ch., 1 d.c. into 2nd ch. from hook, 7 d.c. into ring, s.s. into top of 2 ch.

2nd round: 2 ch., 1 d.c. into same st., 2 d.c. into each d.c. to end of round, s.s. into top of 2 ch.

3rd round: 2 ch., * 1 d.c. into next d.c., 2 d.c. into next d.c.; rep. from *, s.s. into top of 2 ch.

4th round: 2 ch., 1 d.c. into next d.c., 1 d.c. into each d.c. to end of round, s.s. into top of 2 ch.

5th round: as 4th round.

Brim. 1st row: 2 ch., 1 d.c. into next 18 d.c.; turn.

2nd row: 2 ch., * 2 d.c. into next d.c., 1 d.c. into next d.c.; rep. from * 8 times, turn.

3rd row: 2 ch., * 2 d.c. into next d.c., 1 d.c. into each of next 2 d.c.; rep. from * 8 times; turn.

Join 1st colour and work 1 d.c. into each d.c. to end of brim. Fasten off.

TO COMPLETE

Fit dress to doll, stitching seam on body part. Make shoulder straps by threading 2 strands of 1st colour yarn thr. front of dress, taking strands over doll's shoulders, crossing strands at back and attaching to back of dress.

Make a 9-in. length of chain in 1st colour and thread thr. sides of bonnet behind brim. Tie bonnet firmly on doll's head. Put cover over spare toilet roll, letting doll's legs hang down the centre tube.

Motif apron

(photographed in black and white on page 202)

MATERIALS

3 balls of Robin Casino Crêpe or Tricel-Nylon Perle (see note on wools and yarns, page 22); one crochet hook International Standard Size 3.00 (see page 9).

MEASUREMENTS

16 in. by 12 in. (or adjust size by working extra motifs as required).

TENSION

1 motif—4 in. square when pressed (see note on tension, page 14).

ABBREVIATIONS

See page 20.

MAIN PIECE

Commence with 6 ch., join with s.s. to form a ring.

1st round: * 1 ch., 1 d.c. into ring, 5 ch., 1 h.tr. into 2nd ch. from hook, 1 tr. into each of next 2 ch., 1 h.tr. into next ch.; rep. from * 7 times, s.s. into first d.c.: 8 petals.

2nd round: s.s. into tip of first petal, 1 ch., 1 d.c. into same place as last s.s., * 5 ch., 1 d.c. into tip of next petal; rep. from * 7 times, omitting 1 d.c. at end of last rep., s.s. into first d.c.

3rd round: 8 ch., 1 tr. into same place as s.s., * 6 tr. into each of next 2 loops, 1 tr., 5 ch. and 1 tr. into next d.c.; rep. from * twice, 6 tr. into each of next 2 loops, s.s. into 3rd of 8 ch.

4th round: 5 ch., * 1 tr., 5 ch. and 1 tr. into next loop, 2 ch., miss first tr., 1 tr. into next tr., (2 ch., miss 2 tr., 1 tr. into next tr.) 4 times, 2 ch.; rep. from * omitting 1 tr. and 2 ch. at end of last rep., s.s. into 3rd of 5 ch.

5th round: 2 ch., 2 d.c. into next sp., * 1 d.c. into next tr., work 7 d.c. into next loop, ** (1 d.c. into next tr., 2 d.c. into next sp. **) 6 times; rep. from * but work from ** to ** 5 times only on last rep., s.s. into 2nd of 2 ch.; fasten off. Make 12 motifs altogether. Press each motif to measure 4 in. square. S.s. motifs neatly tog., 4 motifs across and 3 motifs down.

Border. With right side of work facing beg. along top edge.

1st round: 2 ch., * work 1 d.c. into each d.c to approx.

4 d.c. before seam between motifs, * * miss 1 d.c., 1 d.c. into next d.c.; rep. from * * to approx. 4 d.c. after seam; rep. from * to end of top, work 3 d.c. into corner then cont. in d.c. all round outer edge working 3 d.c. into each corner, s.s. to join, 2 ch.

2nd round: work in d.c., working 3 d.c. into each corner, s.s. to join.

Work 6 rows in d.c. along top edge only to form waistband, working 2 turning ch. at end of each row. Fasten off.

TIES (make 2 alike).
With No. 3.00 hook make 66 ch.
Work 6 rows in d.c.
Fasten off.

TO COMPLETE
Stitch ties neatly to waistband of apron. Press work on wrong side using a warm iron over a damp cloth, being careful not to stretch motifs.

Toy ostrich

(photographed in colour on page 191)

MATERIALS
3 balls Robin Vogue Double Knitting, Casino Crêpe, Tricel-Nylon Double Knitting or Bri-Nylon Double Knitting in pink, 1 ball in white (see note on wools and yarns, page 22); crochet hook International Standard Size 4.00 (see page 9); 24 in. of swansdown; 60 pipe cleaners for stiffening; oddments of blue, black and pink felt for features; approx. ½ yd. white ribbon; kapok for stuffing; tissue paper; transparent self-adhesive tape; glue (optional).

MEASUREMENTS
35 in. tall approx.; body 8 in. wide at widest point.

TENSION
5 sts. and 6 rows to 1 in. over d.c. (see note on tension, page 14).

ABBREVIATIONS
See page 20; P., pink; W., white.

BODY PIECE
With P. make 12 ch.
Next row: miss 2 ch., 1 d.c. into each ch. to end, 2 ch.; turn: 10 d.c.
Next row: 2 d.c. into each of first 2 d.c., 1 d.c. into each d.c. to last 2 d.c., 2 d.c. into each of last 2 d.c., 2 ch.; turn:

Hostess apron made from separate motifs — instructions on page 201.

14 d.c.
Rep. the last row 3 times more: 26 d.c.
Next row: 2 d.c. into first d.c., 1 d.c. into each d.c. to last d.c., 2 d.c. into last d.c., 2 ch.; turn: 28 d.c.
Rep. last row twice more.
Next row: 2 d.c. into next d.c., 1 d.c. into each d.c. to last 2 d.c., 2 d.c. into each of last 2 d.c., 2 ch.; turn: 35 d.c.
Next row: 2 d.c. into each of first 2 d.c., 1 d.c. into each d.c. to last d.c., 2 d.c. into last d.c., 2 ch.; turn: 38 d.c.
Next row: 1 d.c. into each d.c. to last 2 d.c., 2 d.c. into each of last 2 d.c., 2 ch.; turn: 40 d.c.
Work 9 rows straight.
Next row: miss first d.c., 1 d.c. into each d.c. to end, 2 ch.; turn.
Next row: 1 d.c. into each d.c. to last d.c., 2 ch.; turn: 38 d.c.
Rep. the last 2 rows once more: 36 d.c.
Next row: miss first d.c., work 26 d.c., 2 ch.; turn.
Next row: miss 2 d.c., 1 d.c. into each d.c. to last 2 d.c., 2 ch.; turn: 22 d.c.
Rep. the last row 3 times more: 10 d.c. Fasten off.

NECK
With right side of work facing, rejoin P. yarn to 8th d.c. from left side, d.c. to end, 2 ch., turn. Work 38 more rows straight on these 8 d.c. ending at front edge.
Shape Head. Next row. 2 d.c. into each of first 2 d.c., 1 d.c. into each d.c. to end, 2 ch.; turn.
Next row: 1 d.c. into each d.c. to last 2 d.c., 2 d.c. into each of last 2 d.c., 2 ch.; turn: 12 d.c.

Rep. these 2 rows once more and the first row again: 18 d.c.

Next row: 1 d.c. into each d.c. to last d.c., 2 d.c. into last d.c., 2 ch.; turn.

Next row: 2 d.c. into first d.c., 1 d.c. into each d.c. to end, 2 ch.; turn: 20 d.c.

Work 9 rows straight ending at front edge.

Next row: miss first d.c., 1 d.c. into each d.c. to last d.c., 2 ch.; turn: 18 d.c.

Rep. the last row 5 times more: 8 d.c. Fasten off.

TO COMPLETE

Join pieces tog. neatly along ch. edge of body to top of neck. Join other side of neck neatly, leaving rest of body seam open.

Twist 3 pipe cleaners tog. and join to 3 more twisted pipe cleaners, thus making one long length. Place this stiffening down front seam of neck, fastening securely at each end. Make 5 more pieces with pipe cleaners as before and place in neck, one down back seam and the others spaced evenly between neck seam, stitching securely at each end. Stuff neck very firmly with kapok. Join part of head leaving open a section at top. Stuff head very firmly, join rest of seam.

Join body seam leaving a part open at back for stuffing. Stuff body very firmly, join rest of seam.

Legs (make 2 alike). With P. make 80 ch. Work 4 rows in d.c. Fasten off.

Twist 4 pipe cleaners tog., rep. this twice more. Now join each piece tog. to form leg, approx. 16 in. long. Make another leg in the same way. Cover with tissue paper and secure with transparent self-adhesive tape, leaving portion at top free to insert into body. Place leg inside crochet strip and stitch along seam firmly.

Rep. for other leg.

Make 2 P. tassels and attach to lower part of each leg. Insert legs into body and stitch securely. Cut ribbon in two, and tie one piece round each ankle.

Feathers. With W. stitch rows of loops with double yarn around body. Leave space in centre for strip of swansdown. Stitch swansdown round as shown in picture on page 191, one piece round base of neck, one in space allowed in centre and short piece as a tail.

Eyes and beak. Cut out pieces in felt for 2 eyelids (blue), 2 eyelashes (black) and 1 beak (pink) as shown in picture. Stick with glue or sew on to head of ostrich.

Bend neck and legs as desired.

Doll's outfit

(photographed in colour on back cover and page 192)

MATERIALS

1 ball Coats Mercer-Crochet No. 20 (20 grm.) pink (624), 2 balls in yellow (582) and 2 balls in brown (579) (see note on wools and yarns, page 20); one steel crochet hook International Standard Size 1.25 (see page 9); 7 press studs; little cotton wool; approx. 15 in. shirring elastic.

MEASUREMENTS

To fit a doll approx. 13 in. tall.

TENSION

7 cross sts. to 1 in.; first 7 rows of patt. to 1 in.; 13 tr. and 6 rows of tr. to 1 in. (see note on tension, page 14).

ABBREVIATIONS

See page 20; P., pink; B., brown; Y., yellow.

PANTIES

FRONT

With P. make 10 ch. and leave aside. With separate yarn (in P.) make 11 ch.

1st row: 1 tr. into 4th ch. from hook, 1 tr. into each ch., 3 ch.; turn.

2nd row: miss first tr., 1 tr. into each tr., 1 tr. into next ch., 3 ch.; turn.

3rd row: 2 tr. into first tr., 1 tr. into each tr., 3 tr. into next ch., 3 ch.; turn.

4th row: 1 tr. into first tr., 1 tr. into each tr., 2 tr. into next ch., 3 ch.; turn.

Rep. last row 3 times more ending last row with 12 ch.; turn.

8th row: 1 tr. into 4th ch. from hook, 1 tr. into each ch., 2 tr. into next tr., 1 tr. into each ch., 2 tr. into next ch., attach length of ch. already worked to same place as last tr., 1 tr. into each ch., 3 ch.; turn.

9th to 11th rows: as 2nd row.

12th row: miss first 2 tr., * 1 h.tr. into next tr., 1 ch., miss next tr.: rep. from * ending with 1 h.tr. into next ch. Fasten off.

BACK

Make 7 ch. and leave aside.

1st row: attach yarn to first foundation ch. on Front, 3 ch.,

1 tr. into same place as join, 1 tr. into each of next 7 ch., 2 tr. into next ch., 2 tr. into next ch., 3 ch.; turn.

2nd and 3rd rows: as 3rd and 4th rows of Front.

Rep. last row 5 times more ending last row with 9 ch.; turn.

Rep. 8th to 12th rows of Front.

Join row ends of last 5 rows of Back and Front.

TO COMPLETE

Leg Edgings (both alike). 1st row: with right side facing attach yarn to base of side seam, work an even number of d.c. all round ending with 1 s.s. into first d.c.

2nd row: into same place as s.s. work 1 d.c., 2 ch. and 1 d.c. (a picot made), * miss next d.c., a picot into next d.c.; rep. from * ending with 1 s.s. into first d.c. Fasten off. Thread 2 rows of elastic thr. sps. at top.

VEST

MAIN SECTION

With P. make 75 ch.

1st row: 1 tr. into 4th ch. from hook, 1 tr. into each ch., 3 ch.; turn.

2nd row: miss first tr., 1 tr. into each tr., 1 tr. into next ch., 3 ch.; turn.

Rep. last row 7 times more omitting turning ch. at end of last row.

Front Shaping. 1st row: 1 s.s. into each of first 6 tr., 3 ch., leaving the last loop of each on hook work 1 tr. into each of next 2 tr., y.o.h. and draw thr. all loops on hook (a dec. made), 1 tr. into each of next 22 tr., a dec. over next 2 tr., 1 tr. into next tr., 3 ch.; turn.

2nd and 3rd rows: miss first tr., a dec. over next 2 sts., 1 tr. into each tr. to within last 3 sts., a dec. over next 2 sts., 1 tr. into next st., 3 ch.; turn.

Neck Shaping. 1st row: miss first tr., a dec. over next 2 sts., 1 tr. into each of next 3 tr., a dec. over next 2 tr., 1 tr. into next tr., 3 ch.; turn.

2nd row: as 2nd row of Front Shaping.

3rd row: miss first tr., 1 tr. into next st., a dec. over next 2 sts., 1 tr. into next st., 3 ch.; turn.

4th row: miss first tr., a dec. over next 2 sts., tr. into next st., 3 ch.; turn.

5th row: miss first tr., a dec. over next 2 sts., 2 ch.; turn.

6th row: miss first st., 1 tr. into next st., 26 ch. (strap). Fasten off. Miss 4 tr. for centre, attach yarn to next tr., 3 ch., a dec. over next 2 tr. and complete to correspond with first side.

TO COMPLETE

Edging. 1st row: with wrong side facing attach yarn to first s.s. on Front Shaping, work an uneven number of d.c. across top edges having 1 d.c. into each ch. of strap, 3 d.c. into last ch. and 1 d.c. into other half of each ch. and ending with 1 ch.; turn.

2nd row: * a picot into next d.c., miss next d.c.; rep. from * ending with a picot into last d.c. Fasten off. Sew 3 press studs in position on open side having front edge overlapping back. Sew 1 press stud on each strap to fasten under edge at centre back.

DRESS

BACK AND FRONT (both alike)

With B., make 53 ch.

1st row: 1 d.c. into 2nd ch. from hook, 1 d.c. into each ch. to within last ch., insert hook into next ch. and draw yarn thr.; drop B., pick up Y. and draw thr. 2 loops, 3 ch.; turn. (*N.B.* Always change colours in this manner.)

2nd row (right side): working over B. in order to conceal it, miss 2 d.c., * 1 tr. into next d.c., inserting hook from behind, 1 tr. into previous d.c. (cross st. made), miss 1 d.c.; rep. from * to within last st., y.o.h., insert hook into next d.c. and draw yarn thr., y.o.h., and draw thr. 2 loops, drop Y., pick up B. and draw thr. rem. 2 loops, 1 ch.; turn.

3rd row: working over Y. in order to conceal it, 1 d.c. into each st., drop B., pick up Y., 3 ch.; turn.

2nd and 3rd rows form patt.

Work in patt. for 15 rows more, or for length required, ending with a 2nd patt. row.

19th row: insert hook into first st. and draw yarn thr., (insert hook into next st. and draw yarn thr.) twice, y.o.h. and draw thr. all loops on hook (a dec. made), 1 d.c. into each st. to within last 3 sts., (insert hook into next st. and draw yarn thr.) 3 times, y.o.h. and draw thr. all loops on hook (another dec. made), drop B., pick up Y., 3 ch.; turn.

20th to 22nd rows: work in patt.

23rd to 25th rows: as 19th to 21st rows, omitting turning ch. at end of last row.

Armhole Shaping. 1st row: 1 s.s. into each of first 5 sts., 3 ch., work in patt. to within last 5 sts., 1 tr. into next st., drop Y., pick up B., 1 ch.; turn.

2nd to 4th rows: as 19th to 21st rows.

Neck Shaping. 1st row: miss first st., (a cross st. over next 2 sts.) 6 times, 1 tr. into next st., drop Y., pick up B., 1 ch.; turn.

2nd to 5th rows: as 19th to 22nd rows.

Rep. last 4 rows once more.

10th row: 1 d.c. into each of first 3 sts., 1 s.s. into each of next 3 sts. Fasten off.

Miss 4 d.c., attach yarn to next d.c., 3 ch., and complete to correspond with first side.

TO COMPLETE

Sew side seams.

Lower Edging. With B. and right side facing, attach yarn to any side seam and work to correspond with Leg Edgings of Panties.

Armhole, Shoulder and Neck Edging. 1st row: with B. and right side facing, attach yarn to left underarm seam and work an even number of d.c. round armhole, across shoulder, along each side of front neck and cont. in this manner all round ending with 1 s.s. into first d.c.

2nd row: as 2nd row of Leg Edging.

Sew 1 press stud to each shoulder.

CAPE

MAIN SECTION

With Y. begin at neck with 48 ch.

1st row: 2 d.c. into 2nd ch. from hook, 2 d.c. into each ch.,

3 ch.; turn.

2nd row: miss first d.c., * a cross st. over next 2 d.c.; rep. from * ending with 1 tr. into last d.c., 1 ch.; turn.

3rd row: 1 d.c. into each of next 17 tr., 2 d.c. into each of next 2 tr., 1 d.c. into each of next 56 tr., 2 d.c. into each of next 2 tr., 1 d.c. into each of next 17 sts., 3 ch.; turn.

4th row: as 2nd row.

5th row: 1 d.c. into each st., 3 ch.; turn.

6th row: as 2nd row.

7th row: 1 d.c. into each of next 18 tr., 2 d.c. into next tr., 1 d.c. into each of next 2 tr., 2 d.c. into next tr., 1 d.c. into each tr. to within last 22 sts., 2 d.c. into next tr., 1 d.c. into each of next 2 tr., 2 d.c. into next tr., 1 d.c. into each of next 18 sts., 3 ch.; turn.

Last 4 rows form patt.

Work in patt. for 31 rows more or length required ending with a 6th patt. row.

39th row: 1 d.c. into each st., 1 ch.; turn.

TO COMPLETE

Edging. Work edging round lower edge, centre front openings and neck edge, as for Leg Edgings of Panties.

Button (make 2). With B. make 4 ch., join with a s.s. to form a ring.

1st row: 6 d.c. into ring.

2nd to 4th rows: 1 d.c. into each d.c.

Cut yarn leaving sufficient to lace thr. last row, fill shape with cotton wool, draw up yarn and secure.

Loop. With B., attach yarn to base of either button, 20 ch., 1 s.s. into same place as join. Fasten off. Sew to cape at neck edge to fasten (see picture on page 192).

HAT
MAIN SECTION

With B., make 6 ch., join with a s.s. to form a ring.

1st row: 3 ch., 11 tr. into ring, 1 s.s. into 3rd of 3 ch.

2nd row: 2 d.c. into same place as s.s., 2 d.c. into each st., 1 s.s. into first d.c., drop B., pick up Y.

3rd row: 3 ch., working from behind, 1 tr. into last d.c. worked (a starting cross st. made), * a cross st. over next 2 sts.; rep. from * ending with 1 s.s. into 3rd of 3 ch., drop Y., pick up B.

4th and 5th rows: as 2nd and 3rd rows.

6th row: 1 d.c. into same place as s.s., * 2 d.c. into next tr., 1 d.c. into next tr.; rep. from * omitting 1 d.c. at end of last rep., 1 s.s. into first d.c., drop B., pick up Y.

7th row: as 3rd row.

8th and 9th rows: as 6th and 7th rows.

10th row: 1 d.c. into same place as s.s., 1 d.c. into next tr., * 2 d.c. into next tr., 1 d.c. into each of next 4 tr.; rep. from * omitting 4 d.c. at end of last rep., 1 s.s. into first d.c., drop B., pick up Y.

11th row: as 3rd row.

12th row: 1 d.c. into same place as s.s., 1 d.c. into each tr., 1 s.s. into first d.c., drop B., pick up Y.

Rep. last 2 rows twice more then 11th row again.

18th row: 1 d.c. into same place as s.s., 1 d.c. into next tr., * a dec. over next 2 sts., 1 d.c. into each of next 4 tr.; rep. from * omitting 4 d.c. at end of last rep., 1 s.s. into first d.c., drop B., pick up Y.

19th row: as 3rd row.

20th and 21st rows: 1 d.c. into same place as s.s., 1 d.c. into next st., * a dec. over next 2 sts., 1 d.c. into each of next 4 sts.; rep. from * omitting 2 d.c. at end of last rep., 1 s.s. into first d.c.

22nd row: into same place as s.s. work 1 d.c., 2 ch. and 1 d.c., * miss 1 st., into next st. work 1 d.c., 2 ch. and 1 d.c.; rep. from * ending with 1 s.s. into first d.c.

Fasten off.

TO COMPLETE

Button for Hat. With B., make 2 ch.

1st row: 6 d.c. into 2nd ch. from hook, 1 s.s. into first d.c.

2nd row: 2 d.c. into same place as s.s., 2 d.c. into each d.c., 1 s.s. into first d.c.

3rd row: 1 d.c. into same place as s.s., 1 d.c. into each d.c., 1 s.s. into first d.c.

Rep. last 2 rows once more then 2nd row again.

7th row: 1 d.c. into same place as s.s., * 1 ch., miss 1 d.c., 1 d.c. into next d.c.; rep. from * omitting 1 d.c. at end of last rep., 1 s.s. into first d.c. Fasten off leaving sufficient yarn to lace through last row. Fill shape with cotton wool (or use button), draw up yarn and secure.

Sew button to top of hat.

Index